CIVIL WAR
Small Arms
of the U.S. Navy and Marine Corps

by John D. McAulay

ANDREW MOWBRAY PUBLISHERS • P.O. Box 460 • Lincoln, Rhode Island 02865 USA

LIBRARY OF CONGRESS
CATALOG CARD NO.: 99-074227
    John D. McAulay
      Civil War Small Arms of the U.S. Navy and Marine Corps
  Lincoln, RI: ANDREW MOWBRAY INCORPORATED—*PUBLISHERS*
      pp. 184

ISBN: 0-917218-87-6

©1999 by John D. McAulay

All rights reserved. No part of this book may be reproduced in any form or by any means without permission in writing from the author and the publisher. To order more copies of this book, call 1-800-999-4697.

Printed in the United States of America.

This book was designed and set in type by Jo-Ann Langlois. The typeface chosen was Galliard.

Front Cover: The USS *Congress* burning after being attacked by the CSS *Virginia*. (Original painting by Tom Freeman)

Back Cover: The USS *Miami* crew firing on the CSS *Albemarle*. (Original painting by Tom Freeman)

1 2 3 4 5 6 7 8 9 10

In memory of one of my best college friends,
P.F.C. Dick Dusseau, USMC
killed in action, March 5, 1969.

Foreword

by Norm Flayderman

This sixth published work by John McAulay is a highly significant addition to the lore of American arms history. The widespread use and reliability of his earlier writings have firmly established the author among the preeminent researchers of weapons of the American Civil War. The great wealth of factual material afforded here, much of it newly reported, is certain to lead to a better understanding and appreciation of American naval weapons and their use by the sea services during the war years and the decade that preceded it.

Collecting American naval firearms and edged weapons, especially those of the Civil War, never lacked for devotees; their monetary values certainly kept pace with commensurate increases in all historic American arms. However, it has been a source of puzzlement why collectors of naval weapons have been so few in number as compared to those who prize Army-issue weapons. Despite all the scholarship devoted to the Civil War era and Civil War weapons, there is a very noticeable difference between the vast amount of published literature about arms made for and issued to various branches of the U.S. Army and works on naval arms, which are few and far between. Attributing the disparity to the metaphoric "which came first, the chicken or the egg" (in this case, should there first have been good reference books to stimulate collecting naval arms) is likely an oversimplification. The culprit very likely is the fact that the majority of naval arms do not bear easily identifiable "U.S.N." or "U.S.M.C." markings, for they certainly do not lack for important historical associations nor physical attributes.

Although a few arms were made specifically for the Navy and were so marked (such as the Jenks carbines and rifles, the Ames Model 1843 percussion pistol and various cutlasses) the vast majority were the same as those in service for the Army and were often procured through identical sources. It was not until August of 1864 that the Navy Bureau of Ordnance actually issued instructions detailing how inspector markings were to be applied to various arms. And judging from specimens viewed, there is a strong suspicion that those instructions may not have been followed to the letter.

Important developments and innovations in naval weapons introduced in the 1850s have been thoroughly covered in this new book. The author's well-documented account of their use by Marines and Naval forces in various foreign expeditions and actions in the decade preceding the Civil War causes them to be viewed with far greater respect than formerly. The role of that earlier period was highly significant to naval weapons. This era is discussed at far greater length than the book's title implies, much to the credit of the author.

The author has meticulously assembled a wide range of data, much never previously published, convincingly documenting actual shipboard use of a very wide variety of weapons. Collectors will possibly be surprised, if not delighted, to learn about the many arms not formerly thought to have been in use on American warships or in naval inventories. The British flintlock "Brown Bess" and later percussion Enfield muskets as well as the Remington Maynard conversion muskets are excellent examples of such firearms. Arms historians and collectors alike will find that the author's method of coupling the story of naval weapons procurement and issuance along with a chronological account of naval engagements 1850–1865 tends to lend added relevance to the subject. Especially intriguing are those lesser-known encounters in foreign waters where American Marines and sailors were deployed. The naming of the U.S. vessels involved with detailed listings of the varied type, make and model firearms, cutlasses, boarding pikes and battle axes in each of their respective arms lockers lends a new dimension to the manner in which naval arms are viewed and collected — one certain to heighten their interest.

Civil War Small Arms of the U.S. Navy and Marine Corps is the singularly most important book yet written on the subject. Its influence in the world of collecting American arms is certain to be felt in these coming years, as it assumes its rightful position as the cornerstone for understanding this subject. The author and this book have made a major contribution to the lore of American historical weaponry.

- *Staff Arms Consultant to Springfield Armory Museum by Appointment U.S. Army Corps of Ordnance*
- *Arms Consultant to the Marine Corps. Historical Center, Washington, D.C., by U.S. Marine Corps appointment*
- *Member, Board of Overseers of U.S.S. Constitution Museum, Navy Yard, Boston*

Introduction

In undertaking this project, it was my intent to give the reader an overview of the small arms associated with the Navy and Marine Corps for the period 1851–1865. The concept of each chapter is to discuss the procurement, small arms aboard ships and in military service for both branches of service.

The period of 1851–1865 was chosen because, at the beginning of the period, both services were completing the transition from flint to percussion. The close of the Civil War in 1865 was a convenient and logical place to conclude this study. The story is told by time frames to give the reader a better understanding of the impact that the various arms had on Naval and Marine military operations. The first two chapters give the story of the decade of the 1850s. In the first chapter, the reader will learn about Perry's trip to Japan as well as the Marine detachment assigned to the frigate "Old Ironsides" *Constitution* on her voyage from December 1852 to June 1855. The second half of the decade was a period of forced modernization for both services. The reader will find the small arms inventory for the Navy as of December 1858 and the Marine procurement of the M1855 rifle musket in 1860. Throughout the book, the Marines' story is interwoven with the Navy's since most of their operations were in support of the naval forces. An exception was the Battle of Manassas in July 1861, when the Marine battalion was attached to the Army.

Each of the Civil War years is presented in a separate chapter. Just a few of the events that the reader will encounter are the Marines with DuPont in 1861, the yearly procurement of NCO swords and accouterments obtained for the Marines, the serial numbers for Sharps & Hankins rifles received at Washington in 1862 and Whitney revolvers received in 1864, the Spencer rifles sent to the Mississippi Squadron in 1863 plus a few serial numbers for Army Spencer rifles obtained in the fall of 1863. The stories of the *Monitor* and *Merrimack*, Mobile Bay and Fort Fisher are also covered. The last chapter covers the partial list of small arms on board nearly 400 vessels during the war. A similar chart for the 1850s can be found at the end of the second chapter.

Each chapter starts with the theme of the chapter followed by other areas of overall interest. The second part of each chapter covers procurement and military operations. In this section, the text is divided into four parts: Muzzleloaders; Breechloaders; Pistols/Revolvers; and Edged Weapons. These categories are further divided by type of small arms.

It is my hope that the reader will come away with a better appreciation for the small arms used by sailors and Marines during this critical period in our nation's military history.

John D. McAulay

Acknowledgments

I am greatly indebted to the following individuals and organizations for making this book a reality:

Mr. Steve Selenfriend for his great assistance in making available his large collection of naval documents and books plus photos from his collection; Mr. Rick Peuser of the Navy Branch, National Archives, for his considerable help in locating vast amounts of naval records stored at the Archives including the 150 ship's daily logs — one being the original log of the 1852–1855 cruise of the USS *Constitution*; Mr. Jerry Rinker for use of the sailor photos from his collection; Mr. Peter Schmidt for his photos on the Hall rifle and Hall M1833 carbine; Mr. Hubert Lum for photos of the Navy Perry carbine; Mr. Jim Stamatelos for allowing his collection of Marine Corps accouterments and NCO sword to be photographed for the book, Mr. Paul Johnson for photos of his Remington/Maynard musket; Mr. David Sullivan for his suggestions on locating Marine Corps data; Mr. Kenneth Smith-Christmas, Curator of Material History Marine Corps Museum, Quantico, Virginia, for his help in the Civil War procurement of Marine accouterments and the photo of the museum's Navy Spencer rifle; Mr. Jack McCormick for the photo of the Marine detachment at the Brooklyn Navy Yard; Mr. Will Gorges for the photo of his M1852 Officer's sword and thanks to Mr. Jack Weiser of Time-Life Books for allowing the use of photos taken by Mr. Larry Sherer in *Echoes of Glory: Arms & Equipment of the Union*; Gettysburg National Military Park for the photo of the M1842 Musket with rear sight; photos were also obtained from the U.S. Military Academy, U.S. Naval Academy, Smithsonian Institution, U.S. Military History Institute; Library of Congress and the National Archives; the photo section of the Naval Historical Center at the Washington Navy Yard was most helpful in providing assistance in obtaining photos from their collection; Mr. Mike O'Donnell for his photos of items from the author's collection; special thanks to my sister, Mrs. Jill Hedley, for typing and reviewing the manuscript; and Mr. Norm Flayderman for his kindness in providing the foreword.

TABLE OF CONTENTS

Part One • The 1850s

Chapter 1 Land of the Rising Sun, 1851–1855

- Perry's Trip to Japan, 1853–1854 13
- Navy Yard Small Arms Inventories 18
- Ringgold-Rogers Expedition 20
- Procurement and Sea Service 21
    - Muzzleloaders 21
        - Navy 21
        - Marine 23
    - Breechloaders 24
        - Hall Rifles and Carbines 24
        - Jenks Carbines 25
    - Pistols/Revolvers 28
        - Single-Shot Pistols 28
        - Colt Revolvers 30
    - Edged Weapons 31
        - M1852 Naval Officer's Swords 31
        - Battle Axes 32

Chapter 2 Drifting Towards War, 1856–1860

- John Brown's Raid on Harpers Ferry 33
- Navy 1858 Small Arms Inventory 34
- Procurement and Sea Service 34
    - Muzzleloaders 34
        - Prewar Plymouth Rifles 34
        - Navy and Marine Corps Alterations (Rifled Muskets), 1856 ... 38
        - 1857–1858 40
        - 1859–1860 43
        - Marine Corps 43
        - Model 1855 Rifle Musket 44
    - Breechloaders 45
        - Jenks Carbines 45
        - Perry Carbines 46
        - Sharps Carbines and Rifles 47
        - Other Breechloaders, 1859–1860 49
    - Revolvers 50
        - M1851 Colt Revolvers, 1856–1858 50
        - Paraguay Expedition 51
        - 1859–1860 52
        - North-Savage Revolvers 53
    - Edged Weapons 54
        - Marine Corps Swords and Accouterments 54
- Small Arms Inventory, 1851–1860 55

Part Two • The Civil War Years

Chapter 3 Forming the Blockade, 1861

- Vessels Outfitting for Sea April 1861 59
- Running the Blockade 60
- Marines at Bull Run 62
    - July 21, 1861 62
- Union Defense Committee 62
    - New York 62
- 1861 Procurement and Sea Service 65
    - Muzzleloaders 65
        - Navy Muskets and Plymouth Rifles 65
        - Marine Corps Muzzleloaders 66
        - Port Royal Operations 66
        - Sea Duty 68
        - Amphibious Operations, 1861 69

- Breechloaders ... 69
    - Jenks Carbines ... 69
    - Joslyn Rifles ... 71
    - Sharps & Hankins Rifles and Spencer Rifles ... 71
    - NM1859 Sharps Rifles ... 71
    - John Mitchell's Sharps Rifle Contract ... 72
- Pistols/Revolvers ... 73
    - Single-Shot Pistols ... 73
    - Colt Revolvers M1860 ... 74
    - New Model 1861 ... 74
    - Galveston Raid, November 17, 1861 ... 74
    - Joslyn Revolvers ... 76
    - North-Savage Revolvers ... 76
    - Starr Revolvers ... 76
- Edged Weapons ... 78
    - Model 1861 Ames Naval Cutlass ... 78
    - Marine Corps Swords and Accouterments ... 79
    - Battle Axes and Boarding Pikes ... 81
    - Dahlgren Bowie Knives and Saber Bayonets ... 81
    - Saber Bayonets for Mitchell's Sharps Rifles ... 82

Chapter 4 The Clash of the Ironclads, 1862

Monitor vs. *Merrimack* ... 83
Clash with CSS Ram *Arkansas*, July 15, 1862 ... 85
Porter's Mortar Squadron ... 85
  Ordnance for the South Atlantic Blockading Squadron ... 87
1862 Procurement and Sea Service ... 87
- Muzzleloaders ... 87
    - Navy ... 87
    - Marine Corps ... 88
    - Plymouth Rifles ... 89
    - Enfield Rifles ... 90
- Breechloaders ... 91
    - Sharps Rifles ... 91
    - Spencer Rifles ... 92
    - Sharps & Hankins Rifles and Carbines ... 92
- Pistols/Revolvers ... 93
    - Colt Revolvers ... 93
    - Remington Revolvers ... 94
    - Pistols at Sea ... 95
- Edged Weapons ... 98
    - Marine Corps Swords and Accouterments ... 98
    - Boarding Pikes ... 98
    - Model 1861 Ames Cutlasses ... 99

Chapter 5 Opening the Mississippi, 1863

Small Arms for the Mississippi Squadron ... 101
Spencer Rifles for the Mississippi Squadron ... 103
Capture of USS *Satellite* and CSS *Atlanta* ... 105
Mare Island ... 106
1863 Procurements and Field Service ... 106
- Muzzleloaders ... 107
    - Marine Corps ... 107
    - Plymouth Rifles ... 107
- Breechloaders ... 109
    - First Model Maynard Carbines ... 109
    - Sharps Rifles and Carbines ... 109
    - Sharps & Hankins Carbines ... 110
    - Spencer Rifles ... 113
    - Spencer Army Rifle Inspection Report ... 114
- Edged Weapons ... 115
    - Bowie Knives and Ames Cutlasses ... 115
    - Marine Corps Accouterments and Swords ... 115

TABLE OF CONTENTS *(Continued)*

        Revolvers 117
            Colts 117
            Remington 118
            Whitney 119

Chapter 6 — Mobile Bay, 1864

August 5th Action, Mobile Bay 121
Albemarle Raid 123
Issues of Small Arms to Vessels 124
Table of Allowance, Changes For 1864 126
Accouterments 126
        Navy 126
        Marine Corps 128
Small Arms Inspections 128
1864 Procurements and Field Service 129
        Muzzleloaders 129
            Navy 129
            Capture of CSA Muzzleloaders 130
            Marine Corps 130
            Enfield Rifles 132
            Act of Treason 132
            Plymouth Rifles 133
            Tulifinny Crossroads, December 9 134
        Breechloaders 134
            Sharps Carbines and Rifles 134
            Small Arms of the USS *Kearsarge* 135
            Sharps & Hankins 135
            Smith Carbines 137
            Spencer Rifles 138
            Favorable Reports 138
            Unfavorable Reports 138
        Revolvers 140
            Remington 140
            Marine Corps Sentry Revolvers 140
            Whitney 140
        Edged Weapons 142
            Ames Cutlasses and Bowie Knives 142
            Marine Corps NCO and Musician Swords 142

Chapter 7 — Fort Fisher, January 15, 1865

Capture of Fort Fisher 143
1865 Procurements and Sea Service 146
        Muzzleloaders 146
            Marine Corps Muzzleloaders and Accouterments 147
        Breechloaders 150
            Sharps & Hankins 150
            Lincoln in Richmond 151
            Marine Corps Sharps & Hankins 151
            Sharps & Hankins Cartridges 152
            Spencer Rifles 152
        Revolvers 152
            Remington and Whitney 152
        Edged Weapons 153
        Decommissioning of Vessels 154
        Weekly Returns of Ordnance Stores (December 1, 1866) 158

Chapter 8 — Small Arms Inventories, 1861–1865

Record Group #24: List of Logbooks of U.S. Navy Ships and Miscellaneous Units, 1801–1947 ... 161
Ship Inventory for Nearly 400 Vessels 164

Endnotes 173
Bibliography 177
Index 179

Part *One*

The 1850s

Chapter 1
Land of the Rising Sun, 1851–1855

Perry's Trip to Japan, 1853–1854

The goal of the United States for many years was to establish open trade markets with countries in the Far East, especially with the closed society of Japan. In 1852, Matthew C. Perry received command of the East India Squadron. Included in this territory was Japan. Perry's orders were to deliver a letter from the President of the United States to the Emperor of Japan. The president's letter would request that the Japanese treat our shipwrecked sailors and Marines with care, allow United States vessels to obtain provisions and supplies from their ports, and establish a free trade policy with the United States.

In preparation for his trip, Perry wrote to the Secretary of the Navy on March 27, 1852, for permission to take government stores as gifts. He would request small arms no longer of practical naval use, but highly valuable as presents for foreign military authorities. Perry asked for the following small arms from the New York Navy Yard: 48 Hall carbines — percussion, 48 Hall carbines — flint and bayonets, 92 Jenks carbines — percussion with bayonets (long), and 5 Bowie knife pistols percussion.[1] The flintlock Halls were actually Hall rifles. The Jenks carbines were the 30-inch barrel rifles, while the Bowie knife pistols were the Elgin Cutlass pistols delivered to the Navy in the late 1830s. While Perry requested these arms, it appears he did not take them, but instead took ordnance stores provided by the Army.

Lieutenant Bent in the *Mississippi's* first cutter, forcing his way through a fleet of Japanese boats while surveying the Bay of Yedo (Tokyo), Japan, July 11, 1853. Bent's men were armed with muskets, pistols and cutlasses, plus every other sailor was also issued a pike.
Perry Order #8.
(Illustration by W.T. Heine, U.S. Naval Historical Center)

Engraving of the side-wheel frigate *Susquehanna* riding out a gale. The *Susquehanna* was one of Perry's ships to travel to Japan in 1853. (U.S. Naval Historical Center)

The Army stores included:

Army Ordnance Stores[2]
Issued to USS *Mississippi*
April 1852

From New York Arsenal
40 Hall rifles with 4,000 cartridges
20 Percussion pistols and
2,000 cartridges

From Watervliet Arsenal
20 Artillery swords

From Frankford Arsenal
20 Muskets with Dr. Maynard percussion locks

From Washington Arsenal
40 Light cavalry sabers
60 Strips of Maynard primers

Perry's flagship, the side-wheel frigate *Mississippi*. (USAMHI)

Chapter 1 • Land of the Rising Sun, 1851–1855

On June 16, Commodore Charles Morris, Chief of Ordnance and Hydrography, contracted Samuel Colt for 100 of his revolvers for Perry's trip. By July 10, the 100 revolvers were received on board the frigate *Mississippi*.³

Perry left the States on November 24, 1852, for the Far East, arriving at Hong Kong on April 6, 1853.⁴ The balance of his squadron, the frigate *Susquehanna* and sloops *Plymouth* and *Saratoga* were already on station in the area when Perry arrived in the *Mississippi*. Upon Perry's arrival, he found the *Susquehanna* on station at Shanghai, China, watching over American merchants and missionaries. At this time, China was in the midst of civil war. To protect the Americans, the *Susquehanna* delivered to the American Episcopal Mission four carbines and 50 rounds of ammunition for their defense. Twelve carbines were sent to the House of Russel & Co. and six muskets to the American Volunteer Company at the American Consulate. The ship's Marine orderly sergeant was sent ashore to drill the company of volunteers. The carbines delivered were the Jenks, while the muskets were altered smoothbore percussion. In August, the frigate *Powhatan* sent to the American Consulate at Hong Kong for their defense 25 muskets and a number of single-shot pistols.⁵

As of April 1853, the *Susquehanna* had been on station for nearly two years. With harsh discipline aboard ship, the crew's morale was extremely low. Before returning to the states in early 1855, several of the crew were court-martialed for a variety of causes. One incident occurred while at Shanghai on April 24, 1853. Fourteen men were given shore leave, including forty-year-old Marine Sergeant Bernard Doriss of West Chester, Pennsylvania. Sergeant Doriss was acting as Master of Arms for the ship on this cruise. One of his fellow Marines, holding a grudge against the sergeant, came up behind him on a narrow Shanghai street and hit him over the head with a beer bottle. He then proceeded to kick him and throw stones at the

Commodore Perry meeting the imperial commissioners at Yokohama, Japan. *(Illustration by W.T. Peters, U.S. Naval Historical Center)*

The deliveries of American gifts at Yokohama, Japan, in March 1854. Note the Marine sentry. The Marine detachment was armed with .69 caliber altered smoothbore muskets.
(Illustration by W.T. Heine, U.S. Naval Historical Center)

sergeant's face and head and left him for dead. Sergeant Doriss was found by other members of the crew and taken to the ship. He recovered from his wounds, but was unable to perform his duties sufficiently. Sergeant Doriss was sent to the United States Navy Hospital at Macao, China, for further tests. The attacker involved in this incident was court-martialed and discharged from the service.[6]

Perry took his squadron to Naha, Okinawa, in May 1853 to establish a temporary base of operations for his trip to Japan. The deck logs of the fleet for their stay in Okinawa showed a daily exercise with small arms and with the ship's cannons. The Marines were also receiving drill on shore while at Okinawa. On June 11 and June 16, at 5:30 a.m., the Marine guard of the *Mississippi* spent two hours on shore at drill.[7] A large quantity of the ordnance stores brought from the States aboard the *Mississippi* were distributed to the other ships. The *Saratoga* received in this matter 10 muskets with bayonets and cartridge boxes, 10 cutlasses with scabbards, 10 boarding pikes, 10 pistols with belts and frogs, plus a quantity of ammunition. Delivered to *Susquehanna* were nearly half of the 100 Colt revolvers, 20 pistols,

The American squadron in Shimoda.
(Illustration from The Journal of John Glendy, Sproston, U.S.N., *Library of Congress)*

20 Hall rifles and 20 muskets. The *Susquehanna* in turn would send five of the Colts to the *Plymouth* upon arriving in Japan. The revolvers were intended for the use of the *Plymouth's* officers.

Finally, on July 2, the fleet set sail for Japan and, on the tenth of the month, arrived at what is now Tokyo Bay. Perry's order number eight of April 14, 1853, stipulated that each sailor assigned to boats going ashore be armed with a musket, pistol and cutlass, and that every other sailor also be issued a pike. Each individual was also issued a musket and pistol cartridge box.[8] On Thursday, July 14, at about 9:00 a.m., Perry went on shore to meet with authorities sent by the Emperor. His force consisted of about 250 sailors and Marines. The flagship *Mississippi* sent its first and second cutter and barge containing 52 sailors, 10 bandsmen and 54 Marines as part of the American presence. After presenting the letter from President Fillmore, Perry stated that he would return in the spring for an answer. He returned to his ships at about 11:30 a.m. One side note to this date: the deck log of the *Susquehanna* reflects that its crew on this day consumed 220 pounds of beef and bread, 450 gallons of water, and 4 gallons of whiskey.[9]

The American fleet left Japan and returned to Okinawa and Hong Kong. From Hong Kong, a detachment of Marines from the *Mississippi* was sent to Canton, China, to guard the U.S. store ship *Supply*. In September, Major Jacob Zeilin, ranking Marine Corps officer of the squadron, was sent with 23 Marines from the *Susquehanna* to relieve the Marines from the *Mississippi*. Zeilin took with him a field piece with ammunition.[10]

The Americans returned to Japan in February 1854. The parties agreed to hold talks at Yokohama. While off the coast of Yokohama, the frigate *Powhatan* received a large quantity of ordnance stores from the *Susquehanna*.

The flintlock Hall rifles presented to the Japanese as gifts were from the New York Arsenal. The arsenal had delivered 40 Hall rifles with 4,000 cartridges to Perry's flagship *Mississippi* in April 1852.

Transfer of Ordnance Stores[11]
from *Susquehanna* to *Powhatan*
March 3, 1854

19 Colt Revolvers — Army	1 Box of Muskets w/Maynard Locks (20)
32 Colt Revolvers — Navy	2 Boxes of Hall Rifles (39)
6 Colt Revolvers — Small	1 Box of Cavalry Sabers (49)
1 Box of Army Pistols (19)	1 Box of Artillery Swords (17)
4 Boxes of Rifle Cartridges	2 Boxes of Pistol Cartridges
5,000 Percussion Caps	

From the above ordnance stores, Perry would draw his gifts for the Japanese authorities. At 10:00 a.m. on the morning of March 12, Captain Abbott, with an escort of several boats and a detachment of Marines from the *Powhatan*, landed with gifts for the Emperor of Japan and other Japanese individuals.[12] The box of gifts for the emperor was stamped "EMPEROR". The small arms presented were:

Emperor	To Other Individuals
5 Hall Rifles	10 Hall Rifles
3 Maynard Muskets	—
12 Cavalry Sabers	11 Cavalry Sabers
6 Artillery Swords	—
1 Carbine	3 Carbines, Cartridge Boxes and Belts, 180 Cartridges
20 Army Pistols	1 Box Containing 11 Pistols

After the signing of the treaty on March 31, Perry and his squadron

The small arms presented to the Japanese were delivered on shore from the side-wheel frigate *Powhatan*. (U.S. Naval Historical Center)

toured other areas of Japan to show the flag. The Japanese dignitaries were presented gifts at several of these stops. These gifts, like the previous gifts, were taken from the *Powhatan*. These gifts consisted of 8 Hall rifles, 4 Colt revolvers, 3 pistols and 5 cavalry sabers. Later in the year, Perry sailed back to the States to a hero's return.

The sloop *Plymouth* returned to Shanghai after the signing of the treaty. On the evening of April 3, 1854, the *Plymouth* was at anchor in the harbor. In the evening, she observed signals of "Want of Assistance" coming from the British and American consulates. The *Plymouth* landed 60 men armed with muskets and bayonets under the command of Navy Lieutenant Guest. Finding the area surrounded by Chinese imperial troops, the lieutenant and eleven men were posted at the American consulate while the remainder returned to the ship. At one o'clock the next morning, the decision was made to send in a combined British/American force to drive the imperial force away from the foreign settlements. The American force of sailors and Marines from the *Plymouth* was led by her Captain, Commander John Kelly. In the skirmishes that drove the Chinese away from the two consulates, ordinary seaman George McCorkle was killed and two Marines wounded. To protect the consulates, 35 men were stationed there, while at the U.S. Mission, an additional eleven men were posted.[13] A year later, the *Powhatan* would repeat this action all over again.

Navy Yard Small Arms Inventories

During this period, a number of reports were submitted by the various Navy yards on small arm inventories. The first report reflects a partial listing of small arms on hand at New York.

Small Arms Inventory[14]
October 21, 1852
New York Navy Yard

Flintlock Muskets

Lockplate	Quantities	Manufacturer
1826–1827	34	M.T. Wickham, Philadelphia
1837	34	Eli Whitney
1838	18	Springfield
1827–1831	8	Harpers Ferry

Flintlock Pistols

1827–1831	1,087	Valley Forge and S. North

Carbines

	48	Hall Carbines

A year later, New York received authorization to sell these obsolete small arms:

Ordnance Authorized for Sale[15]
New York Navy Yard
August 1853

73	Flintlock Tower Muskets w/Bayonets	4	Flintlock Rifles returned from Franklin Expedition
135	Flintlock U.S. Muskets w/Bayonets	2	Brass Flintlock Blunderbusses
104	Flintlock U.S. Pistols	4	Iron Flintlock Blunderbusses
6	Pistols w/Knives	20	Old Style Bayonets

The next chart is interesting as it shows what was in inventory at Norfolk in 1852 and again in 1854:

Small Arms Inventory[16]
Norfolk Navy Yard

	1852	1854
Muskets — Brown	118	—
— Bright	511	415
— Flintlock	174	144
Jenks — Improved	290	289
— Short	749	605
— Long	315	254
Halls — Short	35	15
— Long	2	1
Pistols — Bright	701	533
— Brown	107	91
— Short	48	—
— Flintlock	73	—
— Revolvers (Colts)	5	4
Swords — Ames-Pattern	122	122
— Roman	300	300
— Cutlasses	—	10
Boarding Pikes	—	48
Battle Axes — Old	—	592
— New	—	88

The last chart is from the Washington Navy Yard. Note the interesting types of rifles shown:

Small Arms in Serviceable Condition[17]
Washington Navy Yard
July 20, 1852

Muskets — Percussion	40	dated 1844 and 1845
— Flintlocks	45	dated 1810 and 1812
— Self Priming	1	dated 1818
Carbines — Jenks	84	dated 1845

Rifles and Shooters

Hall Patent Rifles to load at the breech	1
Ketland & Co. Five Shooters of different patents	2
Henry Rifle	1
Cooper Rifle	1

On March 24, 1853, sixty Model 1851 Sharps carbines along with 40,066 Maynard tape primers were received on board the sloop *Vincennes* at the Brooklyn Navy Yard. *(Steve Selenfriend collection)*

U.S. Arsenal Harpers Ferry dated 1804 and 1809		2
Colt Six Shooters		2
Pistols — Percussion	115	dated 1844, 1845 and 1849
— Flintlock	25	dated 1827
— Colt	1	
Cutlass — Roman	147	
— Curved	26	
— Straight	1	
Battle Axes	106	
Boarding Pikes	135	
Spare Bayonets	23	

Ringgold-Rodgers Expedition

In the fall of 1852, Commander Ringgold started organizing his survey expedition to the China Seas. He placed the following request on October 11, 1852, with the Chief of Bureau of Ordnance:

Ordnance Stores Requested[18]
Ringgold China Sea Expedition

60 Sharps Carbines Rifles	150 Stands of Ships Carbines
60 Marston Carbine Rifles	150 Stands of Ships Pistols
60 Marston Medium Pistols*	250 Navy Swords
3 Fowling Pieces	

*Colt revolvers were substituted for the Marston pistols.

The flag ship for the Ringgold expedition was the eighteen-gun sloop *Vincennes*. During the spring of 1853, she was being outfitted for the voyage from the Brooklyn Navy Yard. Six boxes of Sharps rifles, one box of fixtures, and 40,066 Maynard primers were delivered to the *Vincennes* on March 24. Two weeks later, on April 9, 30 five-inch barrel pistols and 20 six-inch barrel pistols plus 50 powder flasks and 44 pistol belts were brought on board.[19]

The 60 Sharps rifles were actually Sharps carbine M1851 with the Maynard tape primer system. They are stamped on the buttplate "USN". The pistols delivered were of the .31 caliber M1849 Colt revolvers. Prior to sailing, ten of the Sharps carbines were sent from the *Vincennes* to the storeship *John P. Kennedy* and one each to the steamer *John Hancock* and *Porpoise*. Later in Hong Kong, six Sharps were sent by the *Vincennes* to the *Fenimore Cooper* and six Colts to the *Porpoise*.[20]

The Marine detachments assigned to the expedition were armed with the altered smoothbore muskets.

Marine Guard Detachments[21]
Ringgold Expedition
July 1853

	Vincennes	*Porpoise*	*John Hancock*
2nd Lieutenant	1	—	—
Sergeants	2	—	—
Corporals	2	2	2
Drummer	1	—	—
Fife	1	—	—
Privates	<u>20</u>	<u>10</u>	<u>10</u>
Total	**27**	**12**	**12**

Chapter 1 • Land of the Rising Sun, 1851–1855

Ringgold proceeded to arrive on station as part of Perry's East India Squadron at Hong Kong. In 1854, Ringgold's ships would be part of Perry's fleet that went to Japan. While at Hong Kong, Lieutenant Rodgers replaced Ringgold. In December, while on station, the *Vincennes* arrived at Napa Kiang Roads, Island of Loo Choo. Here, a little after noon on the 12th of the month, along with the 1st, 2nd and 3rd divisions of sailors from the *Vincennes*, the Marine guard went ashore. The sailors were armed with Sharps & Jenks carbines and Colt revolvers. They also brought a twelve-pound howitzer with them. The Americans proceeded to the palace, which they completely surrounded. Lieutenant Rodgers went inside for discussion with the local authorities regarding infractions of the treaty by the locals. Being assured of their future compliance with the treaty, the Americans returned to the *Vincennes*. To show his goodwill, Rodgers gave as gifts to the local authorities two carbines, two Colt revolvers along with two cartridge boxes and a small quantity of ammunition.[22] The expedition would continue on to the Bering Strait and the Aleutian Islands before returning in 1855.

One of the Model 1851 Sharps carbines delivered to the *Vincennes* is stamped "U★S★N" on the buttplate and serial numbered 371.
(Steve Selenfriend collection)

Procurements and Sea Service

MUZZLELOADERS

Navy

By the late 1840s, the Navy had started to convert, from flint to percussion, all of their muskets aboard ship. These altered .69 caliber smoothbore percussion muskets are the cone-in-barrel conversions. The USS *Flint* at Norfolk in March 1851 had 32 flintlock pistols and 165 flintlock muskets condemned. By early 1852, the forty-four gun frigate *Savannah* had replaced all her flintlock muskets with the altered percussion muskets.[23] In April 1853, the steamer *Massachusetts* turned in 55 flintlock pistols, 26 flintlock muskets, and 3 Jenks carbines. As late as November 1855, the

On April 9, 1853, the *Vincennes* received on board 30 Model 1849 Colt revolvers with five-inch barrels and 20 Model 1849 Colts with six-inch barrels. Shown is a six-inch barrel Colt Model 1849 revolver of the type delivered to the *Vincennes*.
(Steve Selenfriend collection)

receiving ship *North Carolina* at the New York Navy Yard still had 40 flintlock pistols and muskets on board for general service use. In 1852, the Norfolk Navy Yard had notified the Bureau of Ordnance that they had kept 150 flintlock muskets on hand for general use but sold all excess flintlock muskets. This practice had been ongoing since 1849.[24]

In late 1851, three vessels were being outfitted for sea at Boston. Each ship was issued the altered percussion muskets, single-shot pistols, and Jenks carbines. The ammunition received was:

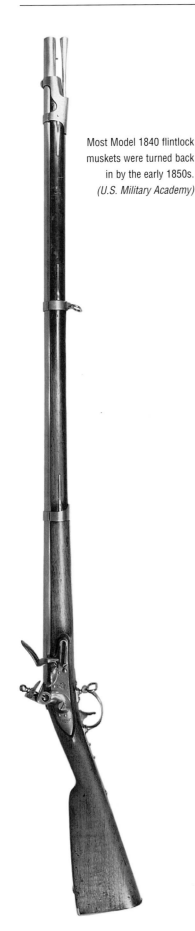

Most Model 1840 flintlock muskets were turned back in by the early 1850s. *(U.S. Military Academy)*

Ship Ammunition Request[25]
October–December 1851
Boston Navy Yard

	USS *Portsmouth*	USS *Princeton*	USS *Cumberland*
Musket Ball Cartridges	4,000	3,000	6,000
Percussion Caps	25,000	18,900	37,800
Carbine Ball Cartridges	2,600	3,750	4,000
Pistol Ball Cartridges	3,000	2,240	5,000

With the conversion to percussion arms, a large quantity of flintlock small arms were placed in storage. On November 4, 1852, the Navy contacted the Ordnance Department to request permission to send their flintlocks to the Watertown Arsenal for conversion to percussion. Permission was granted and the first 250 muskets, 50 carbines (actually Hall rifles), and 1,200 pistols were sent from Boston Navy Yard by December.[26] Additional arms were sent for conversion, and by April 1853, Major Edward Harding, commanding officer at the arsenal, could report that 6,027 muskets, rifles and pistols belonging to the Navy had been altered to percussion.[27] Also in 1852, the Army sent to the Naval Academy two hundred cadet muskets with brown barrels. These cadet muskets had been supplied from the Watervliet Arsenal.[28]

The altered smoothbore muskets were aboard the frigate *Columbia* in January 1855. While at sea, the *Columbia* exercised the crew in musket practice. In the two-day exercise, 634 rounds were fired at a 24-inch square target at 48 yards. Only one in four shots hit the target and only three pierced the "ball eye." Each member of the crew fired two rounds each with Private Henry L. Braun of the Marine guard having the best shots. The results of the firing:

Musket Practice[29]
USS *Columbia*
January 11–12, 1855

Ship's Crew	Shots Fired	Hits
1st Division	124	31
2nd Division	142	27
3rd Division	122	22
4th Division	64	13
5th Division	62	19
Master Division	38	18
Marine Guard	82	26
Total	**634**	**156**

In August 1855, halfway around the world near Hong Kong, the sailors and Marines of the frigate *Powhatan* saw action. A combined American/British force attacked the pirate stronghold at Ty-Ho Bay on August 4. In the all-day action, they captured many pirates and 17 junks. One of the largest junks was destroyed by the pirates. In the fight, three American sailors, James A. Halsey, Isaac Coes and John Pepper, were killed and seven wounded. The Marine casualties included privates Samuel Mullards and B. Adamson, who were both mortally wounded. When the naval force returned to the *Powhatan*, an inventory listed 17 muskets, 2 carbines, 2 cutlasses, 3 ramrods, 7 cartridge boxes, and 8 belts lost in the fight with the pirates.[30]

Marine Corps Muzzleloaders

At the start of 1851, the Marine Corps' authorized strength was about 1,200 officers and men. As of September 1852, over 750 or 60 percent of the Corps' total strength was aboard 28 ships.[31] In December 1852, Lieutenant Charles Henderson was ordered to proceed to New York and take command of the Marine guard detachment assigned to the frigate *Constitution*. "Old Ironsides" was to be the flagship for the African Squadron.

Marine Guard Detachment
USS *Constitution*
December 1852

Deployment Locations	Lieutenants	Sergeants	Corporals	Privates	Musicians
Headquarters	1	0	3	30	2
Philadelphia	0	1	0	0	0
New York	0	2	0	10	0
Total	**1**	**3**	**3**	**40**	**2**

One of the sergeants from New York, James Darey, had been recently promoted from private to sergeant. On the day the Marines reported aboard December 22, 1852, the ship was placed in commission by Commander John Rudd. In addition to the Marine guard, the crew consisted of 14 officers, 64 seamen, 110 ordinary seamen, 66 landsmen and 32 boys. The sailors were from the receiving ship *North Carolina*.

On this voyage, "Old Ironsides" was at sea for nearly two-and-one-half years before returning to the States in June 1855. On the voyage, the Marine guard was exercised with their .69 caliber altered percussion muskets both at sea and on land. While at the Bay of Porto Grande, Island of St. Vincent, on January 27, 1854, the Marine guard, howitzer crew, 74 small arms men, and 40 riflemen went ashore for target practice. Six months later, at the same location, the Marines again went on shore to drill. The *Constitution*

USS *Constitution* "Old Ironsides" off Philadelphia in 1876. The Marine detachment on her last military voyage of 1852–1855 consisted of one officer, three sergeants, three corporals, two musicians, and forty privates. The detachment was armed with the altered .69 caliber smoothbore cone-in-barrel muskets.
(U.S. Naval Historical Center)

At the beginning of the period, both branches of service were mainly armed with the .69 caliber smoothbore altered cone-in-barrel conversion muskets. (U.S. Military Academy)

returned to the Portsmouth Navy Yard in June 1855 and was placed out of commission on June 14. Sometime after 4:00 p.m. on this date, the Marine guard left the ship for the Marine barracks at Portsmouth.[32]

The Marine guard detachment at the beginning of this period was armed with the .69 caliber smoothbore percussion cone-in-barrel musket. In April 1851, the Corps received 1,000 of these altered muskets from the Washington Arsenal. The first of the new Model 1842 percussion muskets were delivered to the Marines in October 1853.[33]

In 1853, sailors and Marines of the flagship *Albany* were both armed with the altered percussion muskets. The Marines were armed with 21

The Marines received their initial delivery of 1,000 Model 1842 percussion smoothbore .69 caliber muskets in October 1853. (U.S. Military Academy)

muskets, and the sailors were issued 60. They found that the percussion caps would not ignite the paper cartridge without difficulty. It took the Marines 41 percussion caps to set off 34 cartridges, while 94 percussion caps were needed by the ship's crew to ignite 42 cartridges. After a close inspection of the muskets, it was found that the vents of the muskets were covered with lacquer. After the nipples were cleaned, the muskets worked just fine.[34]

In 1855, the Marine detachment on the *Powhatan* consisted of about 45 men. As of March, the ship was on station at Shanghai, China. Desertion was a problem aboard all ships. On March 31, Boatswain William Whiting and 12 men from the *Powhatan* went on shore to apprehend several deserters. A Marine, in the attempt to break down a door with the butt of his musket, had it accidentally discharge. The bullet from the musket struck and killed Whiting, who was buried with full military honors at the European burial grounds in Shanghai. At sea, the Marines were also used as a burial detail. On August 6, 1855, at 10:00 a.m. aboard the frigate *Congress*, the body of ordinary seaman John Rodgers was committed to the deep. The remains were received on deck by the corporal of the guard. The order to present arms was given, and after three rolls of the drum, a final three shots were fired over the body. The Marines, at this time, were armed on the *Congress* with the Model 1842 musket.[35]

BREECHLOADERS

Hall Rifles and Carbines

Between September 1827 and July 1828, the Navy had taken delivery of 1,041 flintlock Hall rifles.[36] These rifles have the barrel bands held in place by the conventional band springs. The breechblock is marked with an 1824 date. By the 1850s, these old flintlock Halls were well past their service life. To make them more acceptable for naval service, 48 Hall rifles were sent from Boston in December 1852 to Watertown Arsenal for alteration to percussion. They were in such poor condition that they were returned and

Five hundred Model 1833 Hall carbines were delivered to the Navy in September of 1841. *(Peter A. Schmidt collection)*

sold at auction.[37] In June 1852, Dahlgren at the Washington Navy Yard had six Hall rifles converted to take the standard nipples at a cost of 90 cents each.[38] It is probable that some Halls were converted to percussion, since the Watertown Arsenal totals include alterations of rifles for the Navy. (For the Halls with Perry, see the earlier section on Perry's trip to Japan.)

The Hall carbine had been in naval service since September 1841, when 500 carbines were received from the Army.[39] These .52 caliber Hall carbines are believed to be the Model 1833 with the ramrod bayonet. In the early 1850s, two vessels known to have been issued the Hall carbines were the 18-gun sloop *St. Louis* and the 20-gun sloop *St. Mary's*. Commander David Farragut, Assistant Inspector of Ordnance at Norfolk, stated that the Hall carbine was greatly preferred to the Jenks by most naval officers.[40] The New York Navy Yard in July 1853 had 20 Hall carbines of the first pattern, without the manufacturer's name stamped on them, that were beyond repair. Thirteen carbines had defective locks, six had broken locks and stocks, and one had several missing parts.[41] A year before, in June 1852, Norfolk had sent to Washington 323 Hall carbines plus 10 Remington/Jenks carbines. That same month from Norfolk, the sloop *St. Louis* was receiving 4,000 musket ball cartridges, 6,300 percussion caps, and 1,000 Hall carbine cartridges. After leaving the Norfolk Navy Yard in 1852, the sloop *St. Louis* was stationed in the Mediterranean. While on station, the crew was exercised with the Hall carbine in Marseilles, France, near Malta and at Alexandria, Egypt.

A "fouled anchor" (pointed downward) scratched into the underside of the butt behind the triggerguard of an 1824-dated Hall rifle. During the 1820s, the Navy obtained 1,041 Hall rifles, most of which were of the 1824 model with the barrel band held by the conventional band springs.

(Peter A. Schmidt collection)

Jenks Carbines

In 1854, the Navy found that they were having a problem with the size of the cones on the Jenks. Many of the Jenks cones would not take the percussion cap. The solution chosen was to size them all to one size at a cost of about four cents each. The Boston Navy Yard submitted this report on their Jenks arms:

Boston Navy Yard[42]
February 1854
Cone Thread Sizes on Jenks Arms

Quantity of Carbines by Year	Year Mfg.	Thread Size Threads Per Inch	Remarks
270	1844	22	New
20	1844	24	New
140	1845	22	New
240	1845	22	New
120	1846	22	New
1	1842	24	Have Been Issued
7	1845	24	Have Been Issued
4	1845	24	Have Been Issued
26	1845	22	Have Been Issued
3	1846	24	Have Been Issued
Total 831			

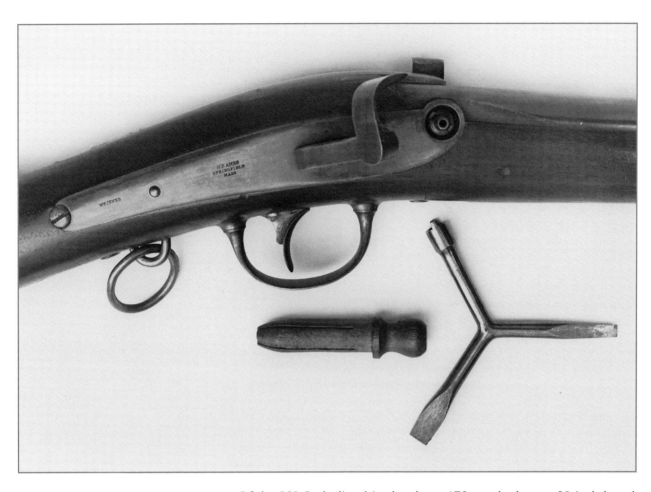

Close-up of the Jenks lock. The percussion nipple is mounted through the lockplate. The combination tool and tompion for the Jenks are also pictured.

The 30-inch barrel Jenks rifle and 24-inch barrel carbine were purchased by the Navy during the 1840s. One thousand Jenks rifles and 4,200 carbines were obtained for sea service.

Of the 831 Jenks listed in the chart, 473 are the longer 30-inch barrel Jenks rifles. The chart does not distinguish between the two (carbine vs. rifle).

A second problem faced by the Navy in that year was the lack of sufficient quantities of Maynard tape primers for the improved Jenks carbines (Remington/Jenks). Norfolk had requested primers for the Jenks as early as 1852. The New York Navy Yard stated in October 1854 that 400 of the improved Jenks carbines were on hand but lacked Maynard primers for them. To alleviate this problem, the Navy ordered from the Army 200,000 Maynard primers at 42 cents per thousand.[43] Deliveries were made for 50,000 primers each at Boston, New York and Norfolk and 25,000 each for Philadelphia and Portsmouth.[44] With the large supply of Maynard primers on hand, it does appear that large quantities of the Remington/Jenks carbines were placed in service.

When the sloop *Jamestown* was outfitted for sea in May 1854 at Philadelphia, her small arms consisted of Jenks carbines, single-shot pistols, altered smoothbore muskets and cutlasses.
(U.S. Naval Historical Center)

The Jenks carbine was the standard breechloader in the Navy at the time. In December 1852, when the frigate *Constitution* was outfitted for sea at New York, she received about 70 of the regular Jenks carbines. During the voyage, which lasted until June 1855, the 4th division of the *Constitution* crew was mainly exercised with the Jenks carbines. Aboard the frigate *Congress*, the apprentice seamen were exercised in both setting the sails and small arms, including the Jenks.[45] The following list reflects a few of the vessels issued Jenks carbines during the period:

**Small Arms Issued
1851–1855**

	San Jacinto	*Levant*	*Water Witch*	*Jamestown*	*John Adams*
Percussion Muskets	54	50	20	54	54
Pistols	80	70	20	72	72
Jenks Carbines	80	42	10	22	42
Swords	100	75	22	93	—
Pikes	100	50	—	—	—
Battle Axes	—	22	—	—	27

The sloop *Levant* was outfitted at Boston in October 1855 and assigned to the East India Squadron. Sometime after September 18, 1860, she disappeared enroute to Panama from Hawaii.

A violent riot broke out in Greytown, Nicaragua, in May 1854. During the riot, the American consul was arrested by British officials for threatening to shoot the rioters. After his release, he went to Washington to complain about his harsh treatment by the British. Commander George Hollins of the 22-gun sloop *Cyane* was directed to sail to Greytown. He was to extract an apology from the local officials and collect for damages to American property.

On June 6, while being outfitted for this trip, the *Cyane* received on board at the New York Navy Yard 18 Jenks carbines and 12 single-shot pistols to complete the ship's small arms inventory.[46] She set sail from New York on June 19, 1854, and arrived at Greytown on July 11. When the town refused to give in to Hollins' demands, a party of 15 sailors and about 18 Marines were sent ashore to disarm the town. The Marines were probably armed with the altered percussion muskets. The sailors were issued 2,200 percussion caps, 1,100 musket ball cartridges, 14 muskets and cutlasses, plus one Jenks carbine. The shore party was under the command of Navy Lieutenants Pickering and Fauntlerey. They seized from the town three field pieces, a few muskets, and destroyed a quantity of powder. No casualties were reported in this action. On July 13, at 8:50 a.m., the Marine drummer boy beat the crew to quarters. *Cyane* opened fire on Greytown at 9:00 a.m. In the first forty minutes, 16 paicchan shells and seventy 32-pound round shots were sent into the town. After a short cease-fire, an additional 88 shots and shells were fired at the town. At 3:00 p.m., Hollins sent his party on shore to set fire to and destroy Greytown. The party returned to the ship at 7:30 p.m., having completed their task. Before leaving the area on July 17, *Cyane* left 20 muskets, 2 Jenks carbines, and a small quantity of ammunition with Vanderbilt's agent of the Accessory Transit Company.[47]

On May 7, 1854, the sloop *Fenimore Cooper* landed on one of the South Sea islands to explore it. In the search of the island, two seamen became lost from the rest of the landing party. A search party was sent out to look for them. Over the next two days, the searchers built fires on the beach and combed the beaches for the lost men without success. Over 200 rounds of Jenks carbine ammunition and 30 pistol rounds were fired to try to get the attention of the lost seamen. Finally, on the third day of the search, May 9, they were informed by local natives that the missing men were safe in a village on the north side of the island. While the *Fenimore Cooper* crew was armed with the Jenks carbine at this time, a little over three months later, while at Hong Kong, she was to receive six Sharps M1851 carbines from the flagship *Vincennes*.

PISTOLS/REVOLVERS

Single-Shot Pistols

The Navy started 1851 with the .54 caliber single-shot percussion pistol as its standard sidearm. The inventory listed the Navy pistol with six-inch barrel manufactured by N.P. Ames and the eight-and-a-half-inch barrel Army model by Aston. The quantity of pistols issued to a ship is shown below:

Table of Allowance[48]

Vessel	Pistols Quantity	Pistol Ball Cartridges	Bullet Moulds	Screwdrivers
Ship of the Line —				
Three Deck	360	14,000	1	15
Two Deck	270	11,000	1	11
Razees	186	7,000	1	6
Frigates —				
1st Class	140	6,000	1	6
2nd Class	136	5,000	1	5
Sloops —				
1st Class	90	4,000	1	4
2nd Class	70	3,000	1	4
3rd Class	60	2,000	1	3
Brigs	35	1,000	1	2
Steamers —				
1st Class	80	3,000	1	4
2nd Class	60	2,000	1	4

In September 1853, Commodore Morris wrote to the Secretary of the Navy stating that if all ships were to be outfitted for sea, the Navy would be deficient 3,125 pistols. Morris did not see this as a problem since the pistols could be obtained from the Army.[49] No pistols were procured during this period.

As the Table of Allowance chart shows, a frigate the size of "Old Ironsides" would be entitled to 140 pistols.

On her voyage of 1853 to 1855, the *Constitution* was issued Navy pistols stamped "NP Ames, Springfield, Massachusetts" and dated 1844. Her ship logs are unclear on the number of times that the pistols were used. It does show that shortly before going out of commission on June 14, 1855, the crew did exercise with all ordnance including pistols.[50]

One of Perry's vessels assigned to his squadron that entered Tokyo Bay in 1853 was the sloop *Saratoga*.

On June 8, 1853, she received from the ordnance ship *Supply* at Napa Roads 40 pistols, 20 pistol cartridge boxes and belts, plus 20 muskets with bayonets. On the voyage to Japan from Okinawa, the 2nd, 3rd, and 4th divisions of the *Saratoga* crew took target practice with their pistols.[51] The frigate *Powhatan* at anchor at Yokohama, Japan, on March 18, 1854, received from the frigate *Susquehanna* 90 muskets, 100 pistols, and 12 cutlasses. The storeship *John P. Kennedy* at Hong Kong transferred to the sloop *Macedonian*:

During the 1850s and later, the ship-of-the-line USS *North Carolina* was the receiving ship at the New York Navy Yard. In November 1855, the *North Carolina* still had in inventory 40 flintlock pistols and a like quantity of flintlock muskets for the use of the ship.
(U.S. Naval Historical Center)

Ordnance Stores Received[52]
USS *Macedonian*
October 30, 1855

- 19 Carbines (Jenks)
- 10 Muskets with Bayonets
- 26 Pistols
- 1 Sharps Patent Rifle (Carbine)
- 25 Swords
- 10 Pikes
- 2 Revolvers (Colts)

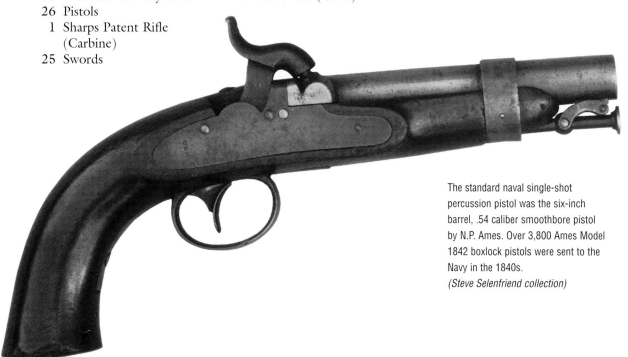

The standard naval single-shot percussion pistol was the six-inch barrel, .54 caliber smoothbore pistol by N.P. Ames. Over 3,800 Ames Model 1842 boxlock pistols were sent to the Navy in the 1840s.
(Steve Selenfriend collection)

Colt Revolvers

In response to the letter of June 23, 1852, from Colt's agent, stating that the price of the Colt Dragoons and M1851 revolvers was $25.00 each and $19.30 for the other models, the Navy gave this response:

> Bureau of Ordnance and Hydrography
> June 25, 1852
>
> Sir:
>
> *Commander Perry has forwarded to this Bureau a letter addressed to him on the 23rd instant from your agent, giving the prices of certain Revolving Pistols.*
>
> *Commander Perry has informed the Bureau that he wishes to have of the different descriptions, the following number viz:*
>
> 25 Army Pistols — *brass mounted*
> 50 Navy Pistols — *plated*
> 6 Four-inch barrel — *plated*
> 6 Five-inch barrel — *plated*
> 13 Six-inch barrel — *plated*
>
> *The Bureau will agree to take the above number of each kind, at the prices named in the letter from your Agent of the 23rd inst., and the necessary spare parts, provided they should be delivered in the order, and by the time specified in the letter from the Bureau to you of the 16th instant.*
>
> *Respectfully*
> *Your Obt. Servt.*
> *C. Morris*
> *Chief of Bureau*[53]

Sam'l Colt Esq.
Hartford
Connecticut

The 100 Colt revolvers were delivered to the frigate *Mississippi* by the tenth of July. (See Perry's trip for further details.)

Chief of Naval Ordnance Commodore Morris was not a strong proponent of revolvers in naval service. He wrote to the Secretary of the Navy James Dobbin on June 21, 1854, stating:

> *It has not been considered advisable heretofore, to purchase Colts revolvers for general service. Some have been purchased for special purposes, as for the "Mississippi" when she sailed from the United States for Japan and for the vessels under Commander Ringgold.*

He went on to say,

> *Pistols can seldom be used with effect in the Navy, except when boarding vessels, with the view to their capture, which very rarely occurs. At such time, the contest soon becomes hand to hand when swords or boarding hatches could be used by seamen, with equal, if not greater certainty and effect, than pistols.*[54]

He concludes that, since revolvers cost four times more than pistols and are more liable to get out of order, they should not be purchased for general naval service. The revolver was never highly regarded by Navy officials.

A Second Model 1851 Colt revolver of the type delivered to the *Mississippi* in July 1852. At this period in time, Colt revolvers were being purchased only for special naval operations.
(Author's collection)

As late as November 1864, Henry Wise, then Chief of Naval Ordnance, was in favor of adopting a single-shot pistol to replace the revolver. Wise, like Morris, was of the opinion that revolvers were mostly useless for service issue and generally a dangerous arm for the sailor. It should be noted that, after the Civil War, the Navy did adopt a single-shot metallic cartridge pistol as their standard sidearm.

EDGED WEAPONS

Model 1852 Naval Officer's Swords

Five hundred sword belts and a like number of cartridge box belts were received in February 1851 from Joseph T. Bell of New York City. The sword belts were probably for the M1841 naval cutlass. The officer's sword at this time, the M1841 Officer's Sword, was about to change with the adoption, on March 8, 1852, of the new pattern M1852. The M1852 Officer's swords were to have blade lengths ranging from 26 to 29 inches with half-basket hilt, grips white, and mounting of yellow gilt. The scabbards were of black leather. On March 31, the Navy placed an order with T.J. Ames of Springfield, Massachusetts, for 500 of these new officer's pattern swords at $17 for the sword and $5.50 for the belt and mountings. Deliveries to be made as follows:

Proposed Delivery Dates[55]
M1852 Officer's Swords

Location	Total Deliveries	Delivered by June 1st
Charlestown, Massachusetts	100	35
Brooklyn, New York	125	45
Philadelphia, Pennsylvania	75	45
Washington, D.C.	75	30
Gosport, Virginia	125	45
Total	**500**	**200**

Ames accepted the order on April 6, but changed the deliveries of the first 300 to on or before August 31, 1852. The Navy accepted Ames proposal.

On June 8, Ames was notified that Lieutenant Robert B. Hitchcock would inspect the swords when ready for inspection. By December, 420 Model 1852 Officer's swords had been delivered with the last 80 swords sent to New York in January 1853. The following invoice is for officer's swords received at the Boston Navy Yard in July 1852:

Boston Navy Yard[56]
M1852 Officer's Sword Delivery
July 19, 1852

12 New Regulation Navy Officer's Swords 29 inches in length	$204.00
11 New Regulation Navy Officer's Swords 27½ inches in length	187.00
12 New Regulation Navy Officer's Swords 26 inches in length	204.00
35 Belts and Clamps	192.50
2 Packing Boxes	4.50
Paper	1.75
Total Invoice	**$793.75**

By January 3, 1853, the yard had sold 26 of these swords to naval officers at a cost of $535.00.

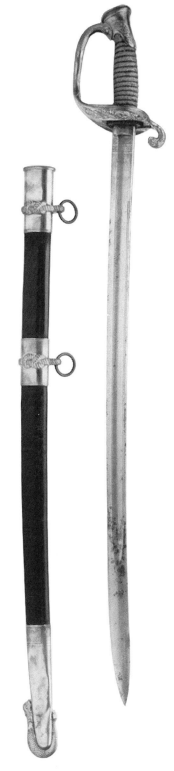

In April 1852, the Navy placed an order for 500 of the new pattern Model 1852 Officer's swords from Ames. *(Will Gorgas collection from* Echoes of Glory: Arms and Equipment of the Union, *photograph by Larry Scherer, c.1991 Time-Life Books Inc.)*

Battle Axes

While Ames was delivering the M1852 Officer's swords to the Navy, he was given an order for 900 battle axes. The order of October 25, 1852, called for deliveries of 300 each at Boston, New York, and Norfolk. The price was set at $1.12½ each. The first 100 battle axes were to be sent to Boston plus three to the Bureau to be used as a pattern. Ames was directed to stamp the axe on one side with their name and the other side with "US Navy". The pattern hatchets were received at the bureau in January 1853, and the go-ahead was given to commence deliveries. In April, 150 battle axes were sent to each of the three Navy yards.[57] Half of the axes sent to Norfolk did not pass inspection.

Mr. Torree at the Boston Navy Yard inspected the 149 battle axes delivered to Boston. He placed them in the yard's ordnance stores without further inspection. Torree did state in his April 5, 1853, report that the battle axes delivered were the same quality as the pattern that had less than a half inch of steel on them. Because of this lack of steel, he felt that after a few hard blows on the standing rigging, the hatchets would become worthless.[58] All 450 hatchets delivered by Ames were rejected by the Navy. In July, Ames made further deliveries of which 171 passed inspection at Norfolk and 137 at New York. Records do not indicate the number of hatchets sent to Boston that passed inspection.

The Boston Navy Yard made their own contract for battle axes.

The Model 1852 Officer's sword was the standard officer's sword during the war. This ensign is shown with his Model 1852 Officer's sword. *(Jerry Rinker collection)*

A battle ax and belt with pistol frog, cartridge box, and frog for a battle ax. *(James Stamatelos collection, from* Echoes of Glory: Arms and Equipment of the Union, *photograph by Larry Scherer, c.1991 Time-Life Books Inc.)*

The Model 1841 Officer's sword was the adopted sword for naval officers at the start of this period. Shown is a Navy captain during the war with the Model 1841 eagle head Officer's sword. *(Jerry Rinker collection)*

On November 23, 1853, they entered into an agreement with Underhill Edge Tool Company for 1,200 hatchets. Deliveries were to be made by May 1, 1854. Underhill notified them that they could not meet the schedule date. They sent their first 527 battle axes to the yard in July; however, 271 failed inspection. By March 22, 1855, the company had delivered 1,009 hatchets, all of which had passed inspection, but an additional 30 dozen battle axes had been rejected for a variety of reasons. Later in the year, 264 hatchets were received, of which 184 passed the test. The order was accepted as completed.[59] During the first half of the decade over 1,500 battle axes had been obtained by the Navy.

The second half of the decade would see both the Navy and Marine Corps more actively appropriating funding to modernize their small arms inventory. The period would also lead the country down the path to all-out civil war.

Chapter 2
Drifting Towards War, 1856–1860

The second half of the decade saw the nation slide further and further towards all-out civil war. The events of October 1859, in which the Marines played a major role, would accelerate this process.

On the evening of October 16, 1859, at about 10:30 p.m., the Harpers Ferry Arsenal was seized by 18 men led by the Kansas abolitionist John Brown. Shortly after noon on October 17, 1st Lieutenant Israel Greene was called to the office of the Commandant of the Marine Corps and informed that he was to lead the Marine detachment of 86 men to help retake the arsenal. His orders stated:

John Brown's Raid on Harpers Ferry

> *Headquarters*
> *October 17, 1859*
>
> Sir:
> *You will take command of a detachment of Marines, and proceed by the 3:20 p.m. train, to Weaverton, Maryland. On your arrival there you will communicate with the senior officer of the Army, who will either be there or in the vicinity, for such instructions as he may have to give you in carrying out his orders from the President of the United States.*
>
> *You will take with you two twelve pound howitzers, with such ammunition as may be necessary to serve them efficiently, in case of their being required for use.*
>
> *Very Respectively Yours,*
> *John Harris*
> *Colonel Commandant*[1]
>
> Lt. I. Greene
> *Commanding Detachment*
> *Headquarters*

With the help of Major William Russell, Paymaster of the Corps, Greene had his men equipped and ready to go by early afternoon. The men had drawn their M1842 muskets and cartridges and rations for the trip to Harpers Ferry. At 3:30 that day, the Marines left on the Baltimore & Ohio train for the arsenal.

The government forces were led by Lieutenant Colonel Robert E. Lee of the Second U.S. Cavalry. His aide was Lieutenant Jeb Stuart, Company "G," 1st U.S. Cavalry. At 6:30 a.m. the next morning, Lieutenant Greene was given his orders by Lee. His instructions were to storm the engine house where John Brown was holding the villagers that had been taken hostage. Greene was only to attack if Brown refused to surrender.

The surrender terms were handled by Jeb Stuart, and when Brown refused the terms, the Marines went forward. The storming party consisted of 24 men plus three others with sledgehammers to batter down the door. The first Marine to enter the building was Lieutenant Greene followed by Major Russel. The third and fourth Marines were either killed or wounded.

At the age of 66, with 45 years in the Corps, Colonel John Harris became the sixth Commandant of the Marine Corps in 1859 upon the death of Archibald Henderson. On October 17, 1859, Harris sent 1st Lieutenant Israel Greene and 86 Marines to help recapture Harpers Ferry from John Brown. *(National Archives)*

These were the only casualties suffered in the attack. In three minutes of fighting, the Marines had taken possession of the house and wounded Brown. John Brown was tried for treason, found guilty and hanged at Charleston, Virginia, on December 2, 1859.

Navy 1858 Small Arms Inventory

As the year 1858 was coming to a close, the Navy was reflecting the following small arms in their inventory. The inventory had been compiled for J.S. Phelps, Chairman of the House of Representatives Ways and Means Committee.

Small Arms Inventory[2]
U.S. Navy
December 1858

	In Navy Yard	On Board Vessels	Total
Jenks Carbines	4,093	1,359	5,452
Hall Carbines	480	—	480
Perry Carbines	3	35	38
Sharps Carbines	28	60	88
Percussion Rifled Muskets	842	2,760	3,602
Blunderbusses	2	—	2
U.S. Rifles	3	—	3
Sharps Rifles	37	175	212
Army Pistols	1,417	636	2,053
Navy Pistols	1,962	1,944	3,906
Colt Revolvers	781	1,309	2,090
Marstons Revolvers	13	14	27
Swords	2,868	2,965	5,833
Pikes	3,287	1,785	5,072
Battle Axes	1,274	643	1,917
Cutlasses	123	—	123

Note that the schedule does not reflect any quantities of smoothbore muskets. The Hall carbines listed may include some Hall rifles, since the Navy had a tendency to track them as carbines.

Procurements and Sea Service

MUZZLELOADERS

Prewar Plymouth Rifles

The year 1856 saw Navy ships armed with the altered .69 caliber percussion smoothbore musket. The first step taken to develop a rifle musket for the Navy is found in a letter dated February 7, 1856, from Commander John Dahlgren to the acting chief of the Bureau of Ordnance and Hydrography. Dahlgren stated that at the present time the Navy did not possess a single rifled musket in its inventory. He requested approval to have a sample rifled musket prepared for trial to determine the proper rifle musket for naval service. Permission was granted, and by early March several firms had been contacted regarding their interest in developing a model rifle musket for the Navy. The only firm to respond to Dahlgren's inquiries was Eli Whitney of New Haven, Connecticut. Dahlgren's letter to Whitney reads:

Ordnance Office
U.S. Navy Yard
Washington, March 3rd, 1856

John Dahlgren shown in command of the South Atlantic Blockading Squadron during the war. Dahlgren is in the center of the photo.
(U.S. Naval Historical Center)

Eli Whitney Esq.
Office of the Whitneyville Armory
New Haven. Conn.
Sir:

I have been authorized to have made some sample Rifled Muskets for Naval service, and will be pleased to hear from you if inclined to submit proposals for furnishing an arm made on the following general conditions.

The Musket is to be load at the muzzle, — with a Minie shot weighing from 750 to 830 grains, — the form of which is to be cylindro-conical, channeled at the base like the French, and fore-part not too acute — Barrel, decarbonized steel preferred, about 34 inches long. Weight about four and a half pounds — Bore, in diameter that of the U.S. Musket, (Smoothbore). viz: — 0.69 in — The finished musket (without bayonet) not to weigh more than the U.S. Percussion musket, say 10 lb. — The lock to conform to that of most approved construction made at the U.S. Arsenal. — The Bayonet, an elongated Bowie knife, weighing about 1¾ lbs. Fixed and carried like the new French yataghan bayonet, but bearing more of a resemblance to a Bowie knife — the number and depth of grooves, the general character, etc., you will suggest.

If so disposed, you will please address me on the subject, with explanatory drawings, and state when such a sample can be finished and delivered, its cost, etc. also at what rate you would engage to furnish a number of such pieces.

An immediate answer is requested.

Very respectfully
Your Obt. Servant
Jno. A. Dahlgren
Commander
In charge of Ordnance
Department in Yard[3]

Whitney responded four days later by stating that he would supply a sample gun for approximately $25. The gun arrived at the Washington Navy Yard on April 16. After inspecting Whitney's rifle musket, Dahlgren rejected it for a number of reasons. The barrel was too short and too light to take the heavy charge that was contemplated for it. The lock did not conform to the Army's Maynard tape primer lock. Whitney's gun was also equipped to take the saber bayonet and not the Bowie knife. Having rejected the Whitney arm, the Navy asked if he either wanted the rifle musket back or if he wanted them to make payment. Whitney requested payment and was paid $24.75 on September 15.[4]

During the summer of 1856, Dahlgren developed his own model gun. He used the pattern of the French Model 1846 Carabine a Tige for his design. The length of the barrel, sights, bands, position of the sling swivels, and the heavy ramrod corresponded respectively to the French arm. Dahlgren believed that the shorter 34-inch barrel and the .69 caliber bore would be more effective for the Navy than the standard Army .58 caliber rifle musket. Since the sailors would not generally be called on to carry their rifles on long marches, the extra weight of the .69 caliber rifle would not present a major problem. While Dahlgren was developing his rifle, the Navy received correspondence from one of their naval officers assigned to the Pacific Squadron. The officer stated that he had visited a French vessel in a South American seaport where he was shown a Model 1846 Carabine a Tige. The carbine was equipped with a rear sight graduated to 1,200 yards and was superior to any musket in the Navy's arsenal.[5]

In August, Dahlgren submitted his rifle to Harpers Ferry for rifling. Dahlgren's model gun used the standard Model 1842 stock and percussion lock. The 34 3/16-inch barrel had been forged from a bar of steel. The lock was stamped "Harpers Ferry" and dated 1854. The barrel bands, triggerguard and bow, buttplate, sideplate and lower swivel bar were of brass. The rear sight was non-graduated. The Bowie knife bayonet submitted with the rifle had been manufactured by the surgical instrument maker Schively of Philadelphia, Pennsylvania.[6] The Navy inquired of Harpers Ferry the cost to produce 3,000 of Dahlgren's rifles with either the M1842 percussion lock or the Maynard tape priming lock used on the new .58 caliber Army rifle musket. Henry W. Clove, Superintendent of the U.S. Armory at Harpers Ferry, put the price tag at $15 each, which included the rear sight and Bowie knife bayonet if the M1842 lock was used plus machinery cost of $2,000. The cost with the use of the Maynard tape priming lock increased to $20 per rifle plus $12,000 for tooling-up costs.[7]

Dahlgren set the number of rifled muskets to be manufactured for trial at 100.

With the national armories gearing up for production of the new M1855 rifle musket and the civilian market unwilling to manufacture such a small order, the Navy made the decision to contract out for the various parts of the rifle musket. The cost was put at $14.13.

Estimate to Manufacture[8]
Plymouth Rifle — 1856

Barrel (decarbonized steel from Remington)	$4.50
Breech Screws	.163
Lock	1.546
Bands	.653
Guard Plate	.492
Swivels	.505
Ramrod	.396
Stock	.874
Knife or Sword Bayonet	5.00
Total Cost	**$14.13**

On April 9, 1857, E. Remington and Sons were given an order for 150 musket barrels. Nine days later, Ames was contracted to supply 75 sword bayonets and 75 Bowie knives. Ames' contract called for the pattern by June 1 and the balance soon thereafter. Dahlgren was to supply the pattern bayonets to Ames.[9] Springfield Armory was requested to supply various parts of the M1842 musket, which were to be used on the new Navy rifle musket.[10] Dahlgren was able to proceed with his rifle musket design since $2,000 had been appropriated for this purpose in March. Dahlgren was to receive disturbing news from the Springfield Armory when he learned that the armory did not manufacture the Maynard tape priming lock in .69 caliber. They directed him to Remington, who was manufacturing this lock for the altered rifled muskets being altered at Frankford Arsenal. On April 18, the Navy placed an order with Remington for 100 locks. To their surprise, the Navy was informed that the Remington .69 caliber Maynard tape primer lock would only apply to the U.S. Model 1822 bolster and not to the Model 1842 barrels being supplied by the company to the Navy. Dahlgren had no choice but to cancel the order for the Maynard locks and go with the standard M1842 percussion lock.[11] It would appear that the barrels and bayonets previously ordered were delivered. On May 23, Ames had been directed to send his pattern bayonets to Dahlgren by express and the rest by less expensive means.[12]

During this period, the sloop *Plymouth* was in the process of being outfitted as an ordnance vessel at the

Chapter 2 • Drifting Towards War, 1856–1860

Boston Navy Yard. One of the major goals of the *Plymouth* when she was set to sail in June was to test the latest of heavy naval ordnance. Dahlgren was to command the *Plymouth* and was anxious to have some of the new rifled muskets on board when it sailed. With time drawing short before the *Plymouth* sailed, Dahlgren proposed on April 20 to have only 50 of his rifled muskets assembled by using the standard M1842 lock. The barrels would be sent to Ames at Chicopee, Massachusetts, for installing breech plugs, sights and bayonet lugs. The Army would only fine bore and rifle the barrels.[13] Even with the reduced request, the rifled muskets were not available when the *Plymouth* sailed on June 24, 1857.

After returning from the voyage in November, Dahlgren went back to his work at the Washington Navy Yard. The 150 barrels and the bayonets from Ames were probably waiting for him when he returned. The lock and the stocks for the rifle musket were obtained from Harpers Ferry. The standard M1842 percussion locks were stamped "HARPERS/FERRY" dated 1854 or 1855. The source of the brass fittings for the rifle musket may have been produced at the navy yard. On February 17, 1858, Dahlgren notified Captain Ingraham that he had some of his new barrels ready to be rifled and requested that the work be handled by Harpers Ferry. Two days later, Colonel Craig from the Ordnance Department notified the Navy that "the superintendent of Harpers Ferry has been instructed to have rifled such guns barrels as Commander Dahlgren may sent him for that purpose."[14]

Dahlgren's 1856 Plymouth rifle model gun. The model arm has a Model 1842 Harpers Ferry lockplate dated 1854. The rifle has a 34 3/16-inch steel barrel with a non-graduated rear sight. The furniture is of brass. *(Smithsonian Institution)*

During the 1858 cruise of the ordnance ship *Plymouth*, the latest in heavy ordnance — IX- and XI-inch guns plus the Model 1855 Sharps rifle and Plymouth rifles — were tested. *(U.S. Naval Historical Center)*

In 1856, Harpers Ferry delivered to the Navy 1,800 caliber .69 rifled and sighted rifled muskets. These rifled muskets were of the cone-in-barrel design. (Author's collection. Photo by Mike O'Donnell)

The barrels on these 1858 pattern rifle musket were marked "PLYMOUTH/PATTERN/1858".

When the *Plymouth* left on its second cruise on May 29, 1858, Dahlgren's Plymouth rifles were aboard. The number of rifles on board is found in the *Plymouth* ship logs stating that 54 Plymouth and 22 Sharps rifles and accouterments had been turned in at the end of the cruise.[15] In target practice firing at an eighteen-inch diameter target at 74 feet, the following results were recorded:

USS *Plymouth*[16]
Small Arms Practice
August 11, 1858

1st Division (Plymouth Rifles)	12 hits of 30 shots
2nd Division (Sharps Rifles)	17 hits of 22 shots
3rd Division (Plymouth Rifles)	14 hits of 32 shot
Marine Guard (Muskets)	22 hits of 44 shots

The major reason for the voyage was to test the naval heavy ordnance of Dahlgren IX- and XI-inch guns. On August 30, both types of cannons were fired with these results. The XI-inch gun was fired at a target of 13' x 30' at a distance of 600 yards. Twenty rounds were fired with five hits. The IX-inch gun was fired at the same distance at a 13' x 20' target with all ten rounds striking the target.[17] The next day, the IX-inch was fired at the same distance with 11 of 14 rounds hitting the target. After sailing the Caribbean for several months, the *Plymouth* returned to Washington in early December. Dahlgren returned to his duties at the Ordnance Bureau, and it appears that the Plymouth rifles were placed in storage at the Navy Yard.

Navy and Marine Corps Alterations (Rifled Muskets), 1856

During the period that Dahlgren was developing his pattern rifle musket, the Navy was obtaining rifled muskets from the Army for their immediate use. Each .69 caliber altered percussion Model 1840 musket delivered to the Navy had been rifled, equipped with a rear sight, and the barrels were browned for naval use. The cost to the Navy for these rifled muskets was set at three dollars each.[18] The arrangements made by the Navy for these altered rifled muskets is shown in the letter dated April 9, 1856, from Craig to Ingraham. The letter states:

I have to acknowledge the receipt of your letter of the 8th inst. respecting an exchange of 1,500 muskets and in answer to state that 300 rifled muskets and 20,000 elongated balls, suitable for such arms, have been ordered to be sent to the Commandant of the Washington Navy Yard. The muskets were ordered today from the Washington Arsenal to which place they were dispatched yesterday from Harpers Ferry Arsenal. The balls were ordered from the Allegheny Arsenal... The residue of the rifled muskets (1,200) will be delivered from time to time as they may be called for, at such place or places as you may designate. When the whole shall have been supplied, bills for the actual expense incurred by the Department in making the exchange will be rendered and the 1,500 Navy muskets will be received from the New York Navy Yard.[19]

By the end of October, the Army had made deliveries of 1,600 rifled muskets. Two hundred rifled muskets were delivered in November for a total quantity turned over to the Navy of 1,800 rifled muskets. The Army submit-

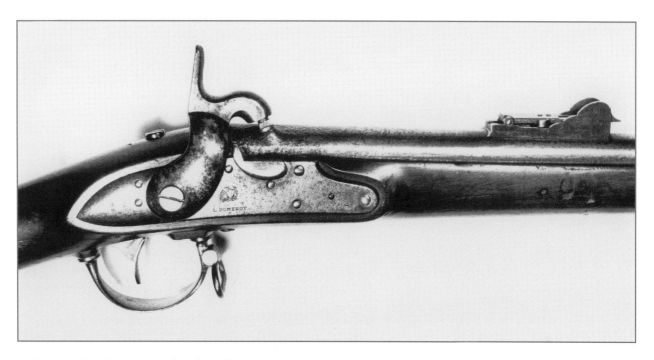

A close-up view of the lock and rear sights on the altered cone-in-barrel rifled muskets delivered to the Navy. *(Author's collection)*

ted their bill of $5,114.92 for the rifling, sighting, and browning of 1,800 muskets plus the cost for cartridges and spare parts. The Navy sent their old altered smoothbore muskets to Brevet Major Hagner at Frankford Arsenal.[20]

The rifled muskets delivered to the Navy in 1856 by Harpers Ferry were the cone-type alteration. This alteration from flint to percussion is better known as the cone-in-barrel conversion. The cone-type conversion on the M1822 musket was the standard alteration performed by the arsenal during the early part of the 1850s. The muskets of this conversion, delivered to the Navy by Harpers Ferry, had been rifled, rear sights added, and the barrels brown. Two vessels to receive these altered rifled muskets were the side-wheel frigate *Susquehanna* and the sloop *Portsmouth*.

Small Arms Issued[21]

USS *Susquehanna* May 16, 1856	USS *Portsmouth* April 1856
54 Rifled Muskets w/4,000 Musket Cartridges	60 Rifled Muskets w/6,000 Musket Cartridges
80 Single-Shot Pistols w/3,000 Pistol Cartridges	90 Pistols w/4,000 Pistol Cartridges
86 Carbines (probably Jenks) w/6,000 Carbine Cartridges	54 Carbines w/4,000 Carbine Cartridge
100 Swords	86 Swords

The *Portsmouth* was assigned to the East India Squadron and took part in Commodore Andrew Foote's attacks on the "Barrier Forts." These forts guarded the approach to Canton, China. In the landing of the sailors and Marines of the *Portsmouth* on the morning of November 20, 1856, two apprentice boys were killed when one of the altered rifled muskets accidentally discharged.[22]

In the month of May, the screw frigate *Merrimack* received 117 altered rifled muskets after turning in their old smoothbore muskets. The *Merrimack* was being fitted out at the Washington Navy Yard. On July 18, the sloop *St. Mary's* located at Panama was issued 80 rifled muskets as well as 50 Colt revolvers. Being issued new arms and not knowledgeable on their use, they requested instructions on the use of the rifled musket. Prior to their arrival, the old smoothbore muskets and the 30 Hall carbines had been fired in

The sloop *Portsmouth* photographed in 1909. In 1856, the *Portsmouth* received on board 60 rifled and sighted .69 caliber rifled muskets. In the landing at the Barrier Forts at Canton, China, in November 1856, two apprentices were killed when one of their rifled muskets accidentally discharged.
(Detroit Photographic Co. — Library of Congress)

In 1857, both the Navy and Marine Corps took delivery of the .69 caliber Remington/Maynard conversion rifled musket. Their rifled muskets were equipped with a long-range rear sight, while this musket lacks one.
(Paul Johnson collection)

practice while anchored at Panama. It took 155 percussion caps to fire the muskets and Hall carbines. In September, with their new rifled muskets, the crew fired all 80 muskets with 50 rounds, striking the target. The distance of the target was not stated.[23] Later in the year, the *St. Mary's* placed a request for 30 bayonets and 20 cartridge boxes for their rifled muskets.[24] A year later, the sloop *John Adams*, also assigned to duty at Panama, delivered 50 of these early altered rifled muskets to the sloop *Decatur* plus 3,740 musket ball cartridges and 10 Colt revolvers.

The Quartermaster of the Marine Corps in 1856 was Major George F. Lindsay. In 1856, Lindsay obtained from the Ordnance Department only ammunition for the Marine detachments aboard the *Wabash* and the *St. Lawrence*. The percussion musket in use with the Marine Corps at the start of the period was the .69 caliber smoothbore Model 1842. It weighed in at just over nine pounds and had an overall length of 58 inches. The 42-inch barrel is equipped to take an angular bayonet. The lockplates are stamped either Springfield or Harpers Ferry. When the Marines of the *Portsmouth*, *Levant* and *San Jacinto* attacked the Chinese forts with Commodore A.H. Foote in November 1856, they were armed with M1842 muskets. In the attack of November 20, the Marines held off a determined Chinese counterattack. That night, the Marines remained in the fort to prevent its recapture. By November 22, all the forts leading to Canton had been occupied. In several days of battle, the Americans suffered casualties of 6 killed and 20 wounded.[25]

1857–1858

In 1857, the Navy placed only one order with the Ordnance Department for rifled muskets, which was the Remington/Maynard conversion. Frankford Arsenal was performing the conversion of these muskets. The Maynard tape primer locks were supplied by Remington & Sons along with the patented bolster. The muskets were rifled and sighted at the arsenal. On June 19, Navy Secretary Isaac Toucey was notified by the Ordnance Department that 600 Remington/Maynard conversion rifled muskets were being sent to the commandant of the Philadelphia Navy Yard. In exchange, the Navy sent an equal quantity of their old pattern smoothbore muskets to the Frankford Arsenal. The Navy received 75,000 Maynard primers for the rifled musket. The old muskets sent to the Army were delivered from the navy

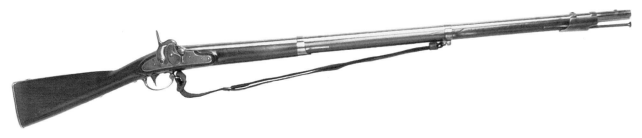

yards of New York and Philadelphia.²⁶ The Remington/Maynard conversion altered muskets were issued to the frigate *Minnesota* and the sloop *Preble*. The *Preble* received 30 altered muskets and the *Minnesota* received 121.

In 1858, the 44-gun screw frigate *Wabash* was making its second cruise. She was to be the flag ship for the Mediterranean Squadron and was under the command of Captain Samuel Barron. His crew consisted of 22 officers, 138 seamen, 132 ordinary seamen, 113 landmen, 27 apprentices, 10 musicians, 27 firemen and 22 coal heavers. The detachment of Marines of 3 sergeants, 3 corporals, 2 musicians and 51 privates was led by Major Jacob Zeilin. They were armed with the .69 caliber Remington/Maynard rifled muskets.²⁷ The ship's small arms consisted of .69 caliber rifled muskets, Jenks carbines, M1855 Sharps rifles, Colt revolvers and the M1841 cutlass.

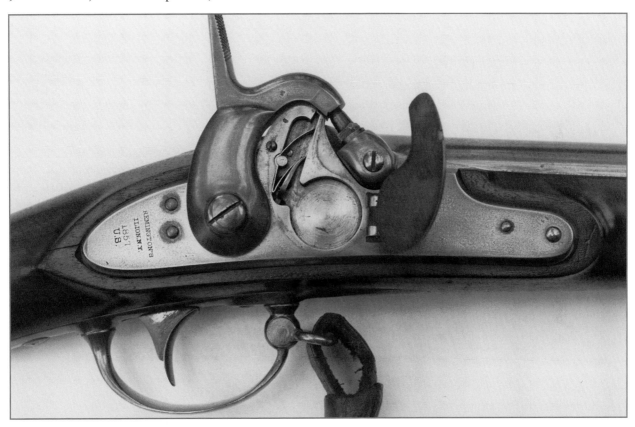

A close-up view of the Maynard tape primer system on the Remington/Maynard rifled musket.

The following exercise routine was developed for the cruise:

Division Routine for Cruise²⁸
Small Arms Exercise
USS *Wabash*
1858–1859

Division	Tuesday	Wednesday	Thursday	Friday
1st	Muskets	—	—	Single Sticks
2nd	—	Muskets	—	Single Sticks
3rd	Muskets	Single Sticks	—	—
4th	—	Single Sticks	—	Sharps Rifles
5th	Single Sticks	Muskets	—	—
6th	Carbines	Single Sticks	—	Carbines
7th	Carbines	—	—	Single Sticks
Marines	Company Drills	—	Company Drills	Company Drills

The year 1858 saw the Navy receiving their third type of altered rifled muskets. These deliveries were the .69 caliber rifled and sighted M1842 percussion musket manufactured at Harpers Ferry. By the end of 1858, Harpers Ferry had delivered to the Navy over 2,400 rifled and sighted M1842 muskets. One ship to receive these rifled and sighted muskets was the frigate *Congress*. In April, the *Congress* turned in 120 old smoothbore muskets for a like number of altered rifled muskets.[29] As would be expected, the accuracy of the rifled musket was superior to the old smoothbore muskets. Early in 1856, during target practice aboard ship with the smoothbore musket, only one shot in four hit the target at a distance of 48 feet. Two years later, on February 4, 1858, men aboard the frigate *Saranac* at Panama fired rifled muskets at a board the size of a man at the distance of 80 feet. The results were that the head and breast of the target were literally cut to splinters.[30] The men of the frigate *Mississippi*, on station in the East China Sea as of May 1858, fired their rifled muskets at a target at a distance of 200 yards. The number of hits was not recorded.

Deliveries of Rifled Muskets[31]
U.S. Navy 1856–1858

Order Date	Quantity	Delivery Location
April 1856	54	Philadelphia
April 1856	246	Washington
May 1856	500	Washington
Aug. 1856	1,000	Washington
June 1857	600	Philadelphia
March 1858	120	Philadelphia
April 1858	200	Washington
May 1858	200	Boston
May 1858	200	Norfolk
June 1858	200	New York
Sept. 1858	200	Brooklyn
Oct. 1858	300	Boston
Oct. 1858	250	New York
Oct. 1858	250	Norfolk
Dec. 1858	500	Brooklyn
Total	**4,820**	

In 1857, Major Lindsay placed the first order for rifled muskets for the Marines. On April 10, 1857, the Marines were sent 200 rifled .69 caliber Maynard tape primer muskets from Frankford Arsenal. Three hundred additional rifled muskets with the Maynard primer locks and 7,500 primers were sent to Major Lindsay at Marine Headquarters on May 23.[32] In January of the following year, 300 musket wipers were supplied by the Army for the Remington/Maynard rifled muskets. Payment was made out of the Marine appropriations for military stores.[33] Most of the Marines' ammunition was supplied by the Navy. The following chart shows small arms ammunition requested for the Marine detachments aboard ship:

Small Arms Ammunition Issued[34]
Marine Detachments
For the Remington/Maynard Rifled Muskets
1857–1858

Vessel	Cartridges	Maynard Primers	Percussion Caps
Germantown	2,000	2,500	—
Saranac	4,000	3,000	—
Powhatan	2,000	8,000	—
Saratoga	2,000	2,000	2,000
Merrimack	9,000	20,000	—
Macedonian	4,000	—	5,000
Mississippi	3,000	5,000	2,500
Wabash	4,000	—	8,000

In 1858, the *Macedonian* Marine guard had 43 Remington/Maynard rifled muskets on board. While the muskets were issued with the Maynard tape primer, the Marines preferred to use the percussion cap when in action because of better results.[35] In 1858, the frigate *Niagara* laid the first transatlantic cable. The Marine detachment for the *Niagara* came on board on February 24, at New York. The guard of 3 sergeants, 4 corporals, 40 privates and 2 musicians were under the command of Lieutenant William Boyd. Boyd's Marines were most likely armed with Remington/Maynard rifled muskets. In October of that year, the Marine guard attached to the frigate *Merrimack* was exercised with their rifled muskets while at Honolulu, Hawaii.[36]

In July 1858, Colonel Henderson placed an order for 500 of the new Model 1855 .58 caliber rifle muskets from the Ordnance Department. Two hundred of them were sent from the Springfield Armory in July. The balance of the order was issued in September 1858. These rifle muskets were sent to Major D.J. Sutherland at Marine Corps Headquarters in Washington. Sutherland had assumed the duty of Quartermaster of the Corps from Lindsay. These 500 caliber .58 Springfield rifle muskets are stamped on the lockplate with the date 1858 and "US/SPRINGFIELD". The 40-inch barrel is equipped with the long-range sight. However, within a few days of the last delivery, Colonel Henderson was informed that the Army needed them back for their own use. The rifle muskets were turned over to Major George Ramsey at the Washington Arsenal on September 18. The Marines were issued from the Washington Arsenal an equal quantity of .69 caliber rifled muskets.[37]

1859–1860

In September 1859, Captain Duncan N. Ingraham, Chief of Bureau of Ordnance, officially set the caliber of small arms at .58. This was the standard caliber of their Army rifle muskets. While the caliber may have been set at .58, there is no record of any such arms obtained by the Navy prior to the outbreak of the war. The .69 caliber rifled musket was still the standard arm of the Navy at the start of the war. Note that the term "rifled musket" refers to smoothbore percussion .69 caliber muskets, which were rifled by the government during the mid-1850s, while "rifle muskets" were the new .58 caliber Model 1855 long arms.

The small quantity of Plymouth rifles fabricated in 1858 remained in storage. In July 1859, one Plymouth rifle, along with the Bowie knife, saber bayonet, plus cartridges and percussion caps was sold for $37.50 from the Washington Navy Yard. A year later, as the *Niagara* was being outfitted for a voyage to Japan, one Plymouth rifle was supplied to the government of Japan.

Cost of Plymouth Rifle for Japan[38]
June 1860

1	Plymouth Rifle Musket Pattern	$25.00
1	Knife Bayonet (Bowie)	5.00
1	Sword Bayonet	5.00
1	Belt with 2 Frogs	1.96
100	Ball Cartridges	1.80
500	Balls for the Musket	6.24
700	Percussion Caps	1.93

Marine Corps

On January 6, 1859, Archibald Henderson died after serving 39 years as the Commandant of the Marine Corps. When news of Henderson's death reached the fleet, several ships fired a 13-gun salute in his memory. His successor was the next most senior officer of the Corps, Lieutenant Colonel John Harris. Harris, at 66, had served 45 years in the Corps, having started as a second lieutenant in 1814. His record showed action in the War of 1812 and the Mexican War plus twenty years of duty at sea. One of the new commandant's first requests for small arms occurred on April 20. The letter to Colonel H.K. Craig at the Ordnance Department states:

> *Headquarters, Marine Corps*
> *Washington, April 20, 1859*
>
> Sir:
> *I will thank you to furnish for the use of the Marine Corps 500 altered rifled muskets — caliber .69 inch — to be delivered as follows: 150 to brevet Lieutenant Colonel Dulany commanding marines, Navy Yard Boston, 150 to Captain Brevoort commanding marines, Navy Yard, New York and 200 to Major Sutherland Quartermaster Marine Corps, Washington City.*
> *Major Sutherland will receipt to you for 500.*
>
> *Very Respectively Yours*
> *John Harris*
> *Colonel, Commandant*[39]

Three days later, Craig wrote back stating that the rifled muskets would be sent from the Springfield Armory to the locations requested in Harris' letter. These altered muskets were the rifled and sighted Model 1842 muskets

By September 1858, the Marines had received 500 Model 1855 Springfield .58 caliber rifle muskets with the long-range rear sights. Since the Army was in need of them, they were turned in and exchanged for the .69 caliber rifled musket from the Washington Arsenal. *(U.S. Military Academy)*

In 1860, the Marine Corps took delivery of 1,000 Model 1855 Harpers Ferry rifle muskets with the Maynard tape primer system. They are found equipped with an iron patchbox and two-leaf rear sight. This rifle musket was the major arm of the fleet Marines at the outbreak of the war. *(Smithsonian Institution)*

manufactured at Springfield. During the year, the Marines aboard the *Lancaster, John Adams, Constellation, San Jacinto, Sumter, Mystic, Mohawk, Wyandotte, Congress, Narragansett, Levant* and *Iroquois* received ammunition for their rifled muskets.

Model 1855 Rifle Musket

By November 1859, the Marines had decided to adopted the Army .58 caliber Model 1855 rifle musket equipped with Maynard tape primer system as their standard arm. Therefore, the November requests from Warrington, Florida, for 60 muskets and the Norfolk order for 40 muskets were turned down. These locations were told that the Corps intended to dispense with the old .69 caliber muskets and adopt the Army's .58 caliber rifle musket. They would have to wait until the new rifle muskets were received. On February 27, 1860, Major Sutherland, with Harris' approval, made a formal requisition in triplicate for 500 percussion rifle muskets. On March 21, Colonel Craig contacted the Marines on the type of muskets that they were requesting. Hearing no answer from Harris, Craig notified the Marines on April 6 that 500 percussion muskets rifled and sighted of .69 caliber were being sent from Harpers Ferry to the Washington Arsenal where they could be picked up. The cost to the Corps for these muskets came to $1,134.35.[40] The next day, Harris wrote the following letter to Craig:

Headquarters, Marine Corps[41]
April 7, 1860

Sir:
I duly received your letter in relation to supplying 500 rifled muskets for the use of the Marine Corps, and did not reply at once as we wished to test the qualities of the caliber 69 and 58, which we have done and find the former defective. I will, therefore, thank you to supply us with 500 of caliber 58.

Very Respectfully Yours
John Harris
Colonel, Commandant

The order for the 500 caliber .69 muskets was canceled and replaced with the above request. As of April, the Marine Corps had in inventory the .69 caliber smoothbore Model 1842 percussion musket, the rifled and sighted Model 1842 and the Model 1822 Remington/Maynard conversion. It was Harris' plan to return to the Army all the old .69 caliber muskets as soon as the new .58s were issued.[42] The order was increased to 1,000. On May 3, the Secretary of the Navy Isaac Toucey was notified that the Marine's 1,000 rifle muskets of .58 caliber would be supplied as soon as possible from Harpers Ferry.[43]

Harpers Ferry was substantially backlogged in filling requests for rifle muskets. As of July 7, they had orders of 1,000 rifle muskets with the Marines and with Allegheny and St. Louis Arsenals. Craig contacted Harris to see if the Marines still had a need for the 1,000 rifle muskets. Harris responded that they still needed the arms, but if they could not obtain them all at once, they would settle for 500 for immediate use. In August, the Marines received 500 brass tip caliber .58s and 500 iron tip Model 1855 rifle muskets. These rifle muskets were stamped "U.S./Harpers Ferry" on the lockplate with 1859 for the brass tip arms and 1860 for the iron tip arms. They are equipped with an iron patchbox and a two-leaf rear sight on the 40-inch barrel. Needing ammunition, an order was placed with the Army for 30,000 caliber .58 ball cartridges and 50,000 percussion caps. Their request was delivered from the

Washington Arsenal on September 5. The first Marines to be issued the 58s were the Marine guard aboard the *Allegheny*, *Pensacola*, and *Susquehanna*.[44] The steamer frigate *Susquehanna*, which was being outfitted for sea service to the Mediterranean Marine guard, was commanded by Captain Young. Since 35 of his Marines were recruits and had never before fired a musket, Young requested that he be given an additional quantity of ammunition for target practice.[45] The rifle muskets issued up to this time were of the iron-mounted tip model. On September 7, Craig requested that the last 500 be returned, since the Army was in need of them. Harris responded that he would honor the request if he was given assurances that he would receive a like number by the first of December. On the 19th of the month, the Marine Quartermaster turned in 500 rifle muskets with the brass tip to Major Ramsey at the Washington Arsenal.[46] The 500 were replaced from Harpers Ferry on November 19. Twenty of these rifle muskets were forwarded to the Marine guard on the sloop *Macedonian*. In October, the commandant ordered three sergeants, three corporals, thirty privates and one musician be sent to the frigate *Cumberland*. They were to be issued the new uniform complete and the new rifle musket.[47] In December, the new rifle muskets were also being issued to the Marines on the *St. Mary's*. As the year 1860 came to a close, the Marine Corps was in the process of rearming with the .58 caliber Model 1855 rifle musket. However, a larger quantity of the old .69 caliber muskets were still in active service.

BREECHLOADERS

Jenks Carbines

All of the new screw frigates, the *Merrimack*, *Wabash*, *Colorado*, *Niagara* and *Minnesota*, when outfitted for sea between the years 1856 and 1858, were issued Jenks carbines. It is believed that all the issued Jenks were of the improved Model (Remington/Jenks) since the Navy had such a large quantity of Maynard tape primers for the carbines. One vessel being outfitted with the Jenks during this period was the *Preble*.

Small Arms Issued[48]
USS *Preble*
May 1857

60 Single-Shot Pistols	30 Altered Rifled Muskets w/Bayonets
70 Swords	3 Battle Axes
42 Carbines (probably Jenks)	

Other ships issued Jenks during the period were the *Congress*, *Cumberland*, *Susquehanna*, *Portsmouth* and *Saranac*. The *Wabash*, *Minnesota* and *Merrimack* were each to receive 70 Jenks carbines. As previously shown, the 6th and 7th divisions of the *Wabash* were exercising with the Jenks during their voyage to the Mediterranean. Company E of the frigate *Colorado* was issued Jenks carbines for small arms drills. While at Port-au-Prince on December 8, 1857, the second cutter crew of the sloop *Cyane* fired at a target with their Jenks carbines. The results were not reported. As of December 1858, the Navy had in service 1,359 of their 5,400 Jenks carbines.[49]

Between the years 1859 and 1860, ten new sloops were placed in naval service. At least two of these vessels were to receive Jenks carbines. They were the *Lancaster* and *Iroquois*. The *Lancaster* was on station at Panama, where the crew was exercising as skirmishers with their Jenks. After they had been fired four or five times, the carbines became worthless. In 1860, the

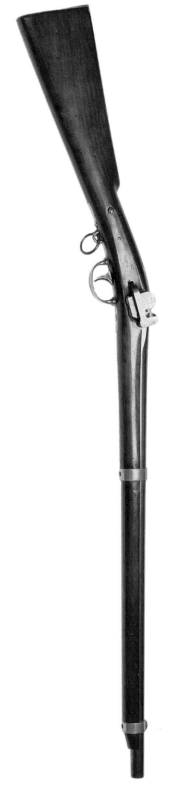

The side hammer Remington/Jenks carbine equipped with the Maynard tape primer system. The new screw frigates being outfitted for sea were equipped with these Remington/Jenks carbines. *(Author's collection)*

In September 1860, the Washington Navy Yard received 294 Jenks/Merrill carbines for Inspection. Several problems were uncovered during the inspection, and 240 carbines were returned to the factory for the necessary repairs. *(Author's collection)*

Iroquois was attached to the Mediterranean Squadron. While at the Bay of Naples and later at Palermo, Italy, the crew was exercised at target practice with their Jenks. The *Iroquois* remained in the Mediterranean until the summer of 1861, when she returned to the States and the war.[50]

During 1858, the Navy made several tests with the Merrill breechloading system on the Jenks carbines. The results were favorable, and on September 20, 1859, James Merrill was granted a contract to alter 1,000 Jenks carbines to his breechloading system. The cost was set at $10 each. In September 1860, Merrill made his first delivery of 294 of the altered Jenks/Merrill carbines for inspection. Dahlgren's report on their inspection stated that the carbines did not effectively ignite the paper cartridge. The breech levers were found not to stay closed when the butt of the carbine was smartly tapped, as in order arms. The weapons were returned for the necessary repairs. The carbines were returned in January and passed inspection. The balance of the contract was canceled.[51]

Perry Carbines

In February 1856, Dahlgren received permission to purchase 200 Sharps and 200 Perry arms. A fund of $10,000 was appropriated for the procurement of these breechloaders. On March 19, Dahlgren entered into an agreement with J.M. Quimby, President of the Perry Patent Arms Co. at Newark, New Jersey, for 150 Perry carbines. The price was set at $25 each with deliveries starting in 30 days.[52] The deliveries called for 50 of the Second Model Perry carbines with the tip-up breech to be sent to Norfolk and the balance to New York. In September, the first 50 were received for inspection. When the carbines were inspected in November, nearly a third of them failed inspection. The entire lot was sent back to the factory for repairs. By March 18, 1857, the 50 carbines were returned and passed inspection.[53] The balance of the order for 100 carbines was canceled for the lack of deliveries within the time frame given. The Perry carbines were placed on board the steam frigate *Roanoke* when she left Norfolk in May 1857. The first cruise of the *Roanoke* lasted but a few months. The second cruise covered the period of August 1858 through May 1860. During this voyage, she was on station in Panama. Included in her small arms inventory were 35 Perry carbines. The ship logs of September 17, 1858, show the 1st and 6th divisions of the *Roanoke* exercising with Perry carbines. At Aspinwall, Panama, in January 1859, Company D of the ship was exercising with Perrys. In May 1860, when the *Roanoke* was to rotate back to the States, the sloop *Lancaster*, also stationed at Panama, requested permission to replace their old Jenks carbines with the *Roanoke* Perrys. The logs of the two ships do not indicate that the transfer was made.

In March of 1857, the Perry Patent Arms Company delivered 50 Second Model Perry tip-up breech carbines to the Navy. Thirty-five Perry carbines were issued to the screw frigate *Roanoke* during her 1858–1860 cruise to Panama. *(Hubert Lum collection)*

Chapter 2 • Drifting Towards War, 1856–1860

Sharps Carbines and Rifles

Five days before the Perry contract, Dahlgren had entered into a contract with John Palmer, President of the Sharps Rifle Mfg. Co. The March 14, 1856, contract called for 150 Sharps rifles with bayonets. The delivery of these $36 rifles was to commence within 20 days. Dahlgren's purpose for the quick turnaround was to place some of the Sharps on the frigate *Merrimack*, which was scheduled to depart shortly. The *Merrimack* set sail without the Sharps and had to settle for the Jenks. Prior to initial delivery in September, the Sharps contract was increased by an additional 50 rifles, making the total contract at 200 rifles. Fifty of the rifles were to be equipped with the self-cocking Rollin White device. In September, 150 Sharps rifles were received and underwent inspection. Of the 50 rifles with the Rollin White device, only 12 passed inspection. Of the 200 Sharps rifles delivered, 57 had to be returned for corrections. All 200 M1855 Sharps rifles were accepted by June 1857.[54] On June 30, the Navy agreed to purchase 100 Sharps rifle carbines at $25 each. These M1855 Sharps carbines were the leftover carbines from the British order. They were equipped with the .577 caliber 18-inch barrel and had the British-style rear sights. The 100 carbines were inspected in July by Commander Stephen C. Rowan at the factory and then shipped to the Brooklyn Navy Yard.[55]

The 200 Model 1855 Sharps rifles were received by June 1857. The screw frigates *Wabash* and *Merrimack* were both issued 35 of the Model 1855 Sharps rifles. *(Author's collection)*

During the year 1857, the Sharps rifles were issued to the frigates *Mississippi*, *Wabash*, *Minnesota* and *Merrimack*. The *Mississippi*, being outfitted at New York for duty in the Far East, had requested Sharps carbines, but ship's logs indicate that they were to receive the rifle instead. The frigate *Merrimack*, being outfitted for her second cruise out of Boston, received the following small arms:

Small Arms Issued[56]
USS *Merrimack*
September 1857

120 Rifled Muskets	140 Pistols
35 Sharps Rifles	25 Colt Revolvers
70 Jenks Carbines	22 Battle Axes

The *Merrimack* was assigned to the Pacific Squadron and sailed as far as Hawaii, arriving there in October 1858. On November 15, three weeks after

One hundred Sharps Model 1855 carbines were sent to the Brooklyn Navy Yard in July 1857. Sixty of these carbines equipped with an 18-inch barrel were sent on the Paraguay Expedition of 1858–1859. *(Author's collection)*

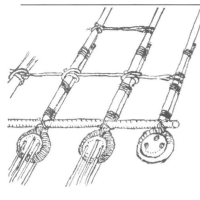

leaving Hawaii, the 5th division of the ship was exercising with Sharps rifles while at sea. She returned to the States in January 1860 and went into drydock at Norfolk for repairs to her engines. While being repaired in April 1861, the *Merrimack* was captured by the Confederates, who took control of the Navy Yard. The *Merrimack* was converted to the ironclad CSS *Virginia*.

In 1857, the frigate *Wabash* was assigned to the home squadron. As previously shown, the 4th division was issued Sharps rifles. In December, Commander Hiram Paulding on the *Wabash* landed at Greytown with 300 sailors and Marines. The men, armed with rifled muskets and Sharps and Jenks carbines, arrested the American William Walker and his men. He and his men were returned to the States. In 1860, Walker arrived in Honduras, was captured, and shot by a firing squad. In 1858, *Wabash* was assigned to the Mediterranean Squadron as the flagship. For a variety of reasons, Flag Officer Lavallette gave three of his Sharps rifles and a few Colt revolvers as gifts during the cruise. When the ship returned to the States in 1859, Lavallette was strongly criticized by naval authorities for overexceeding his authority in presentation of the *Wabash* small arms. Also in 1858, the sloop *Plymouth* was outfitted for sea. (See *Plymouth* section.)

Late in the year 1858, the Navy was outfitting a number of vessels for the Paraguay Expedition. The sloop *Fulton's* inventory of small arms included M1855 Sharps rifles, while the bark *Crusader* and frigate *Sabine* received M1855 Sharps carbines. On the voyage to Paraguay, the 1st and 2nd launch crews of the *Sabine* exercised with Sharps carbines. In January 1859, the *Sabine* sent 1,500 Sharps cartridges to the *Crusader*. In March, *Sabine* received 13 of their Sharps rifles from the *Fulton*. For the balance of the cruise, the *Sabine* was armed with both the Sharps rifles and carbines. Her ship logs of December 29, 1859, list the exercise of Companies C and D with Sharps rifles and carbines.[57]

In July 1860, the Norfolk Navy Yard had only nine Sharps rifles and a few Hall carbines for issue to the sloop *Seminole*. In December of the year, the Portsmouth Navy Yard received 80 Sharps for issue to the sloop *Macedonian*. These Sharps, obtained from Boston, were found to include 32 Sharps carbines. Out of the 32 carbines, sixteen were found to go off at half cock, plus one had a broken lock.[58] A year before, on September 9, 1859, the Navy placed an order for 900 NM1859 caliber .56 Sharps rifles. These 30-inch barrel rifles equipped to take the saber bayonet are found in the serial number range 33000 to 34000. In November 1860, the Sharps factory forwarded 510 of the rifles to the Washington Navy Yard and 120 to Philadelphia. The balance of the order was delivered shortly before the outbreak of hostilities. It was these Sharps rifles that were issued between April and June of 1861.

The bark *Crusader* — one of the vessels on the Paraguay Expedition — was issued the Model 1855 Sharps carbines along with pistols, Colt revolvers and rifled muskets.
(U.S. Naval Historical Center)

One of the 510 NM1859 Sharps rifles delivered to the Washington Navy Yard in November 1860 was serial number 33623. This rifle is of .56 caliber and takes the saber bayonet.
(Steve Selenfriend collection)

Other Breechloaders, 1859–1860

In July 1859, the Washington Navy Yard was the scene of several test breechloader trials. The purpose was to determine their effectiveness for naval service. The July 22 report from Lieutenant H.H. Lewis on the Model 1855 Colt revolving rifles stated that two Colt rifles were each fired 500 times. He continues, "during the trial of these pieces, the firing was deliberate. They were not cleaned and sufficient time only allowed for them to cool when hot. They worked smoothly and easily. None failed to go off, and the cylinders showed less deposits than usual."[59] With favorable tests like the above and others, the Navy appropriated $90,000 for the purchase of breechloading arms. In September 1859, the Navy placed contracts for over 3,000 breechloading arms. (See Sharps and Jenks sections for 1859 procurement.)

(Below) Close-up of the breech section of the Model 1855 Colt revolving rifle. One hundred Colt revolving rifles were received at the Washington Navy Yard in February 1860.

Naval Breechloading Contracts and Deliveries[60]
1859–1860

	Burnside Rifles	Joslyn Rifles	Colt Rifles	Maynard Carbines
Date of Contract	9/9/59	9/9/59	9/13/59	2/23/60
Quantities Ordered	700	500	100	60
Price	$37.50	$37.50	$47.50	$30.00
Model	2nd	M1855	M1855	1st Model w/Tangsights
Dates of Delivery	—	—	2/60	3/60
Quantity Delivered	—	—	100	60

In March 1860, the New York Navy Yard received 60 First Model Maynard carbines from the Maynard Arms Company of Chicopee Falls, Massachusetts. (Author's collection)

The Colt rifles were delivered in February 1860 at the Washington Navy Yard. These .64 caliber M1855 rifles are equipped with the 31 5/16-inch barrels. It appears that they remained in storage until the outbreak of the war. As the above chart reflects, no deliveries were received of the Burnside and Joslyn rifles during this period.

In October 1859, a First Model Maynard carbine was tested at the Washington Navy Yard. In two days of trials, the carbine was fired 602 times. On the first day, 250 rounds were fired at a target at 500 yards with all striking the target. On the second day, 43 shots were fired at a target at 1,300 yards with 15 hitting the target and several shots passing over it. With such great success, the Navy ordered 60 carbines in February 1860. Delivery of the .50 caliber twenty-inch barrel 1st Model Maynard carbines was made on March 3. Some of the Maynards were placed on the sloop *Saratoga*. In addition, the *Saratoga* was issued 32 Colt revolvers, 36 battle axes and 140 rifled muskets.[61]

REVOLVERS

Model 1851 Colt Revolvers, 1856–1858

In 1856, Samuel Colt contacted the Navy, offering to supply them with the Navy size revolvers for $24 each for an order of 1,000 or more or $20 each for 5,000. The Navy responded that their peacetime appropriations did not allow for the purchase of handguns as costly as the Colt. When the price was further reduced to $18 each, 50 were purchased on June 16.[62] As soon as the Colts were received, they were issued to the sloop *St. Mary's* at Panama. On September 10, she sent to the flagship, the frigate *Independence*, twelve of her Colt revolvers for the flagship's use, plus 1,000 percussion caps to go with them. Twenty-five Colts of the earlier deliveries of 1852 were sent to the frigate *Merrimack* on May 3. A year later on May 29, 1857, the frigate *Cumberland*, in the process of being outfitted at Boston, was issued 15 of these Colt revolvers.

On May 21, 1857, the Navy placed an order for 50 Colts for the frigate *Roanoke*, which was being outfitted for sea at Norfolk. These Colts were

An iron frame 4th Model 1851 Colt revolver delivered to the Boston Navy Yard in September 1859. (Author's collection)

sent forward by steamer to Norfolk. An additional eighty Colts were forthcoming by August. Fifty of these revolvers were delivered on board the side-wheel frigate *Mississippi*, then being fitted at New York. The *Mississippi* intended to issue the Colts to officers and the two boat crews.[63] The frigates *Mississippi* and *Minnesota* took part in the allied fleet, including both England and France, that forced China to open its ports to foreign trade.

The sloop *St. Mary's*, photographed c.1900. The 50 Colt revolvers delivered to the Navy in 1856 were sent to the *St. Mary's* then on station at Panama. *(U.S. Naval Historical Center)*

The "U.S." mark stamped on the frame of all prewar contract Colt revolvers. *(Author's collection)*

The second largest procurement of small arms placed by the Navy during the 1850s occurred on September 28, 1857. An order was given to Colt for 2,000 revolvers at a cost of $18 each. The order reads in part: "by direction of the Secretary of the Navy you are authorized to furnish 2,000 of your Navy pistols less 130 already delivered with flasks, bullet moulds, and other appendages complete."⁶⁴ The first 615 Colt revolvers on this contract were delivered to Norfolk on November 9. These Colts had serial numbers from 55782 to 59713. The Norfolk inspector of the Colts was Commander James L. Henderson. His Colts are stamped "USN" over "J.L.H." on the buttstrap.⁶⁵ The second deliveries were received at Boston on December 6, when 667 were sent. Commander George M. Ranson was the inspector of these Colts. The "USN" is stamped on the buttstrap and "GMR" in the wood below the "USN" marking. The balance of the deliveries were sent to New York also in December. The New York Colts were inspected in the same manner as the Boston Colts. The two New York inspectors were Commanders James R. Madison Mullaney and Stephen C. Rowan. The New York Colts are found in the serial number range 61306 to 62300.⁶⁶ The two thousand .36 caliber M1851 Colts delivered on the contract have the small "U.S." on the frame and are equipped with Colt London-type iron backstraps and large iron triggerguard. The barrels are found stamped with an early New York address.

The stamping on the butt of a Model 1851 Colt revolver delivered to the New York Navy Yard in December 1857. The initials "S★C★R" are for Commander Stephen C. Rowan. *(Author's collection)*

Paraguay Expedition

The largest peacetime American punitive expedition up to this time was organized in the fall of 1858 against Paraguay. The expedition was to punish Paraguay for her part in damaging the side-wheel sloop *Water Witch* three years before. In October, the Brooklyn Navy Yard was busy outfitting ships for the expedition. The Army sent 200 rifled muskets there for the use of the sailors. Two of the improved Jenks/Merrill carbines and 1,000 ball cartridges for them were also sent on the expedition. There were sufficient Sharps rifles and carbines in addition to rifled muskets on this trip to arm every sailor that could be landed.[67] The old Jenks carbines that were taken on the expedition were only for back-up purposes. They had been taken along since the Navy lacked funding to purchase new and improved arms. Over half of the Colts delivered in 1857 were issued for the expedition. Each Colt was supplied with a bullet mould and power flask. In addition, nearly a thousand pounds of powder were supplied to make cartridges for the Colts. At 350 rounds per pound, this quantity of powder was sufficient to fight a small-scale war.[68]

The 300 Marines attached to the fleet were commanded by Captain Robert Tansill. Tansill's Marines were armed with their .69 caliber Remington/Maynard rifled muskets and 35,000 cartridges obtained from the Navy out of the 50,000 requested.[69] When Captain Tansill left the states, he was attached to the frigate *Sabine*, but after reaching Paraguay, he transferred to the sloop *Preble*. The Marines were assigned to the *Harriet Lane*, *Sabine*, *Niagara*, *Atlanta*, *Westernport* and the *Caledonia*. When the fleet left late in the year, it consisted of eleven steamers and eight sailing ships with a force of 2,200 sailors and 300 Marines. In January, the fleet arrived in Paraguayan waters. Not knowing if they would have to fight, some of the ships sent their crews on shore to drill with small arms. One such vessel was the sloop *Water Witch*. On January 31, the ship sent her sailors and Marine guard on shore to drill. The expedition was settled peacefully without hostilities. The following chart reflects the small arms aboard three of these vessels:

Paraguay Expedition[70]
Small Arms Inventory
1858–1859

	USS *Fulton*	USS *Westernport*	USS *Crusader*
Colt Revolvers	10	35	20
Pistols	35	40	35
Rifled Muskets	20	40	20
Sharps Rifles	20	—	—
Cutlasses	35	49	—
Boarding Pikes	—	40	25
Carbines (type not stated)	—	30	20 (probably Sharps)
Battle Axes	—	—	9

1859–1860

The last prewar order for the Model 1851 Colt revolvers occurred in August 1859. An order was placed for 600 Navy revolvers at $18 each. Half of the order was sent to the New York Navy Yards and the balance to Boston. For these deliveries, Colt was to receive payment of $11,663.10.[71] The serial numbers of these Colts are found in the range 89000 to 91000. Commander George W. Rodgers inspected the Colts delivered to New York, while the Boston deliveries were not inspected. The revolvers inspected by Rodgers are stamped "USN" on the buttplate and "I" over "G.W.R." below in the wood. In 1860, several vessels that were issued Colt revolvers were outfitted for sea service. One such ship was the sloop *Pawnee*, commissioned on June 11, 1860, at the Philadelphia Navy Yard.

Small Arms Issued[72]
USS *Pawnee*
June 1860

70 Rifled Muskets w/Bayonets	40 Boarding Pikes
28 Colt Revolvers	50 Swords w/Scabbards
45 Navy Pistols	5 Battle Axes

By the end of the decade, the Colt revolvers were becoming standard issue for all vessels being outfitted for sea.

North-Savage Revolvers

The only other revolver received by the Navy during this period was the North-Savage .36 caliber six-shot revolver. In January 1858, Dahlgren test fired a "Figure 8" North-Savage revolver. It was fired 102 times without exerting the least effect on any of its working parts. Dahlgren recommended that they be tested in actual naval service. The order was placed six months later on July 20, 1858, for 300 of North's Patent Pistols at $20 each.[73] The order called for deliveries to commence within eight months. After several extensions, delivery was made in December 1860 with the standard wartime model revolver. Edward Savage received payment on February 12, 1861, in the amount of $6,037.50.

The deck of the *Pawnee* showing the starboard battery. *(Library of Congress)*

EDGED WEAPONS

Marine Corps Swords and Accouterments

It was the practice of the Corps' Quartermaster to go out on bids for the following year's procurements. The successful bidder would supply the Corps for the upcoming calendar year. In 1857, the firms given contracts for accouterments were Mr. Pinchin of Philadelphia for 100 brass waist plates and Henry Dingee of New York City for the balance of their yearly requirements. In the fall of the year, Dingee supplied the following accouterments:

Accouterments Received[74]
Henry Dingee
New York City
October–November 1857

800 Cartridge Boxes	400 Waist Belts
350 Cartridge Box Belts	600 Bayonet Scabbards
400 Bayonet Belts	

The 600 bayonet scabbards were intended for use with the .69 caliber Remington/Maynard rifled muskets. In 1860, when the Marine Corps adopted the Model 1855 rifle musket as standard issue, the firm of Emerson Gaylord of Chicopee, Massachusetts, received the first order for the .58 caliber bayonet scabbards.[75] The sergeant (NCO) and musician swords in use at this period of time were the Model 1840 NCO and Musician swords. Between the years 1857 and 1859, the Philadelphia firm of Horstmann Bros. & Co. of 723 Chestnut Street supplied the Corps' needs for swords.

Horstmann Bros. & Co.[76]
Sword Deliveries
1857–1859

	Sergeant (NCO)	Musicians
1857	12	6
1858	24	—
1859	24	—

The April 23, 1859, contract with Horstmann called for the delivery of 150 sergeant swords of various lengths. Records, however, show deliveries of 24 late in the year. An additional 50 were called for but not received. On October 15, 1859, the Marine Corps adopted the Army's Model 1850 Foot Officer's Sword for both the NCO and officer needs.[77] A sample of the new sword was sent to the Marine barracks in New York and

(Far left) The Model 1840 Musician swords were being purchased by the Marines from the Philadelphia firm of Horstmann Bros. & Co. *(U.S. Military Academy)*

(Left) The Model 1840 NCO sword was the standard issue to the NCOs of the Corps for most of the period. *(U.S. Military Academy)*

Chapter 2 • Drifting Towards War, 1856–1860

Boston and one sword was kept by Captain Maddox at the Philadelphia Depot. The 24 swords delivered by Horstmann on November 23, 1859, were probably these new pattern swords intended for the NCOs.

The sword contract for 1860 was awarded to James P. Ames of Ames Manufacturing Co. in Chicopee, Massachusetts. Ames' contract called for deliveries of sergeant's swords at $5.50 each, while musician's swords were priced at $4.40 apiece.[78] On July 7, 1860, Major Slack ordered from Ames 36 sergeant's swords of the new pattern. Deliveries were not received at Philadelphia until November. The swords were then forwarded to headquarters in Washington. One of the new pattern swords was sent to the Marine guard on board the sloop *Pawnee*.

As 1860 came to a close, the first shots of the war were only months away. South Carolina had already left the Union, and several Southern states were about to follow. The nation was on the brink of all-out civil war.

The Marine detachment assigned to the sloop *Pawnee* in 1860 were issued the Model 1850 Foot Officer's sword for the NCO and the Model 1855 rifle musket. *(U.S. Naval Historical Center)*

Small Arms Inventory, 1851–1860

During the 1850s, the U.S. Navy was extremely small with a total fleet that did not greatly exceed 100 vessels. In September 1852, Colonel Henderson, Marine Corps Commandant, listed that Marine guards were attached to 28 ships. It is likely that no more than 50 to 60 vessels were in commission at any one time. The following schedule gives a partial inventory of small arms aboard about half the fleet during the 1850s. All vessels during the period were receiving the Model 1841 Cutlass.

The inventories were obtained from National Archives Record Groups 24 and 74. See the Civil War inventory section towards the back of this book for details. The muskets and pistols listed are percussion unless stated as flintlock (F/L). The Sharps carbines are both the Model 1851 and 1855. The Sharps rifles are the Model 1855. The Jenks carbines are both the Regular and Remington/Jenks carbines.

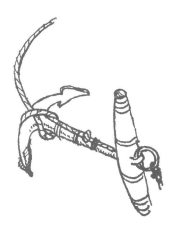

Name of Vessel	Small Arms
Albany	Muskets
Caledonia	Muskets, Pistols, Jenks Carbines, Colt Revolvers
Colorado	Jenks Carbines, Colt Revolvers
Columbia	Muskets
Congress	Muskets, Jenks Carbines, Colt Revolvers
Constitution	Muskets, Pistols, Jenks Carbines
Crusader	Muskets, Pistols, Colt Revolvers, Sharps Carbines

Name of Vessel	Small Arms
Cumberland	Muskets, Pistols, Jenks Carbines, Colt Revolvers
Cyane	Jenks Carbines, Pistols, Muskets
Decatur	Muskets, Sharps Rifles, Colt Revolvers
Dolphin	Muskets, Pistols
Fenimore Cooper	Sharps Carbines, Pistols, Colt Revolvers
Flint	Muskets and Pistols, both were Flintlock
Fulton	Muskets, Pistols, Colt Revolvers, Sharps Rifles
Independence	Muskets, Colt Revolvers
Iroquois	Muskets, Jenks Carbines
Jamestown	Muskets, Pistols, Jenks Carbines
John Adams	Muskets, Pistols, Jenks Carbines, Colt Revolvers
John Hancock	Muskets (F/L), Sharps Carbines
John P. Kennedy	Muskets, Jenks and Sharps Carbines, Pistols
Lancaster	Jenks Carbines, Colt Revolvers
Levant	Muskets, Pistols, Jenks Carbines
Macedonian	Muskets, Pistols, Jenks and Sharps Carbines, Sharps Rifles
Marion	Pistols (Navy)
Massachusetts	Muskets and Pistols both Flintlock and Percussion, Jenks Carbines
Merrimack	Muskets, Pistols, Sharps Rifles, Colt Revolvers, Jenks Carbines
Minnesota	Sharps Rifles, Pistols
Mississippi	Colt Revolvers, Muskets, Pistols, Sharps Rifles
Niagara	Muskets, Pistols, Jenks Carbines
North Carolina	Muskets and Pistols, both Percussion and Flintlock
Pawnee	Muskets, Pistols, Colt Revolvers
Perry	Sharps Carbines
Plymouth	Muskets, Plymouth Rifles, Sharps Rifles, Colt Revolvers
Porpoise	Colt Revolvers, Sharps Carbines
Powhatan	Colt Revolvers, Muskets. Pistols, Jenks Carbines
Portsmouth	Muskets, Pistols, Jenks Carbines, Colt Revolvers
Preble	Muskets, Pistols, Jenks Carbines
Princeton	Muskets, Pistols, Jenks Carbines
Roanoke	Colt Revolvers, Perry Carbines
Sabine	Muskets, Colt Revolvers, Pistols, Sharps Rifles and Carbines
San Jacinto	Muskets, Jenks Carbines
Saranac	Muskets, Jenks Carbines, Colt Revolvers
Saratoga	Muskets, Pistols, Maynard Carbines, Colt Revolvers
Savannah	Muskets both Percussion and Flintlock
Seminole	Muskets, Hall Carbines
St. Mary's	Muskets, Colt Revolvers, Hall and Jenks Carbines
St. Louis	Muskets, Hall Carbines
Susquehanna	Muskets, Pistols, Jenks Carbines, Colt Revolvers
Vandalia	Muskets
Vincennes	Colts Revolvers, Sharps Carbines
Wabash	Muskets, Pistols, Jenks Carbines, Colt Revolvers, Sharps Rifles
Water Witch	Muskets, Pistols, Jenks Carbines, Colt Revolvers
Westernport	Colt Revolvers, Pistols, Muskets
Wyoming	Pistols (Navy)

Part *Two*

The Civil War Years

Chapter 3
Forming the Blockade, 1861

Vessels Outfitting for Sea, April 1861

At the start of 1861, the United States Navy consisted of only 90 ships of war, only 42 of which were in active service. When shots were fired on Fort Sumter in April, the Navy had only the *Brooklyn* and *Relief* available for coastal blockade duty, while ships like the *Niagara* were in far-off Japan. The steam frigate *Merrimack* was in dry-dock at Gosport Navy Yard in Norfolk, Virginia, for repairs to her engines. The United States Navy started the conflict with 1,457 officers and 7,600 sailors. The Marine Corps, under the command of Colonel John Harris, had an actual strength of 1,892.[1]

Forming the blockade (Anaconda Plan) was not the brain child of the Navy, but was developed by Lieutenant General Winfield Scott, Commander in Chief of the Army. In May 1861, Scott went to President Lincoln with his plan. Scott's plan called for blockading the Confederate coastline of the Atlantic and Gulf; maintaining pressure on the Southern armies in Northern Virginia, splitting the Confederacy in two by controlling the Mississippi River, and having the Navy support the Army with naval gunfire and the transportation of troops for amphibious landings. The concept was to strangle the Confederacy by closing all their ports to foreign trade. With modifications, the Navy adopted Scott's plan.

The small arms for the vessels being outfitted for the blockade was the responsibility of the Bureau of Ordnance and Hydrography. Captain

The screw sloop *Brooklyn* was one of only two vessels available for coastal blockade duty at the outset of the war. Her small arms consisted of Colt Model 1851 Navy revolvers, single-shot pistols, rifled .69 caliber muskets, and Model 1841 naval cutlasses.
(U.S. Naval Historical Center)

Andrew A. Harwood was in charge at the outbreak of hostilities. By the start of the war, Harwood had served over 43 years in the Navy.[2] During the first month of the war, Harwood's department received a request from the New York Navy Yard for 600 muskets, 300 Colt revolvers, and 200 swords, while from Philadelphia came orders for 60 Colts, 70 Sharps rifles and 100 rifled muskets. Each location also demanded large quantities of small arms ammunition.[3] The arms scheduled for Philadelphia were intended for the *St. Lawrence*, then in the process of being outfitted for sea. The New York deliveries were placed on board:

Vessels Outfitted for Sea
New York Navy Yard
April 1861

	Wabash	*Roanoke*	*Savannah*	*Potomac*
Rifled Muskets, cal. .69	220	220	160	220
.54 cal. Army Pistols	110	110	76	110
Colt Revolvers	110	110	76	110
Roman Swords	170	170	125	170
Colt Ammunition	11,000	11,000	7,600	11,000
Musket Cartridges	10,400	10,400	7,200	9,400
Pistol Cartridges	11,000	11,000	7,600	11,000
.58 cal. Cartridges for the Marine Guard	12,000	12,000	8,000	10,000

By August 20, the frigate *Wabash* received an additional 8 Navy swords, 4 Army pistols, 4 Colt revolvers, 5 rifled muskets, plus 4 battle axes and a like quantity of boarding pikes.

By June, three of the navy yards were showing in their inventory the following quantities of small arms:

Small Arms Inventory[4]
Navy Yards
June 1–4, 1861

	Boston	New York	Philadelphia
.54 cal. Army Pistols	372	—	23
.54 cal. Navy Pistols	163	—	12
.54 cal. Altered Pistols	647	—	—
.44 cal. Colt Revolvers	250	250	—
.36 cal. Colt Revolvers	—	116	50
.36 cal. Savage Revolvers	77	60	100
Rifled Muskets, cal. .69	150	551	130
Smoothbore Muskets, cal. .69	500	450	—
Jenks Rifles	87	—	—
Jenks Carbines	987	380	100
Sharps Rifles	80	—	—
Sharps Carbines	14	—	—
Battle Axes	206	137	29
Boarding Pikes	261	505	—
Navy Swords	220	550	68

Six weeks prior to these reports, the New York Navy Yard was listing 37 First Model Maynard carbines in storage.

Running the Blockade

Scott's plan called for the Navy to blockade the Southern seaports from Virginia to Texas. The blockade was not too effective in the first year of operations due to a lack of vessels on station. Therefore, the Confederates found it fairly easy to run. Two vessels that ran the blockade during this period were the *Fingal* and the *Gladiator*. In October, the *Fingal* sailed from England with a cargo consisting of 11,340 Enfield rifles, 60 pistols, 24,100 pounds of gunpowder, 550,000 percussion caps, 409,000 cartridges, 500 sabers and other ordnance stores.[5]

The screw frigate *Wabash* shown as the receiving ship at Boston Navy Yard in the 1890s. In April 1861, the *Wabash* was authorized 220 rifled muskets, 110 army pistols, 110 Colt revolvers and 170 Roman swords (1841). The Marine detachment aboard the *Wabash* were issued the Model 1855 rifle musket. *(Detroit Photographic Co. — Library of Congress)*

When the steamer *Fingal* reached Savannah, Georgia, her cargo was sent to both the Confederate armies in Tennessee and Virginia, with a small portion of the stores going to the State of Georgia and Louisiana.[6] The second vessel to get her cargo through the blockade was the steamer *Gladiator*. Her cargo included 1,112 cases of Enfield rifles totaling 22,240 rifles.[7] These types of successes by the Confederates had to be prevented by the Navy if the blockade was to work.

Not all Southern vessels were so successful in running the blockade. On August 5, near Fernandina, Florida, the sloop of war *Jamestown* spotted a vessel attempting to run the blockade and gave chase. The merchant vessel *Alvarado*, registered out of Boston, had recently been captured by the Confederate privateer *Jefferson Davis*. The prize crew from the privateer was attempting to get the *Alvarado* to a Confederate port to unload her cargo of sheep and goat skins, wool, and 70 tons of iron at a value of $70,000. The crew stranded the prize on a bar near shore, abandoned the ship and rowed to shore. The *Jamestown* sent out three launches under the command of Lieutenant Flusser to investigate. Flusser's instructions called for the men to move the vessel off the bar and sail it out, if possible. If this was not possible, he was to burn it. The naval party consisted of 45 sailors and 13 Marines. The sailors were armed with the .56 caliber Sharps rifles, Colt revolvers and the prewar Plymouth rifles, while the Marines were equipped with .58 caliber Model 1855 rifle muskets. When the launches neared the stranded vessel, two six-pound cannons on shore opened up on Flusser's party. No one was hurt in this action, and they proceeded to board the vessel. Finding it impossible to get the vessel off the bar, they set it afire. The sailors and Marines returned to the *Jamestown* without suffering any casualties.[8] A second vessel to be captured by the Union Navy in the early days of the war was the privateer schooner *Savannah*. On June 3, 1861, she was captured by the brig *Perry* after a lengthy chase.

Amongst the items seized by the *Perry* were the *Savannah's* Confederate flag, along with 15 flintlock pistols, 16 smoothbore muskets, 10 cutlasses, 1 Maynard rifle and 3 revolvers.

Marines at Bull Run

July 21, 1861

The first bloodshed by the Marine Corps in the war occurred not at sea but on land. On July 15, Colonel John Harris, the Commandant of the Corps, received the following orders from the Secretary of the Navy:

"You will pleased to detail from the barracks four companies of eighty men each, the whole under command of Major Reynolds, with the necessary officers, noncommissioned officers, and musicians, for temporary field service under Brigadier General McDowell, to whom Major Reynolds will report. General McDowell will furnish the battalion with camp equipage, provisions, etc."[9]

The Marines drew their .69 caliber M1842 muskets from the headquarters ordnance stores. Issued to the battalion were 15,000 ball cartridges for the smoothbore muskets.[10] The battalion was also to receive 350 haversacks and canteens. When the battalion departed the next day to join the Union infantry on their march toward the Confederates camped at Manassas, the battalion consisted of 353 officers and men. Only 16 Marines had prior combat experience, with the balance being raw recruits. In the line of march, the Marine battalion was placed behind Captain Charles Griffin, Battery D, 5th U.S. Artillery.

The battle of July 21 at Bull Run had been engaged for several hours when the Marines were called forward. At about 2:00 p.m., Captains Griffin and Rickett's batteries, consisting of 11 guns, were placed in an exposed position near the Henry House. The Marine battalion and a detachment of New York Zouaves were sent to support the batteries. Just as the action was starting, 2nd Lieutenant Robert E. Hitchcock was struck by a cannon ball and killed. Lieutenant Hitchcock, an 1859 graduate of Norwich University, had been with the Corps only since June 5, the date of his commission. He was the first Marine killed in the war.[11] Across from the Marine's position was a Confederate battery of 15 guns, which took a toll on the Marines. The 33rd Virginia Infantry advanced at length on the Union position. Since they were dressed in blue uniforms, the Marines and the New York Zouaves believed that the approaching forces were Union reinforcements and held their fire. When the Confederates came within 70 yards of the Union lines, they unleashed a volley killing many of the horses and men in the battery. This unexpected volley caused a great deal of confusion in the Marine battalion. Three times the Marines broke and three times Major Reynolds and his officers brought them back in line. One of the junior officers in this engagement was 2nd Lieutenant Robert W. Huntington who, throughout the war, carried a Model 1855 .58 caliber pistol carbine. The next Commandant of the Corps, Major Zeilin, was wounded in the battle. Up and down the Union line, the troops started to retreat, which took the troops all the way back to Washington. The Marine casualties were:

Marine Battalion[12]
Strength and Casualties
Battle of Manassas
July 21, 1861

	Strength	Casualties
Major	3	1 wounded
Captain	2	—
Lieutenant — 1st	1	—
Lieutenant — 2nd	6	1 killed and 1 wounded
N.C. Staff	2	—
Sergeants — 1st	4	—
Sergeants — 2nd	3	—
Corporals	8	1 wounded
Drummers	2	—
Fife	2	—
Privates	320	8 killed, 16 wounded, and 16 missing
Total	353	44

Union Defense Committee

New York

On April 20, five days after Lincoln's proclamation calling for 75,000 volunteers for 90-day service, the Union Defense Committee (UDC) of New York City was formed. With a budget of a million dollars, their task was to help equip and outfit forces being sent for the defense of the Union. A small portion of these funds was earmarked for the Navy, while most of the funding went to the Army. One of the first expenditures for the Navy was on April 25, for the 30-day charter of the *Quaker City,* which was extended an additional 30 days. The *Quaker City* had formerly been operated by the New York, Havana, and Mobile line. After being chartered for 60 days and capturing six prize vessels, she was purchased by the Navy on August 12, 1861, for blockade duty.[13] In addition to chartering the *Quaker City,* UDC also outfitted her

Lieutenant Robert Huntington remained in the Corps after the Civil War, retiring in 1900 with the rank of Colonel. He is shown here in an 1898 photo as the commanding officer of the Marine battalion in Cuba during the Spanish-American War. Sergeant Major Henry Good is looking through the telescope while Lieutenant Colonel Huntington looks on. Good was killed by enemy sharpshooters shortly after this picture was taken.
(Detroit Photographic Co. — Library of Congress)

for sea at a cost of $15,013.75. The ordnance stores placed on board the vessel included:

Ordnance Stores Issued[14]
Quaker City
April–June 1861

Single-Shot Pistols	153	Boarding Swords	100
Sharps Rifles	100	Cutlasses	250
Savage Revolvers	26	Boarding Pikes	4
Hall Carbines	100	Battle Axes	1
Iron Mounted Musketoons	100	6 Pd. Rifled Brass Cannons	2

The Hall carbines issued were the Model 1843 while the iron mounted musketoons were the Model 1847 Sappers and Miners.[15] The cutlasses appear to have been the Model 1840 heavy cavalry dragoon, not cutlasses. The .52 caliber Sharps NM1859 rifles were purchased from W.J. Syms and

On April 27, the Union Defense Committee of New York purchased 100 iron-mounted musketoons (Sappers & Miners) from William J. Syms at a cost of $9 each. The musketoons were turned over to the New York Navy Yard in June.
(U.S. Military Academy)

Brothers on April 27. Two days later, from the same source, the Halls, musketoons and cutlasses were obtained. Late in the year, UDC sent the Navy a letter requesting payment for the small arms placed on board the *Quaker City*. The Navy would question the cost of several of the small arms and the haggling would go on for some time before UDC claims were settled. The day after UDC chartered the *Quaker City*, UDC gave the New York Navy Yard 50 Colt .31 caliber Model 1849 revolvers, free of charge. These revolvers were inspected by Guert Gansevoort and stamped "UDC" on the buttstrap, "USN" on top of the buttstrap, and "P/GG" on the cylinder. By 1864, twenty Model 1849 Colts had been given by the navy yard to the commanding officers of vessels being outfitted for sea. At the end of the war, two of these .31 caliber Colts were in the possession of Commander William W. Reynolds of the *New Hampshire*, the store ship of the South Atlantic Blockading Squadron.[16]

The Navy and Marine Corps records for the war years are very incomplete. The actual quantities of small arms obtained for their separate services cannot be totally determined. However, the discussions in the following chapters will give the reader a good indication of the types and quantities of small arms used by the sailors and Marines during the conflict.

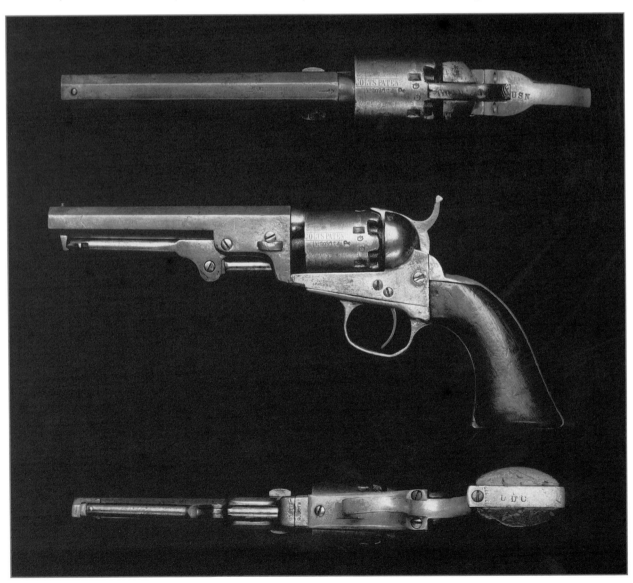

On April 26, UDC turned over to the New York Navy Yard, at no cost to the Navy, fifty Model 1849 pocket revolvers. The Colts were given to captains of vessels being outfitted for sea at the navy yard.
(Steve Selenfriend collection)

1861 Procurements and Sea Service

MUZZLELOADERS

In April, the Navy requested the Army supply them with two hundred .69 caliber muskets and 25,000 musket cartridges. The Army delivered the muskets to the Philadelphia Navy Yard, and the cartridges for the muskets were supplied by Major Ramsay from the Washington Arsenal.[17] By early June, the New York Navy Yard was told that after they outfitted the frigate *Colorado* with the .56 caliber Sharps NM1859 rifles, all future vessels would have to be issued the old smoothbore muskets then being obtained from the Army. The powder charge for these old muskets was set at 100 grain of powder.[18] In July, 100,000 musket cartridges and 100,000 percussion caps were delivered to the Atlantic Blockading Squadron.[19] In September, an additional 1,000 altered .69 caliber muskets were sent by the Ordnance Department to New York, and 420 caliber .69 muskets were delivered to Lieutenant Sanford, the Naval Ordnance Officer for the Mississippi Squadron.[20]

By late in the year, the Navy started to receive from the Army the .58 caliber rifle musket. The first 250 of the .58 caliber rifle muskets were sent to the Washington Navy Yard in November. On November 30, the request went out to the Army for 500 rifle muskets for Porter's mortar squadron, being outfitted at New York, plus a like quantity for Flag Officer Goldsborough at Hampton Roads, Virginia. It appears that the Army supplied the Navy with the .577 caliber Enfield rifle, since Porter's mortar squadron was issued Enfield rifles. By the end of the year, the Army had supplied the Navy in excess of 3,000 muskets of various models.

On December 26, the sloop *Dale* off the coast of South Carolina was notified by the colonel of the 45th Pennsylvania Infantry about a small schooner operating on the South Edisto River. Lieutenant Truxtun in command of the *Dale* sent two cutters to investigate. The sailors were issued muskets, while the Marines carried their .58 caliber rifle muskets. No schooner was found, but upon their return to the *Dale*, they approached the home of Governor Aiken of South Carolina. The naval party was hailed from shore by twelve to fourteen pickets of the 4th South Carolina Infantry. Words were exchanged and a musket volley was fired from shore, but no one was hurt. The sailors and Marines returned the fire, and several shots were fired from the boat howitzer. After the house was destroyed by one of the shells, the Confederates retreated inland. The naval party remained in the area for about half an hour and then returned to the ship.[21] From 1863 to the end of the war, the sloop *Dale* was the ordnance store ship located at Key West, Florida.

Navy Muskets and Plymouth Rifles

Eli Whitney was notified by telegram on May 2 inquiring whether he would be interested in furnishing 3,000 Navy muskets, barrel length 34 inches, and caliber .70 inches. Whitney would produce the muskets if he could use some of the same parts manufactured for his .58 caliber rifle muskets. In June, Captain Hitchcock took one of the 1858 pattern Plymouth rifles to Whitney to use as an example. Whitney, after further discussion with the Navy, agreed to manufacture 10,000 caliber .69 Navy muskets. Whitney

"Sailor on Sentry" by Alfred Waud. The muskets in use by the sailors in 1861 were mainly the smoothbore and rifled musket, caliber .69. *(Library of Congress)*

The rifled and sighted Model 1842 musket. At the outbreak of the conflict, both the Navy and Marine Corps were partially armed with these muskets. *(Gettysburg National Military Park collection, from* Echoes of Glory: Arms & Equipment of the Union, *photograph by Larry Scherer c.1991 Time-Life Books Inc.)*

was allowed to use the standard 1861 lock, iron furnishings and a new Navy pattern rear sight similar to the ones used on the French M1859 rifle.[22] The contract was sent to Whitney on July 15 and called for the rifles to be equipped with saber bayonets at a total cost of $25 each including the saber bayonet. The first 500 rifles were due seven months from the date of the contract signing. The Navy sent Whitney two Springfield rifle muskets from the Springfield Armory to use as patterns for the lock, buttplate, and trigger.[23] Whitney called on Remington to manufacture the barrels for his rifle but was informed that they could not produce the barrels due to their own government orders. Whitney had to look for other sources to manufacture his barrels. By year's end, little progress had been made on the production of the rifles for the Plymouth rifle contract.

The bearded officer standing in the center of the photo is Captain H.B. Lowrey, commander of the Marine detachment aboard the *Wabash*. On November 7, he and his men, armed with their Model 1855 rifle muskets, took possession of the two captured Confederate forts at Port Royal. *(MOLLUS-USAMHI)*

Marine Corps Muzzleloaders

At the outbreak of the war, the standard small arm of the Marines was the .58 caliber Model 1855 rifle musket. The commandant wanted to maintain the .58 caliber in the Corps. On May 9, Colonel Harris wrote to the Secretary of the Navy stating, "I enclosed a requisition for 1,000 rifle muskets of caliber now in use in the Corps and request an order for them on the War Department."[24] The Army was unable to supply the .58 caliber rifle muskets. Therefore, on June 4, Harris ordered five hundred smoothbore muskets. Three hundred of these muskets were sent to Major Slack from the Washington Arsenal in June, and an additional 300 were supplied to the Marines in September. In September, by the request of the Secretary of the Navy, two hundred of these smoothbore muskets were transferred to the Navy.[25]

Port Royal Operations

On September 18, Captain Du Pont wrote to Gideon Welles requesting that a special battalion of 300 Marines be attached to his fleet for the operations at Port Royal, South Carolina. The next day, Colonel Harris was notified he should have this battalion ready to move between October 1 and October 5. Wanting the best arms for his Marines, Harris contacted Welles on September 23 requesting that the War Department supply the battalion with the .58 caliber rifle musket. The official request for the rifle muskets states:

Navy Department, September 24, 1861

Sir:

I have the honor to request that you cause to be issued immediately, for special service, 300 rifle muskets, caliber .58 for the use of the United States Marines, to be delivered at headqurters to Major William B. Slack, quartermaster Marine Corps. A battalion of 300 Marines is to leave with the fleet for important operations connected with the movements of our squadrons, and it is of great importance to furnish them with the same musket which the Marine Corps have heretofore used, viz, the Springfield rifle, caliber .58.

Gideon Welles[26]
Hon. Simon Cameron
Secretary of War

The 300 rifle muskets delivered on this request from Welles were some of the first .58 caliber Model 1861 Springfields manufactured at Springfield Armory. The 1861 Springfield is equipped without the Maynard tape priming system and the patch box in the buttstock. The lock on these rifle muskets obtained by the Marines is dated 1861 with eagles and marked "US/SPRINGFIELD".

In addition to the new rifle muskets, Slack was directed to obtain from the Marine depot at Philadelphia the following items for the battalion:

Battalion Supplies[27]
September 1861

350	Knapsacks	350	Shirts of both Flannel and Linen
350	Haversacks		
350	Canteens	350	Pairs of Drawers
100	Overcoats	350	Pairs of Socks
400	Pairs of Shoes	100	Fatigue Caps

Flag Officer Samuel F. DuPont's naval operations against Port Royal, South Carolina, were the largest naval operations of 1861. The Marine battalion led by Major John G. Reynolds consisted of 19 officers and 330 men. The Marines for this special battalion had been formed from several of the naval stations and were well drilled.[28] The make up of the battalion is as shown:

Battalion Enlisted Strength[29]
October 1861

Marine Location	Sergeants	Corporals	Privates	Musicians
Portsmouth	1	0	15	0
Boston	2	2	40	0
New York	4	4	50	0
USS *North Carolina*	0	0	15	0
USS *Ohio*	0	0	15	0
Lt. Huntington Detachment	1	2	17	0
Lt. Goldsborough Detachment	3	2	36	3
Washington Headquarters	3 - est.	3 - est.	112 - est.	0
Total	14	13	300	3

On October 15, the Marines were directed to embark on the sloop *Pawnee* for Hampton Roads. When they arrived at Hampton Roads, they were sent on board the charter steamer *Governor* out of Boston for the balance of the trip to Port Royal.[30]

The *Governor* left Hampton Roads on Tuesday, October 29, with the Marines on board. On the third day out, a violent storm greatly scattered the Union fleet. The *Governor* started to take on water and was on the verge of sinking. The Marines developed work parties to help pump and bail out the water. The next afternoon, the frigate *Sabine* came alongside and was able to transfer part of the Marines to the *Sabine* before the seas become too violent. The next morning, the remainder of the Marines from the *Governor* jumped into the ocean and were picked up by launches from the *Sabine*. During the two-day transfer, one Marine was killed when he was crushed in two by the collision of the two vessels, and six drowned. All the rifle muskets and about half the accouterments, plus 10,000 rounds of ammunition, were saved. Nearly all the knapsacks, haversacks, canteens and 9,000 rounds of ammunition went down with the ship when it sank a few hours after the Marines had transferred to the *Sabine*.[31]

DuPont started his attack on the two forts at Port Royal on November 7, and by one in the afternoon he silenced the fort's guns. The Marines from the frigate *Wabash*, armed with their M1855 rifle muskets, were sent ashore at 2:45 p.m. to take possession of the forts and prevent the destruction of public property. The Navy quickly converted Port Royal into a major repair and logistics depot for the South Atlantic Blockading Squadron.

RESCUE OF MAJOR REYNOLDS'S BATTALION OF MARINES FROM THE FOUNDERING STEAMER "GOVERNOR."
While being used as a transport, off Cape Hatteras, November 2d, 1861, the steamer *Governor*, Commander Phillips, foundered in the rough sea. Those on board, a battalion of marines under Major Reynolds, were transferred with great difficulty to the *Sabine*. The *Governor* was a sidewheel steamer of 650 tons burden. She was built in New York city in 1846, and was originally intended for river navigation.

Major Reynolds and his Marine battalion arrived on the *Sabine* at Port Royal after its capture. On December 17, Marine headquarters sent to Reynolds the last twenty M1861 rifle muskets in their inventory. The correspondences between Reynolds and Harris indicate that a large number of the arms that the Marines had on hand at Port Royal were the M1855 rifle musket and the M1861.[32]

Sea Duty

Two vessels to which Marines were attached were the *Constellation* and *Pawnee*. In October 1861, while being outfitted for sea at the Boston Navy Yard, the Marine guard aboard the *Constellation* was supplied 5,000 caliber .58 cartridges plus the ship's crew received 3,000 caliber .69 musket cartridges and 10,000 pistol cartridges.[33] When the *Constellation* left port, she sailed the Mediterranean for three years. The sloop *Pawnee*, being outfitted from the Philadelphia Navy Yard, issued the Marine guard 2,000 caliber .58 cartridges.[34] Both detachments of Marine guards were armed with the M1855 rifle musket. The Marine guard aboard the *St. Mary's* at Mare Island, California, pulled night watch on the magazine at the navy yard. The guards were issued the M1855 rifle musket and a Colt M1851 revolver.[35] The *Minnesota*, *Mississippi* and *Wabash* Marine detachments were also armed with the M1855 rifle musket. Marine Corps policy called for each member of the guard to be issued 200 rounds of ball cartridges and 100 blank cartridges.

When the frigate *Minnesota* left for duty in May in the Atlantic Blockading Squadron, she had her full detachment of Marines on board, consisting of one officer, Captain W.L. Shuttleworth, 3 sergeants, 4 corporals, 2 musicians and 40 privates. In a letter to Colonel Harris, Captain Shuttleworth states that he took his men ashore for musket practice. Firing at a target at 250 yards, the Marines hit the target 200 times. He concludes his letter by stating that he would not give one rifle musket for 10 smoothbore muskets.[36]

Not all Marine detachments aboard ship were armed with the new .58 caliber rifle muskets. The Marine guard aboard the frigate *Potomac* and the sloop *Lancaster* was armed with the old .69 caliber muskets. The *Potomac* Marines had the M1842 altered muskets, which were rifled, sighted, and dated 1853.

The screw sloop *Lancaster* in 1899. In 1861, the Marine guard aboard ship were armed with .69 caliber muskets. The *Lancaster* saw service in the Pacific during the war. (Detroit Photographic Co. — Library of Congress)

They reported that after firing five blank cartridges from their altered muskets, the barrels became so hot that they had to cease firing. A request was made for 200 to 300 of the new .58 caliber rifle muskets in exchange for their old muskets.[37] With a shortage of rifle muskets in the Corps, it is unlikely that the *Potomac* Marines received them, since they were aboard a receiving ship and not engaged in combat operations. The Marine guard of the flagship *Lancaster* commanded by Captain James Jones was issued the .69 caliber muskets from the Philadelphia depot. The 40 privates, 4 corporals and three sergeants of the *Lancaster* guard had been taken from the Marine barracks at Washington, Boston and Philadelphia.[38]

Amphibious Operations, 1861

The first amphibious landing of the Marines in the war occurred at Hatteras Inlet on August 28. At 6:00 a.m., the Marines from the *Minnesota*, led by Captain Shuttleworth, arrived on the *Monticello* and were joined shortly thereafter by Marines from the frigate *Wabash*. At 11:45 a.m., the Marines left the *Monticello* and were landed on shore in landing craft from the ships.[39] Because of heavy surf, only 300 Marines and soldiers were able to land before the balance of the landing parties were canceled. Cut off from the fleet, the landing force proceeded to attack Fort Clark. However, the Confederates had evacuated the fort after filling up all their ammunition and proceeded to Fort Hatteras. The Marines entered the fort without a fight and spent the night on the lookout for possible Confederate attacks that never materialized.

In the morning, the fleet continued to pound away at Fort Hatteras until the white flag was hoisted above the fort at about 1:30 p.m. Seven hundred and fifty prisoners of war were taken. In the two-day battle, the Marines suffered no casualties. One of the vessels in the bombardment of Fort Hatteras was the gunboat *Harriet Lane*. On August 29, she became stranded on a shoal and was unable to break free. To lighten the load, shot, shells and coal were thrown overboard as were two First Model Maynard carbines. After nearly 50 hours, the *Harriet Lane* was able to free herself at 2:20 p.m. on August 31.[40]

=== *Breechloaders* ===

Jenks Carbines

By early January, the 240 Jenks/Merrill carbines were ready for final inspection at Baltimore. Lieutenant Wainwright was directed on the 19th of the month to travel to the Merrill plant and inspect the carbines. Wainwright reported back that the latch catch, which had been a problem, had been corrected and that all 240 carbines had passed inspection. The arms were then sent forward by ship to the Washington Navy Yard with the transportation cost being charged to Merrill.[41]

The sloop *Richmond* received about 20 Jenks/ Merrill carbines plus 36 NM1859 .56 caliber Sharps rifles, while the gunboat *Michigan* also received the Jenks/Merrill carbine. In June, while at sea, Captain John Pope commanding the *Richmond* had three of his lieutenants test the Jenks/Merrill for military use. The lieutenants' report of June 10 found the following faults with the carbine:

The main spring of the great number of the carbines are not sufficiently strong to explode a percussion cap by the first blow of the hammer, the half cock does not set the hammer far enough back to put a cap on the nipple, this involving the cocking of the piece to cap it, and the letting down the hammer again after capping — the "Merrill Improvement" is defective-the jar occasioned by dropping the piece in coming to "order arms" will in almost every instance force the spring down, this unfastening the security of the receiver.

In our opinion the Jenks Carbine with the "Merrill improvement" is not adopted to Naval purpose, not even so much as the old Jenk's Carbines.[42]

As more effective breechloaders became available, the Jenks/Merrill carbines were replaced. The arms on the *Michigan* remained on board until November 1864, when they replaced their 25 Jenks/Merrill carbines with 40 Sharps & Hankins carbines.[43] Both the *Michigan* and the *Richmond* remained in naval service well into the twentieth century. The *Richmond* was disposed of in 1919 and the *Michigan* in 1927.[44]

On April 5, Captain Harwood instructed each of the naval yards to inspect their Jenks carbines for their effectiveness for further naval service. It was the universal opinion of the officers in question that the Jenks should be withdrawn from active service. Commander John Dahlgren stated that of the 279 Jenks carbines on hand at the Washington Navy Yard, 19 had been inspected. Each of these carbines was fired 20 times each. Sixty grains of loose powder and a spherical ball were used in the firings. After a few firings, the powder residue built up, causing the breech lever from closing because of the fouling. The Navy percussion caps would not always ignite the cartridge. Since the Jenks were not rifled and were defective, Dahlgren felt that the entire lot should be condemned as unfit for naval service.[45] In April, two Navy yards had these Jenks in inventory:

Jenks Carbines in Inventory[46]
April 1861

	New York	Philadelphia
Remington/Jenks	341	71
Jenks/Merrill	2	0
Jenks Long Carbines	10	0
Jenks Old Style	<u>386</u>	<u>264</u>
Total	739	335

(Right) The screw sloop *Richmond* at Baton Rouge on March 30, 1863. In 1861, the *Richmond* was issued both the NM1859 Sharps rifles caliber .56 and the Jenks/Merrill carbines. *(U.S. Naval Historical Center)*

(Below) A close-up of the action of a Jenks/Merrill carbine. Note that the hammer at half-cock does not allow sufficient space to place a percussion cap on the nipple. This problem was identified in the June 10th report by the officers on the *Richmond*. *(Author's collection, photo by Mike O'Donnell)*

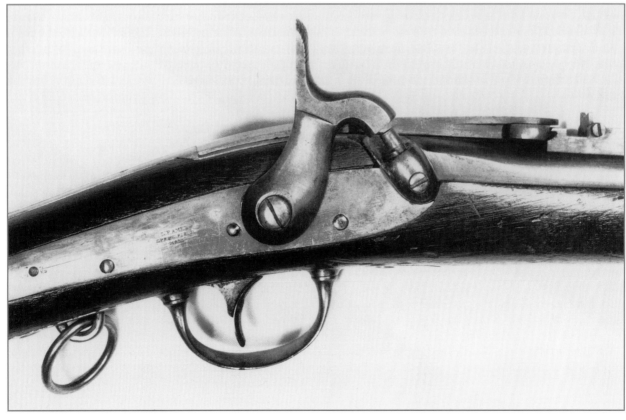

Because of these reports, the Jenks was about to be taken out of service when the war started. The decision was made to issue the Jenks only when no other breechloaders were available. A lack of small arms caused the *Monticello*, *Mississippi* and *Susquehanna* to leave port supplied with the Jenks carbine. In a short period of time, each of these vessels was rearmed with Sharps rifles. On August 27, having a large quantity of Jenks on hand, the Navy sold 2,800 Jenks carbines to A.M. Eastman of Manchester, New Hampshire.[47]

Joslyn Rifles

At the start of the conflict, the 500 Model 1855 Joslyn rifles on the September 9, 1859, contract had never been delivered. When John Q. Adams of Washington, D.C., contacted the Navy that he had 100 Joslyn rifles for sale, the war had been in progress for nearly nine months. On December 23, the Bureau notified Adams that the Navy would take the 100 Joslyn rifles with saber bayonets at $37.50 each plus 10,000 cartridges. Deliveries were directed to the Philadelphia Navy Yard.[48] At this period in time, both the sloops *Brooklyn* and the *Hartford* were being outfitted for sea at Philadelphia. Both vessels were issued a supply of Joslyn rifles. The *Brooklyn* ship logs of February 18, 1862, read: "Exercise boat crew with both rifles and muskets."[49] The rifles in the entry were the M1855 Joslyn. The *Hartford* would have 12 of their Joslyn rifles destroyed when the ship passed the New Orleans forts in April 1862. These two ships are the only vessels known to have had the Joslyn rifles on board.

Sharps & Hankins Rifles and Spencer Rifles

On June 8, 1861, a Spencer rifle was test fired 500 times at the Washington Navy Yard. The results were so favorable that an order was placed for 700 Spencer rifles with saber bayonets at a cost of $43 each. A month later, at the same location, a Sharps & Hankins rifle was also tested with good results. An order was placed for 500 S&H rifles with saber bayonet at $36 each. No deliveries were made on these two contracts in 1861.

NM1859 Sharps Rifles

The last delivery of 120 Sharps rifles on the September 1859 order for 900 was received in April 1861. These .56 caliber Sharps were placed on board the sloops *Vincennes* and *Preble*. The sloop *Jamestown* being outfitted out of Philadelphia received:

USS *Jamestown*[50]
Small Arms Issues
April 16, 1861

60	Colt Revolvers	6,000	Cartridges
70	Sharps Rifles	7,000	Cartridges
70	Muskets w/Bayonets	7,000	Navy Rifle Musket Cartridges (for the prewar Plymouth Rifles)

The only adopted Navy rifle muskets in the Navy at this time were actually the M1858 Plymouth rifles.

By June, all the .56 caliber Sharps had been issued from the New York Navy Yard with the last ones being placed on board the frigate *Colorado*. Philadelphia had issued all of their Sharps by the end of April. The sidewheel frigate *Mississippi* had to leave New York with 80 of the old Jenks carbines, since there was a shortage of Sharps rifles on hand.[51]

One hundred Model 1855 Joslyn rifles were delivered to the Navy in December 1861 and issued to the *Hartford* and *Brooklyn* from the Philadelphia Navy Yard.

CIVIL WAR Small Arms of the U.S. Navy and Marine Corps

In June 1861, John Mitchell, agent for the Sharps Rifle Mfg. Co., received a contract calling for the delivery of 1,500 NMSharps rifles caliber .52. Pictured is one of the Mitchell contract Sharps, serial numbered in the low 40000 range, which had been stored at the Philadelphia Navy Yard prior to its donation to the Smithsonian Institution.

(Below, right) In the fall of 1861, the screw sloop *Pensacola*, being outfitted at the Washington Navy Yard, received on board 80 of the Mitchell contracted Sharps rifles. *(MOLLUS-USAMHI)*

On April 19, 1861, the Secretary of the Navy directed Commander Dahlgren at the Washington Navy Yard to place on board the *Anacostia* sufficient ordnance to be used by the commanding officer at the Norfolk Navy Yard to prevent the capture of the yard by Confederate forces. Included in the ordnance sent were 120 Sharps rifles. This ordnance was transferred to the *Pawnee* before it sailed the next day.[52] By the time the relief fleet reached Norfolk, all the vessels at the yard had been scuttled to prevent their capture. Parties of sailors and Marines from the *Pawnee* were sent on shore to remove or destroy public property so that it would not fall into Confederate control. After the property was destroyed by being torched, the *Pawnee* proceeded to Hampton Roads.

The Confederates shortly thereafter entered the Norfolk facilities and were able to salvage a large part of the yard, including the frigate *Merrimack*, which became the Confederate ironclad *Virginia*. During this same period of time, Dahlgren also outfitted for sea the gunboats *Mount Vernon* and *Pocahontas* with Sharps rifles.

One of the first combat operations in which the Sharps was involved occurred at Mathias Point, Virginia, on June 27. Twenty-three sailors from the *Pawnee* and a similar number from the *Thomas Freeborn* landed at Mathias Point to throw up breastwork of sand bags. Late in the afternoon, the sailors were ordered back to the vessels when they were fired on by Confederate forces. The sailors, armed with their Sharps rifles, returned the fire and then retreated to their vessels. In the exchange of fire, Commander J.H. Ward was killed and four sailors wounded. Eleven of the 21 Sharps rifles belonging to the *Freeborn* were lost in the engagement.[53] The Confederates sustained no casualties in the action.

John Mitchell's Sharps Rifle Contract

With all the Sharps in service by early June, the Navy placed an additional order for 1,500 caliber .52 NM1859 Sharps rifles with Sharps agent John Mitchell of Washington, D.C. Mitchell's order of June 4, called for 150 rifles to be delivered in six days to Boston, Philadelphia and New York. The balance of the contract was to be forwarded to the Navy by the 25th of the month.[54] The order for the saber bayonets was placed the next day with the Ames Sword Company of Chicopee, Massachusetts. Letters uncovered in the National Archives indicate that a large portion of Mitchell's order was received at the Navy yards by late June and early July. The following chart reflects the deliveries made at the Boston Navy Yard on the Mitchell contract:

Boston Navy Yard
Sharps Rifles — Mitchell Contract

Delivery Dates	# of Boxes	Rifles Delivered
June 17, 1861	5	50
June 19, 1861	10	100
July 3, 1861	4	40
July 13, 1861	5	50
July 17, 1861	5	50
July 23, 1861	6	60
July 30, 1861	5	50
August 7, 1861	10	100
Total	**50**	**500**

The first New York delivery by late June was earmarked for the Portsmouth Navy Yard. Deliveries were to be sent as soon as the saber bayonets were received from Ames.[55] On July 8, the sloop *Iroquois*, being outfitted at New York, received 80 of the Mitchell contracted Sharps rifles plus 20 minie muskets and 17 revolvers. A portion of the Sharps rifles sent to Portsmouth were placed on board the sloop *Kearsarge* early the following year. The first rifles delivered to Philadelphia were issued to the *St. Lawrence*. Later, 300 Sharps were sent to William Nelson of Cincinnati, Ohio, for the Mississippi fleet. The sloop *Pensacola*, being outfitted at the Washington Navy Yard, was authorized 80 muskets, 40 Starr revolvers, 80 pistols, 80 Sharps rifles and 130 swords.[56] The serial numbers of the Mitchell Sharps are found in the low 40000 range.

PISTOLS/REVOLVERS

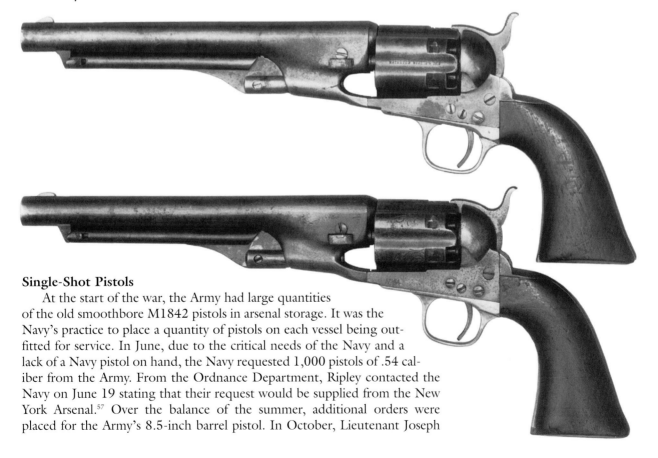

The first Colt revolvers delivered to the Navy during the war were the fluted cylinder .44 caliber Model 1860 Colt Armies. Shown are two Colt Armies serial number 4746 and 4747; both were sent to the Washington Navy Yard in 1861. *(Steve Selenfriend collection)*

Single-Shot Pistols

At the start of the war, the Army had large quantities of the old smoothbore M1842 pistols in arsenal storage. It was the Navy's practice to place a quantity of pistols on each vessel being outfitted for service. In June, due to the critical needs of the Navy and a lack of a Navy pistol on hand, the Navy requested 1,000 pistols of .54 caliber from the Army. From the Ordnance Department, Ripley contacted the Navy on June 19 stating that their request would be supplied from the New York Arsenal.[57] Over the balance of the summer, additional orders were placed for the Army's 8.5-inch barrel pistol. In October, Lieutenant Joseph

Sanford requested the Army send 500 pistols and 500 artillery swords plus 420 muskets to the Mississippi Squadron. Sanford's order was supplied from the Washington Arsenal.[58] In December, the Army supplied 1,000 Army pistols to be divided equally between Porter Mortor Squadron and Goldsborough's fleet. Porter issued about 23 pistols to each of his vessels (see Chapter 4).

In 1861, one vessel to receive the single-shot pistol was the gunboat USS *Dawn*. The gunboat *Dawn* was commissioned into naval service on May 8 at the New York Navy Yard and assigned to the Potomac Flotilla.[59] In addition to her two 32-pound cannons, the *Dawn's* small arms consisted of:

USS *Dawn*[60]
Small Arms
June 1861

Musketoons	30
Pistols	30
Cutlasses	30
Colt Revolvers	1

Colt Revolvers, Model 1860

The first wartime order with Colt occurred on May 2 for the .44 caliber Colt New Model Holster revolvers. The Navy directed Colt to send 250 revolvers to Boston and a similar quantity to New York. The price charged for these .44s came to $25 each. By the end of the month, all 500 revolvers had been delivered. On June 12, an additional 250 revolvers were delivered to Boston, with further orders in August for 200 revolvers at both locations.[61] Two hundred of the .44s were sent also in August to the Washington Navy Yard. Fifty revolvers were selected and tested by Lieutenant Richard Wainwright. During the trials, one of the .44 caliber Colts set off three charges at one pull of the trigger. The cause of the multiple discharge was found to be flaws between the cylinders. Because of the flaws in these fluted cylinder Colts, the Navy had them replaced with .36 caliber NM1861 Colt revolvers on September 28.[62] The .44s were mainly issued to vessels on the Mississippi River. Such ironclads as the *Essex, Cincinnati, Pittsburg, Louisville, Baron deKalb* and the *Mound City* were all armed with the .44 caliber Colt.

New Model 1861

With the exchange of the 200 Colt .44 for a like number of the New Model 1861 .36 caliber Colt revolvers, the .36 caliber became the standard for the Navy and all future orders were in this caliber. Toward this end, the Navy placed orders for and received by year's end 2,000 NM1861 Colts.

NM1861 Colt Revolvers
Deliveries 1861

Navy Yard	Quantities
Washington	600
Boston	500
New York	500
Philadelphia	300
Portsmouth	100
Total	**2,000**

The price paid for the NM1861 Colts was $23 each. Very few of these Colts were stamped by the naval inspectors. The ones that are will be found with "USN" stamped on the bottom of the buttplate.

Galveston Raid, November 7, 1861

One of the most daring raids of the war occurred on the evening of November 7. At 11:40 p.m., Lieutenant James E. Jouett left with two launches from the frigate *Santee*. The lieutenant's mission was to enter the harbor at Galveston, Texas, and if possible, destroy the rebel steamer *General Rusk* anchored in the harbor. To reach the rebel steamer, Jouett's men would first have to slip past the rebel schooner *Royal Yacht*, on guard at the entrance to the harbor, and get past a fort. With their oars muffled to silence the noise, the Union sailors were nearly able to reach the rebel steamer before they were discovered. With the element of surprise gone, they turned back and attacked the lookout schooner *Royal Yacht*. The sailors, armed with M1851 Colt Navy revolvers, .69 caliber muskets and cutlasses, fought their way on board and quickly captured the Confederate crew, which was armed with musketoons, cutlasses and boarding pikes. In the attack, the *Royal Yacht* was struck 37 times by musket fire.[63] Before the struggle was over and 13 Confederate prisoners captured, the Union sailors suffered two killed and seven wounded — one of the wounded being Lieutenant Jouett. Unable to set sail, the Union sailors set fire to the schooner and returned to the *Santee* at 6:15 a.m. They left behind on board the schooner a Colt Navy pistol and a cutlass marked: "26.1 B, 2nd D". For his action in this daring undertaking, Lieutenant Jouett was transferred to New York and given command of his own vessel. One of the sailors, George Bell, would receive the Medal of Honor for his action in this raid. The *General Rusk*, being nearby, came and put out the fire started by Jouett's men. The schooner had suffered substantial damage, but was able to be repaired. It returned to Confederate naval service until it was captured by the *William G. Anderson* on April 15, 1863.[64] In the following year, the frigate *Santee* was turned over to the Naval Academy and acted as a school ship until 1912.

A sailor armed with a fluted .44 caliber Colt Model 1860 revolver with shoulder stock attachment. He is wearing a Dahlgren Bowie knife on his belt.
(Norm Flayderman collection)

The only other .44 caliber revolver obtained by the Navy during the war was the .44 caliber Joslyn. In the fall of 1861, the Washington Navy Yard received 100 Joslyn revolvers. They were issued to both the *Yankee* and *Underwriter*. Both vessels were assigned to the Potomac Flotilla. *(U.S. Army Photograph)*

Joslyn Revolvers

The only other .44 caliber revolver purchased by the Navy during the war was the Joslyn. In June, a five-shot .44 caliber Joslyn revolver was sent to the Washington Navy Yard for testing. The revolver was fired 150 rounds with good results. Dahlgren states in his June 28 report on the Joslyn, "I am induced to request that one hundred of these pistols may be ordered for use in this yard."[65] The order for the 100 Joslyns was placed with Benjamin Joslyn on July 1. The first 50 were delivered in September and the balance in the following month. They are stamped "USN" on the buttstrap, and a small anchor is located on the underside of the barrel. The Joslyn revolvers found their way onto ships being outfitted for service in the Potomac Flotilla. The side-wheel steamer *Underwriter* and the tug *Yankee* were both issued a quantity of Joslyns. As late as 1865, some of the Joslyn revolvers were still in use on the *Yankee*.[66] The *Underwriter* was captured and destroyed by a Confederate boat crew while at anchor in the Neuse River near Berne, North Carolina, on February 2, 1864. If the Joslyns were destroyed with the *Underwriter*, this may be one of the reasons why so few of the naval-stamped Joslyns survived.

North-Savage Revolvers

Only one formal contract was entered for the North-Savage .36 caliber revolvers during the conflict. This order of May 7 with Captain Hitchcock called for the Savage Revolving Fire-Arms Company of Middletown, Connecticut, to supply the Navy with 800 pistol revolvers of North-Savage patent at $20 each. The revolvers were the standard wartime model.[67] Deliveries were as follows: 300 in May, 200 in June, 100 in July, 100 in August, and the last 100 in September. The 100 revolvers received at Philadelphia in May were issued to the frigate *St. Lawrence* then being outfitted for sea.

Small Arms Issued
USS *St. Lawrence*
June 1861

Sharps Rifles	100	North-Savage Revolvers	100
Pistols	35		

The *St. Lawrence* was first assigned to the Atlantic Blockading Squadron. In March 1862, she was one of the Union fleet ships damaged at Hampton Roads by fire from the CSS *Virginia*. She remained in naval service until December 1875 when she was sold. Other vessels to be issued the Savage during the early days of the war were the *DeSoto, James Alger, Stars & Stripes, Unadilla, Valley City* and the *Young Rover*. The most famous vessel to have had Savage revolvers on board was the frigate *Constitution*. At the start of the war, she was the practice ship for the Naval Academy. On February 16, the Boston Navy Yard sent to the academy 50 Savage revolvers.[68] These revolvers would have been on board the *Constitution* when she left with the midshipmen for their new home at Newport, Rhode Island, on April 24, 1861.

Starr Revolvers

Like the North-Savage, only one order was placed for the .36 caliber double-action Starr revolvers. The order of October 12 was for 100 revolvers with 60 being delivered to New York and 40 to Washington. The price was set at $20 per revolver.[69] The revolvers were sent

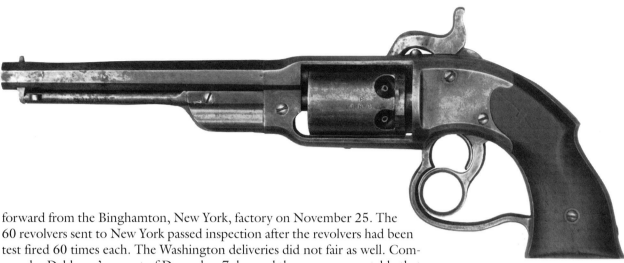

forward from the Binghamton, New York, factory on November 25. The 60 revolvers sent to New York passed inspection after the revolvers had been test fired 60 times each. The Washington deliveries did not fair as well. Commander Dahlgren's report of December 7 deemed them so unacceptable that the entire lot was rejected and returned to the factory. The revolver's rejection was due to the percussion caps catching and prevented the cylinder from rotating. Even when the caps were removed, the cylinder failed to rotate. Of the 40 Starr revolvers tested, only 13 set the percussion caps off every time. They attempted to fire each revolver 12 times.

A total of 800 Savage revolvers were delivered to the Navy in 1861, plus an additional 300 the year before.
(Steve Selenfriend collection)

Test Results of the Starr Revolver[70]
Washington Navy Yard
December 1861

Serial #	# of Times Cap Failed to Explode In 12 Attempts	Serial #	# of Times Cap Failed to Explode In 12 Attempts
2810	3	2721	0
2818	3	2732	1
2825	1	2643	0
2826	2	2710	0
2837	2	2739	0
2821	4	2651	0

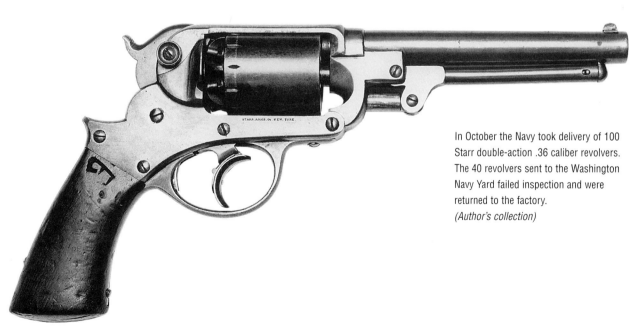

In October the Navy took delivery of 100 Starr double-action .36 caliber revolvers. The 40 revolvers sent to the Washington Navy Yard failed inspection and were returned to the factory.
(Author's collection)

Serial #	# of Times Cap Failed to Explode In 12 Attempts	Serial #	# of Times Cap Failed to Explode In 12 Attempts
2816	1	2731	3
2820	1	2673	0
2813	2	2724	0
2809	1	2667	0
2812	1	2634	2
2823	2	2723	0
2815	1	2730	2
2811	3	2734	1
2819	7	2722	2
2822	1	2662	0
2817	5	2738	0
2814	5	2640	3
2571	1	2733	0
2828	2	2737	0

While the above Starr revolvers were rejected, it had been hoped that they could be issued to the sloop *Pensacola*, then being outfitted for sea at Washington. Some of the Starrs accepted at New York were sent to Philadelphia in January 1862 for issue to the sloop *Hartford*.

EDGED WEAPONS

Model 1861 Ames Naval Cutlass

The Navy's standard cutlass at the start of the war was the M1841 naval cutlass, a.k.a. "the Roman Sword." On May 18, the Navy sent to the Ames Mfg. Co. a drawing of a French sword from which they wanted Ames to produce a sample. About three weeks later, on June 5, the two parties entered into a contract for 8,000 of the new pattern M1861 Ames naval cutlass.[71] The cost to the Navy for this new pattern cutlass was set at $4.53 each.[72] By the second week in July, the first 100 of the M1861 cutlasses were delivered to the Boston Navy Yard. The total deliveries to the various yards had reached 600 by August 7.[73] At this point, Ames was instructed to start stamping serial numbers on the guard and on the upper part of the scabbard for all future cutlasses delivered. The serial numbering was to start at 201 but, since 600 had already been delivered, the numbering started at 601.[74] The cutlasses already delivered were stamped by the navy yard. Serial numbered cutlasses stamped by the Navy are known over 500. When the production reached 1000, the prefix "M" was used. Therefore, the cutlass serial numbered 21049 would be stamped by Ames as "21 M 49".

On December 10, the order for Ames cutlasses was increased to 15,000. By the end of 1861, the Ames factory had sent forward 5,000 cutlasses:

M1861 Ames Navy Cutlasses[75]
Deliveries 1861

Navy Yard	Quantities
New York	1,700
Boston	1,500
Philadelphia	900
Portsmouth	600
Washington	300
Total	**5,000**

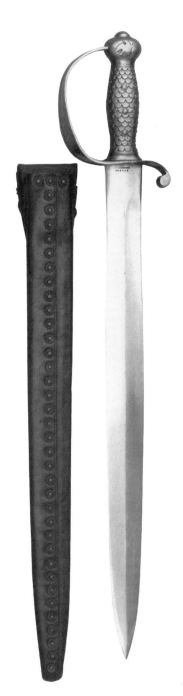

At the start of the war, the standard cutlass of the U.S. Navy was the Model 1841 naval cutlass. During the 1840s the Navy had received over 6,000 of the cutlasses from Ames. (Steve Selenfriend collection)

Marine Corps Swords and Accouterments

On November 28, 1860, the Philadelphia firm of Horstmann Bros. & Co. received the 1861 contract from the Corps for sergeants and musicians swords. The contract called for NCO swords to be delivered at $5.25 each and the musicians swords at a dollar less. Major Slack placed an order on June 3 for 80 sergeants and 40 musicians swords with Horstmann. Slack requested that half of the sergeant sword blades be 31.5 inches in length and the rest of them be 28.5 inches. The musician sword blades on half of the delivery were 26 inches, and the balance at 24 inches. He stated that the standard musician sword blade of 31 inches was much too long for the boy musicians.[76] The swords delivered up to this time were the standard Army M1850 Foot Officer's sword (as the Sergeant Sword). This was to change with this statement: "I should be pleased that the half of the guard on the inside be dispensed with altogether as it only serves to protect the thumb, but is very inconvenient and awkward in wearing the sword both musician and sergeant."[77] Horstmann went along with the changes. On this same date, Slack sent to the Marines at New York five of the standard Army M1850 swords. He told the commanding Marine officer that he would only send five of the new pattern swords since that was all he had, but had just placed an order for more which would have changes to the length of the blade and changes to the guard. In reference to the musician swords, it was the directive of the commandant that the old pattern musician sword be issued first to the musicians going to sea, and this supply was nearly exhausted.

As of December 4, 1860, the New York firms of Henry A. Dingee and Thomas Smith & Sons were awarded 1861 contracts. Dingee's contract called for the delivery of bayonet scabbards for the M1855 rifle musket. Thomas Smith's contract included cartridge boxes, drums, fifes, drum heads, sword frogs and musket slings. In June of 1861, Smith supplied at least 150 cartridge boxes to the Marines.

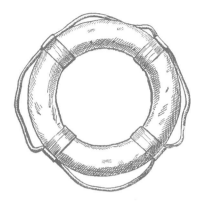

Next to the cannon nearest the camera is a circle of Model 1841 cutlasses. The vessel is the sloop *Pawnee*.
(National Archives)

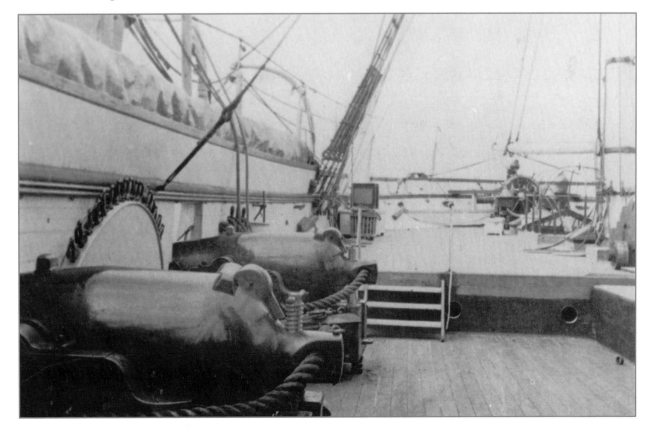

CIVIL WAR Small Arms of the U.S. Navy and Marine Corps

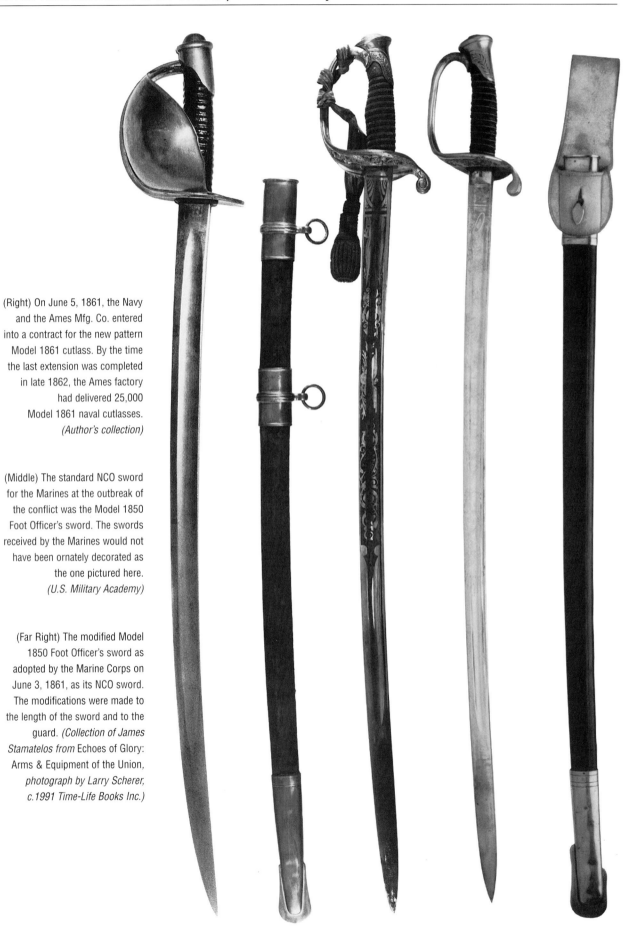

(Right) On June 5, 1861, the Navy and the Ames Mfg. Co. entered into a contract for the new pattern Model 1861 cutlass. By the time the last extension was completed in late 1862, the Ames factory had delivered 25,000 Model 1861 naval cutlasses. *(Author's collection)*

(Middle) The standard NCO sword for the Marines at the outbreak of the conflict was the Model 1850 Foot Officer's sword. The swords received by the Marines would not have been ornately decorated as the one pictured here. *(U.S. Military Academy)*

(Far Right) The modified Model 1850 Foot Officer's sword as adopted by the Marine Corps on June 3, 1861, as its NCO sword. The modifications were made to the length of the sword and to the guard. *(Collection of James Stamatelos from* Echoes of Glory: Arms & Equipment of the Union, *photograph by Larry Scherer, c.1991 Time-Life Books Inc.)*

Battle Axes and Boarding Pikes

The battle ax was supplied to the fireman of the gun crew during enemy action. It was his duty to put out fires caused by the enemy's cannon fire. The battle ax was carried in a case attached to the fireman's belt. To meet the demand for battle axes, the Navy contracted with the Empire Tool Co. of New York City for 1,200 battle axes. The price charged to the Navy was $6.50 per dozen. Deliveries were made on the August 22 order in September.[78]

The nine-foot long boarding pike was used to help repel boarders. With the increased requirements for pikes needed for vessels being outfitted for sea, the Navy placed orders with Richard M. Nichols of New York City. The quantities of boarding pikes supplied by Nichols in 1861 were:

Boarding Pikes Deliveries[79]
Richard M. Nichols
1861

August	1,600
September	1,500
October	1,200
December	500
Total	**4,800**

Dahlgren Bowie Knives and Saber Bayonets

Prior to the war, Commander John Dahlgren had developed a Bowie-style knife bayonet for the Navy rifle musket (Plymouth pattern 1858 rifle). Dahlgren stated that his bayonet "is a short broad and stout knife of the well known Bowie pattern, the principal use of which I designed to be in the hand in close conflict, such as boarding. In campaigning it would also serve many wants: but it may be fixed and used as a bayonet."[80]

The nine-foot-long pikes were used to help repel enemy boarding parties. The pikes in this photo are stored on the side of the ship to the right of the officers.
The photograph was taken aboard the *Kearsarge* at Cherbourg, France, in June 1864. *(U.S. Naval Historical Center)*

81

In the Fall of 1861, the Washington Navy Yard received 500 Dahlgren Bowie knives from Ames. The Bowie knife's principal purpose was to repel boarders. *(Author's collection)*

Several vessels were being outfitted for duty in the Potomac Flotilla. These ships operating in coastal waters would be highly vulnerable to Confederate boarding attack. The Dahlgren Bowie knife would help meet this requirement. On August 14, the Navy telegraphed Ames to forward without delay 200 Bowie knives with belts, frogs and cartridge boxes to the Washington Navy Yard. The order was later increased to 500.

Dahlgren Bowie Knives[81]
Deliveries 1861
Washington Navy Yard

September 28	50 Knives
October 5	150 Knives
October 29	100 Knives
October 31	100 Knives
November	100 Knives
Total	**500 Knives**

Saber Bayonets for Mitchell's Sharps Rifles

The Navy turned to Ames to supply the 1,500 saber bayonets needed for the NM1859 Sharps rifles that were ordered from John Mitchell. The contract for the saber bayonets was signed on June 5 with James T. Ames. The first 100 saber bayonets were received at the Washington Navy Yard on July 23.[82] At year's end, the total deliveries had exceeded 1,300. The balance of the order was received early in the following year.

Ames Sharps Saber Bayonets[83]
Mitchell Contract
Deliveries 1861

Navy Yard	Quantities
Washington	150
Boston	575
New York	386
Philadelphia	200
Total	**1,311**

The saber bayonets received on this contract are stamped "MADE BY/AMES MFG CO/CHICOPEE/MASS" in four lines with the date 1861.

As the year came to a close, the clash of the ironclads was only months away from turning the Navy upside down.

Chapter 4
The Clash of the Ironclads, 1862

A New Age in Naval Warfare Begins

Naval warfare would be revolutionized by the events of March 8 and 9, 1862, off Hampton Roads, Virginia. The age of the wooden ship came to an end. At 11:00 a.m. on March 8, a sunny Saturday morning, the ironclad CSS *Virginia*, formally the *Merrimack*, started down river on her date in history. The *Virginia* first passed the frigate *Congress* firing broadside into her. With the *Congress* heavily damaged, she proceeded on and attacked the *Cumberland* by ramming her. The two ships fired at each other for nearly an hour. All the time, the *Cumberland* was sinking. The *Cumberland* went down losing 121 out of 376 men taken into the fight.[1] The *Virginia* then turned her guns back on the *Congress*. At a distance of 150 yards, the *Virginia* begin to rake the Union ship. For two hours, the *Congress* took the punishment. Unable to fire their big guns at the Confederate ironclad, the Marines and sailors took up muskets and tried to fire volleys at the *Virginia* gunports. With the blood running out of the *Congress'* scuppers, and being on fire, she surrendered. The *Congress* lost 120 out of 434 men in the fight.[2] The *Congress* burned late into the night. The *Virginia* returned to Sewell's Point for the night. The next day, she planned to finish off the Union fleet.

Later that night, the Union ironclad *Monitor* appeared on the scene. The *Monitor* was designed by John Ericsson of New York. Ericsson's *Monitor* was one of three experimental ironclad designs ordered by the Navy in

The sinking of the USS *Cumberland* by the Confederate ironclad *Merrimack* off Newport News, Virginia, on March 8, 1862. (Beverly Robinson collection. Naval Academy Museum, U.S. Naval Historical Center)

83

The deck of the ironclad USS *Monitor* in July 1862. The night watch were issued rifles, probably Enfield or Sharps. On the last day of the year, while under tow, the *Monitor* sank in a gale off Cape Hatteras. *(National Archives)*

1861. The *Monitor*, with the *Galena* and *New Ironsides*, were all placed in service in 1862. The *Monitor* was launched in 100 days as of January 30, 1862, and commissioned on February 28. Its unique design gave the craft the nickname "a tin can on a shingle" or "the cheesebox on a raft." Her revolving central turret held two 11-inch Dahlgren guns. The Dahlgren fired a 166-pound solid shot with a range of one mile, every seven minutes.[3] Forward of the turret was the pilot house. When the *Monitor* left New York harbor for Hampton Roads on March 6, the Navy had invested $275,000 in her success.

Early in the morning of March 9, the *Virginia* started for the *Minnesota*, which was still aground. To the amazement of Captain Van Brunt of the *Minnesota*, the *Monitor* left his side and made straight for the Confederate ironclad. Over the next several hours, the first clash of ironclads took place.

The battle, carried out at point-blank range, caused little damage to either ship. The *Virginia* attempted to ram the *Monitor*, but did little damage. A shell fired from the *Virginia* ten yards away struck the pilothouse. Lieutenant John L. Worden, commanding officer of the *Monitor*, was struck in the face by the shell blast, which blinded him. Lieutenant Samuel D. Greene took command and continued the fight. Shortly after noon, the two warships drew off from each other. The historical battle was finished. No one on either side was killed in the engagement. The fight ended in a tactical draw. It was a major success for the Union cause. The blockade remained in effect. The last real opportunity for foreign powers to intervene for Southern independence had passed.

THE WRECK OF THE IRON-CLAD "MONITOR."

What type of small arms were on board the *Monitor*? No records were uncovered in the National Archives to directly answer this question. However, at the time of her outfitting in March, the Brooklyn Navy Yard was issuing .69 caliber muskets, Colt revolvers, M1861 Ames cutlasses, .577 caliber Enfield rifles and

Sharps NM1859 rifles. Part of the puzzle can be answered by the deck logs of the *Monitor*. The logs were maintained on a daily basis. An entry was placed in the log every four hours. The entry for May 18 for the time period 8 p.m. to midnight reads: "served out rifles to the watch on deck."[4] At the time of this entry, the *Monitor* was near Richmond. The rifles had been given out to the watch to guard against possible Confederate attacks from shore. Since the *Monitor's* logs state that she had rifles on board, this would indicate that the *Monitor* had either Sharps or Enfields.

Clash With CSS Ram Arkansas, July 15, 1862

Out West, in the summer of 1862, the Navy was engaged in the capture of Vicksburg. At 4:00 a.m. on the morning of July 15, the gunboat *Tyler*, ram *Queen of the West* and ironclad *Carondelet*, proceeded up the Yazoo River. After traveling six miles, the Union vessels came upon the Confederate ironclad *Arkansas*. The *Arkansas* was in the process of attempting to run past the Union fleet. The first Union vessel in line, the *Tyler*, fired on the *Arkansas* with musket fire from the 4th Wisconsin Infantry who were acting as sharpshooters on the *Tyler*. The Wisconsin men were armed with the M1842 rifled muskets. One of the casualties on the *Arkansas* from this musket fire was her commanding officer, Lieutenant Isaac Brown, who was wounded. In this uneven fight, the *Tyler* suffered 6 killed and 11 wounded.[5] The *Tyler* maintained her distance from the *Arkansas* and was able to return to the fleet. Fourteen shells struck the *Tyler* with eleven penetrating the vessel.

The next Union ship in line to come under fire from the *Arkansas* was the ironclad *Carondelet*. For an hour, the two ships dueled each other. The *Carondelet* received the worst of the fighting with thirteen shots passing through the ship. The *Carondelet's* loses were four killed, sixteen wounded and ten missing. Small arms lost by the *Carondelet* during the battle were four .44 caliber Colt M1860 revolvers, four short artillery swords, four boarding pikes, one musket caliber .69 and four waist belts and plates.[6] The small arms were lost when several of the men jumped overboard. When it appeared that the *Carondelet* was to be rammed by the *Arkansas*, the crew was called to the hurricane deck to repel boarders. The *Arkansas*, however, made no attempt to board the Union ironclad. The *Arkansas* ran the entire Union fleet and came to rest under Confederate batteries at Vicksburg. In one of the most daring feats of the war, the *Arkansas* suffered casualties of ten killed and sixteen wounded. She remained on the Mississippi River until August 6, when she went aground and was destroyed so as not to be captured.

Porter's Mortar Squadron

Admiral David D. Porter

The entrance to New Orleans was protected by two forts. Commander David D. Porter proposed to send a squadron of converted schooners, each mounted with a 13-inch mortar, to bombard the forts. In November 1861, Secretary of the Navy Gideon Welles gave Porter the go-ahead to form his mortar squadron. By the end of February, Porter had his fleet of schooners at Key West, Florida. The mortar squadron played their part in softening up the fort's defenses to allow the Union wooden ships to get by. After the capture of New Orleans, they, along with the rest of the fleet, proceeded up river to Vicksburg. In July, a dozen of Porter's schooners were reassigned back East. In October, while off the coast of Maryland, several of the mortar squadron were reflecting the following small arms on board:

The thirteen-inch mortar aboard the mortar schooner *Para*. The *Para's* small arms included Colt revolvers, Enfield rifles, muskets, battle axes, pikes and cutlasses. *(Library of Congress)*

Small Arms Inventory of [7]
Porter's Mortar Squadron
October 1862

U.S. Mortar Schooner *Adolph Hugel*
24 Muskets
25 Pistols
25 Enfield Rifles
27 Swords
4   Colt Revolvers

U.S. Mortar Schooner *Dan Smith*
24 Enfield Rifles
23 Army Pistols
4   Colt Revolvers
24 Percussion Muskets
23 Navy Pistols
20 Boarding Pikes

U.S. Mortar Schooner *C.P. Williams*
22 Percussion Muskets
4   Colt Revolvers
21 Navy Swords
23 Army Pistols
20 Boarding Pikes
26 Swords for Drill

U.S. Mortar Schooner *Norfolk Packet*
15 Smoothbore Muskets
4   Colt Revolvers
23 Navy Swords
20 Boarding Pikes
23 Army Pistols
4   Enfield Rifles

U.S. Mortar Schooner *Sophronia*
24 Enfield Rifles
23 Muskets
4   Colt Revolvers

U.S. Mortar Schooner *George Mangham*
4   Colt Revolvers
25 Enfield Rifles
23 Navy Pistols
23 Muskets

U.S. Mortar Schooner *Para*
4   Enfield Rifles
24 Ames Cutlasses
2   Smoothbore .69 cal. Muskets
18 Boarding Pikes — old style
4   Battle Axes
20 Boarding Pistols — old style
5   Colt Navy Revolvers

U.S. Sloop *Oneida*
(Not a mortar schooner but one of the ships to pass the New Orleans forts in April 1862. Date of listing is March 5, 1862)
74 Rifled Muskets cal. .69
26 Sharps Rifles cal. .56
40 Army Pistols cal. .54
40 Colt Revolvers cal. .44

Ordnance for the South Atlantic Blockading Squadron

During 1862, the blockade on the Atlantic coast continued to take shape. In June, a requisition was made to obtain a quantity of small arms ammunition for the squadron. The order consisted of 50,000 revolver percussion caps, 10,000 Colt .44 caliber cartridges, 30,000 Colt .36 caliber cartridges, 10,000 cartridges for the Savage revolvers and a like quantity for the Sharps rifles.[8] Earlier, the South Atlantic Blockading Squadron received from New York:

Small Arms Sent to Port Royal, S.C.[9]
June 2, 1862

300 Ames Cutlasses	50 Army Pistols
200 Enfield Rifles	50 Colt Revolvers

In October, the quantity of small arms on hand at the New York Navy Yard consisted of the following partial list:

Inventories New York Navy Yard[10]
October 23, 1862

56 Cutlasses	30 Muskets (short)	45 Jenks Carbines
10 Rifle Muskets	35 Perry Carbines	205 Smoothbore Muskets
12 Hall Carbines	564 Roman Swords	209 Muskets Bayonets
97 Savage Revolvers		

1862 Procurements and Sea Service

MUZZLELOADERS

Navy

The Navy requested their supply of muskets through the Ordnance Department. On February 18, Captain Harwood wrote to Ripley requesting that the Navy be supplied with 250 rifle muskets and 250 Army pistols. The order was sent to New York.[11] In May, Lieutenant J.P. Sanford, Ordnance Chief at Cairo, Illinois, requested and received from the Army 200 rifle muskets and 100 Colt .44 caliber revolvers.[12] In September, the Ordnance Department forwarded to the Naval Academy 92 cadet muskets pattern 1859. The cadet muskets were received from the Springfield Armory. The Watervliet Arsenal supplied the 12,000 cartridges for the academy order.[13] The next delivery of rifle muskets to the academy was supplied with the Model 1861 Springfield.

In the second year of the war, the smoothbore musket was still on board several vessels. During the year, the *Huron*, *Augusta* and *Philadelphia* all turned in their old smoothbore muskets for the rifle muskets.[14] Rear Admiral DuPont, writing from the frigate *Wabash* in June, complained that some of his ships were still armed with smoothbore muskets. One of his ships, the *Ellen*, was fired upon by the Confederates but was helpless to return fire

In September 1862, the Ordnance Department sent to the Naval Academy 92 cadet muskets, caliber .58, Pattern 1859. In 1864, an additional 144 Pattern 1859 cadet muskets were received at the academy. *(U.S. Military Academy)*

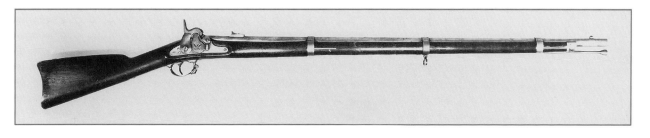

with their old smoothbore muskets.[15] The *DeSoto*, armed with smoothbores, was unable to board a blockade steamer since the Confederate vessel was better armed than they were.[16] As late as March 31, the *Mohican* still had flintlock muskets on board.[17]

The New York Navy Yard outfitted several vessels for sea. The following are but three of those vessels. The quantity of small arms issued, including muskets, were:[18]

USS *Samuel Rotan*	**USS *Commodore Perry***	**USS *Somerset***
10 Smoothbore Muskets	40 Muskets	65 Rifled Muskets w/Bayonets
16 Cutlasses	60 Ames Cutlasses	50 Army Pistols
8 Pistols	40 Pistols	10 Colt Revolvers
5 Colt Revolvers	8 Colt Revolvers	50 Ames Cutlasses
8 Boarding Pikes	10 Boarding Pikes	

The gunboat *Commodore Perry* was assigned to the North Atlantic Blockading Squadron. Her small arms included 40 muskets of .69 caliber. (U.S. Naval Historical Center)

The muskets saw use in several skirmishes on the Mississippi and at New Orleans. When the Union fleet ran the batteries at Vicksburg on July 15, the gunboat *Sciota* armed her sick and disabled with muskets. Their task was to fire on the Confederate riflemen on shore while the ship passed the batteries. When the *Oneida* passed these batteries, the Marines aboard her fired 600 rounds of rifle musket ammunition at the defenders. Earlier, when the fleet was attempting to pass Fort Jackson and St. Phillip on April 24, the Marines on the *Varuna* fired their muskets until water was over the gun trucks before they abandoned ship.[19]

Marine Corps Muzzleloaders

In a letter dated March 12, Major Slack told Colonel George Ramsey at the Washington Arsenal that the Corps' request for muskets would have to be postponed for a couple of months. Slack states in his letter that he had 50 to 60 caliber .58 rifles in storage that could be issued if bayonets were available. The rifles had been turned in from the various expeditions. These rifles were, in fact, the M1855 Rifle Musket. Major Reynolds' battalion from Fernandina, Florida, and the battalion at Port Royal were sent back North in March/April for reassignment. Lieutenant E.A. Smalley, Acting Quartermaster for the battalion at Port Royal, turned in the following equipment upon his arrival at headquarters:

The Marine detachment assigned to the sloop *Kearsarge* armed with the Model 1855 Harpers Ferry .58 caliber rifle muskets. The ship was outfitted for sea at the Portsmouth Navy Yard in February 1862. *(National Archives)*

Equipment Turned In[20]
Marine Battalion, Port Royal, S.C.
April 15, 1862

Rifle Muskets cal. .58	35	Breast Plates	16
Bayonets	12	Waist Plates	14
Scabbards	14	Percussion Cap Pouches	15
Cartridge Boxes	14	Haversacks	27
Swords and Frogs	2	Canteens	40
Waist Belts	14	Musket Slings	11

The 300 rifle muskets ordered the previous December were finally delivered in June. These .58 caliber Model 1861 Springfield rifle muskets were sent from Washington Arsenal and received by Thomas Walter, Chief Armorer, at Marine headquarters.[21] In September, an additional 500 rifle muskets were forwarded by the Ordnance Department to Marine headquarters. From the New York Marine Depot in November, 60 rifle muskets were sent to the Marine guard aboard the flagship *Lancaster* at Panama. After their arrival, the *Lancaster* Marines' .69 caliber muskets were sent to the Marines at Mare Island.

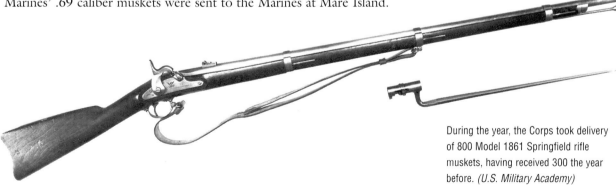

During the year, the Corps took delivery of 800 Model 1861 Springfield rifle muskets, having received 300 the year before. *(U.S. Military Academy)*

Plymouth Rifles

The July 1861 contract called for deliveries to commence by February 16. Whitney contacted the Navy on February 4 to state that he could not meet this schedule. He offered the Navy the right to cancel the contract, which the Navy did not exercise. By June, Whitney had received 2,000 barrels from a subcontractor. However, the barrels were so flawed that they would not stand proof. To correct the problem, Whitney decided to manufacture the barrels with cast steel. This process took several months.

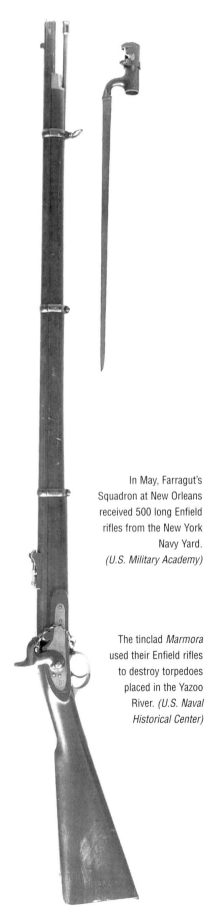

In May, Farragut's Squadron at New Orleans received 500 long Enfield rifles from the New York Navy Yard. *(U.S. Military Academy)*

The tinclad *Marmora* used their Enfield rifles to destroy torpedoes placed in the Yazoo River. *(U.S. Naval Historical Center)*

Finally, in October, five Plymouth rifles were sent forward to the Washington Navy Yard as sample arms. In Dahlgren's report of November 27, he gives the weight of the five rifles sent to him: two rifles at 9.83 pounds, one each at 9.84, 9.68 and 9.80 pounds. The standard Plymouth rifle at the Navy yard weighed 11.5 pounds. Dahlgren's concern about the sample arms was their weight. With the current weight of the arms, the recoil would be too severe for the shoulder. Reducing the powder charge would also reduce the range of the rifle. After further discussions, the lighter weight was accepted. Regular deliveries started in 1863. It appears that the lockplates were some of the first parts manufactured, since a large number are dated 1862.

Enfield Rifles

It appears that the Enfield rifles were obtained from the Ordnance Department. The 500 rifle muskets ordered for Porter's mortar squadron in 1861 were Enfield rifles as shown in the previous charts. In addition to the mortar schooners, other vessels to receive the Enfield in 1862 were:[22]

T.A. Ward	*Restless*	*Arthur*	*Augusta*	*Brooklyn*
Tennessee	*Genesee*	*Daylight*	*Richmond*	*George Washington*

In May, Farragut's West Gulf Blockading Squadron received 500 Enfield rifles. The gunboat *Tennessee* received 50 of them.[23] The gunboat *Genesee* received 30 Enfield rifles in July at the Boston Navy Yard. They found that the percussion caps issued were too small. After the cones were replaced on the Enfields, they performed just fine.[24] That summer, Captain Dahlgren tested both a two- and a three-band Enfield with acceptable results.

One of the first large deliveries of Enfield rifles to reach the Mississippi Squadron at Cairo, Illinois, was in December when 500 were received. The 500 three-band rifles were delivered from New York. On January 2, 1863, 500 additional rifles were received from Boston. This delivery consisted of 380 three-band rifles and 120 two-band Enfield rifles.[25]

One of the mortar schooners to remain in the Gulf was the *Henry Janes*. On November 20, near Matagorda, Texas, a boat crew of nine sailors and the executive officer from the *Henry Janes* went on shore. The purpose of the shore visit was to kill beef for the ship. The crew was surprised by Texas cavalry and taken prisoner. Among the small arms captured were three ordinary muskets and seven Enfield rifles. Two months before, on September 14, at Flour Bluffs, Texas, eight members of the bark *Arthur* were surprised on shore and captured. They lost seven Enfield rifles, seven cutlasses, seven boarding pistols and a Colt revolver. On December 12, the ironclad *Cairo* struck a torpedo and sank. At the time, she was protecting the *Signal* and *Marmora* from Confederate fire. These two vessels were attempting to destroy torpedoes with their Enfield rifles. Ten torpedoes were destroyed in this manner.[26] On board the *Marmora* when it was outfitted in November at Cairo:

USS *Marmora* Issues
November 1862

20 Enfield Rifles	5 Revolvers cal. .36 (probably Remington)	20 Cutlasses
20 Boarding Pistols	20 Boarding Pikes	10 Single Sticks

The ship's log of November 7 for the *Marmora* also stated that the six 24-pound howitzers were serial numbered 228, 229, 230, 233, 234 and 236 while the two 12-pound howitzers were serial numbered 78 and 79.

BREECHLOADERS

Sharps Rifles

With their Berdan contract completed, the Sharps factory offered the Navy 500 rifles of various patterns. The rifles for sale consisted of:

Sharps Rifles for Sale[27]
July 1862

170 NM1859 Sharps Rifles cal. .56 with Saber Bayonets at $40.00 each
80 NM1859 Sharps Rifles cal. .52 with Saber Bayonets at $42.50 each
<u>250</u> NM1859 Sharps Rifles cal. .52 with Angular Bayonets at $41.50 each
500 Total NM1859 Sharps Rifles

A naval shore party armed with NM1859 Sharps rifles. *(National Archives)*

On July 24, Palmer requested the Navy take the 170 caliber .56 rifles if they did not want all of the rifles. It is interesting that the Navy turned down the offer, since only a short time before they were in the market for Sharps rifles. The Sharps factory sold the 80 caliber .52 rifles to the State of Connecticut. Some of the .56 caliber rifles appear to have gone to the State of Pennsylvania, and the angular bayonet rifles were sold to the Ordnance Department in 1865. The Navy did place an order for 10,000 Sharps caliber .52 cartridges on August 29. The Washington Navy Yard received the Sharps cartridges and forwarded the ammunition to the South Atlantic Blockading Squadron.[28]

The Sharps rifles were in sea service throughout the year. On the morning of November 9, Second Assistant Engineer John L. Lay of the gunboat *Louisiana* with 54 men landed at Greenville, North Carolina. Fourteen of Lay's sailors were armed with Sharps rifles. The party arrived at Greenville at 9 o'clock and took possession of the town. Shortly after the occupation of the town, the sailors with the Sharps were attacked by Southern cavalry near the bridge leading into town. After a short fight, the sailors burned the bridge and returned to their ship. One person was killed in the action. When the sailors left Greenville, they took ten prisoners plus six horses and three mules. The animals were turned over to the Army.[29]

Spencer Rifles

On March 11, the Spencer Repeating Rifle Co. delivered to the Navy four handmade Spencer rifles. One rifle went to the Ordnance Bureau, one to the Naval Academy, and two to the Boston Navy Yard.[30] Lieutenant John H. Russell commanding the gunboat *Kennebec* received one of the two Spencer rifles delivered to Boston. The Spencer on board the *Kennebec* was the first Spencer to be placed in military service during the Civil War. During 1862, the *Kennebec* was assigned to Farragut's West Gulf Blockading Squadron and saw action first at New Orleans and later in the year at Vicksburg.[31]

On November 11, the Spencer Repeating Rifle Co. instructed the Navy to return the four handmade rifles. The company would replace them with the standard production Navy rifle. Three of the rifles were replaced, but Russell's Spencer was still at sea.[32] So, when we see 703 Spencer rifles billed in February 1863, the three extra rifles were the three replaced arms. The handmade Spencer rifles delivered in March were unmarked and had no serial numbers. These .52 caliber rifles were equipped with a Sharps NM1859 barrel of 30 inches in length. The rifle's overall length was 47 inches and weighed in at 9 pounds, 12 ounces.[33]

In December, Captain John S. Chauncey and John H. Griffith proceeded to the Boston factory to inspect 600 Spencer rifles that were ready for inspection. Before going to the Spencer factory, Griffith had been inspecting Sharps & Hankins carbines. Their report of Christmas Day stated that each rifle was fired ten times. Of the 6,000 cartridges tried, only four failed to ignite. Out of the 700 barrels proofed, only one failed inspection. The rate of fire was eight rounds in eleven seconds. Five days later, directions were received to send 600 Spencer rifles to the Boston Navy Yard with the balance going to Philadelphia.[34]

Sharps & Hankins (S&H) Rifles and Carbines

The first delivery of 100 S&H rifles was received at the Philadelphia Navy Yard on March 19. In April, 150 rifles were sent to New York, and the Boston Navy Yard obtained deliveries of 150 on May 27.[35] The last 100 rifles were sent to the Washington Navy Yard on June 28. Five days later, on July 3, Samuel Miller, a civilian inspector at the yard, inspected 99 of the S&H rifles. At the start of the inspection, the temperature was 85 degrees and had risen to 101 degrees by the conclusion of the inspection. Each box contained ten rifles, ten saber bayonets and scabbards, ten cleaning rods and two screwdrivers. The serial numbers of these rifles were:[36]

Box 1	Box 2	Box 3	Box 4	Box 5	Box 6	Box 7	Box 8	Box 9	Box 10
562	539	593	525	550	54	295	595	567	558
556	516	534	588	514	577	164	517	594	Letter E
536	529	547	Letter R	551	546	574	543	563	586
560	531	554	Letter S	559	572	538	548	261	571
566	522	569	582	533	576	529	600	551	589
561	509	590	584	515	570	184	549	557	561
592	524	565	553	527	564	269	512	575	Letter J
532	544	583	597	530	599	242	156	587	Letter C
528	264	555	578	537	540	150	580	596	Letter H
573	541	568	585	579	—	520	535	545	Letter D

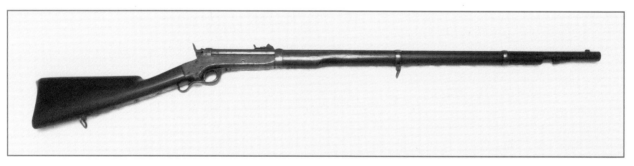

Sharps & Hankins rifle serial number 295 was one of 99 rifles inspected at the Washington Navy Yard on July 3. *(Author's collection)*

The description of the S&H rifles delivered to Washington on June 28 was:³⁷

Weight of Rifle with Bayonet	10.53 pounds
Weight of Barrel	3.98 pounds
Weight of Stock and Bayonet	6.55 pounds
Weight of Bayonet	1.77 pounds
Caliber	.527 inches
Depth of Grooves	.02 inches
Twist of Rifling	One turn in 67 inches

The June delivery was accepted after serial numbers 547, 565, 534 and 568 were replaced. The bill for this delivery came to $3,816.77. One additional delivery was made in September when 100 were sent to Washington. The first issues of the S&H rifles appears to have been issued to the frigate *Wabash* in July from Philadelphia. The rifles delivered were the Old Model with the firing pin in the hammer.

On March 26, 1862, Sharps & Hankins received a contract for 1,000 carbines. These leather-covered carbines, Pattern 1859, were to be delivered with 100 metallic cartridges each. The carbine differed from the rifle in that the carbines were equipped with a floating firing pin in the rear of the receiver. In September, the first 250 of the carbines arrived at Philadelphia. The ironclad *New Ironsides*, being outfitted for sea at Philadelphia, was issued some of the S&H carbines. In October, both New York and Boston received 250 carbines each. After close inspection, they were rejected and sent back to the factory. The reason for their rejection is unclear.

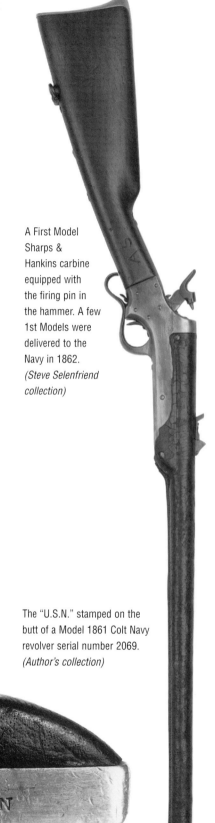

A First Model Sharps & Hankins carbine equipped with the firing pin in the hammer. A few 1st Models were delivered to the Navy in 1862. *(Steve Selenfriend collection)*

PISTOLS/REVOLVERS

Colt Revolvers

By September 4, the Colt factory had made ten deliveries totaling 1,378 M1861 Colt revolvers. Deliveries were received at:

Colt Deliveries — 1862³⁸
Colt Patent F/A Mfg. Co.

Philadelphia Navy Yard	400	Portsmouth Navy Yard	30
New York Navy Yard	498	Boston Navy Yard	100
Fort Monroe	150	Washington Navy Yard	200

The last 200 Colt revolvers were received at Philadelphia in early September. Twelve of the Colts were sent to Baltimore for issue on the Steamer *Mount Vernon*. The *Mount Vernon* also received 30 Ames cutlasses, and six battle axes.³⁹ The *New Ironsides*, also from Philadelphia, was issued a quantity of the September delivery. In February from Portsmouth, the sloop *Kearsarge* was issued both the Sharps rifle and Colt revolvers. In August, New York sent 50 Colts to Farragut care of the naval ordnance depot New Orleans.⁴⁰

On the morning of November 21, at 9 a.m., Acting Master Anthony Chase and five men left the schooner *Maria A. Wood* for a one-hour reconnaissance trip. Chase and his men

The "U.S.N." stamped on the butt of a Model 1861 Colt Navy revolver serial number 2069. *(Author's collection)*

CIVIL WAR Small Arms of the U.S. Navy and Marine Corps

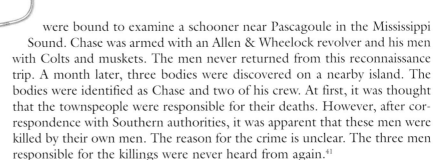

The last wartime delivery of Colt revolvers to the Navy occurred with delivery of 200 Model 1861 Colt revolvers to the Philadelphia Navy Yard in September. *(Author's collection)*

A .44 caliber Model 1860 Colt revolver with rebated cylinder. In June 1862, the Army sent 100 of these Colt revolvers to the Mississippi Squadron. *(Author's collection)*

were bound to examine a schooner near Pascagoule in the Mississippi Sound. Chase was armed with an Allen & Wheelock revolver and his men with Colts and muskets. The men never returned from this reconnaissance trip. A month later, three bodies were discovered on a nearby island. The bodies were identified as Chase and two of his crew. At first, it was thought that the townspeople were responsible for their deaths. However, after correspondence with Southern authorities, it was apparent that these men were killed by their own men. The reason for the crime is unclear. The three men responsible for the killings were never heard from again.[41]

During 1862, the Army was responsible for operations on the Mississippi. The Navy supplied the officers and some of the sailors for the boats on the river. The Army picked up the cost to equip the crews with small arms. In May, Lieutenant Sanford, in charge of the naval ordnance for the Mississippi Flotilla, requested 200 rifle muskets and 100 revolvers from the Army. The 100 revolvers that the Army sent forward were the Colt Model 1860 revolvers caliber .44. The Colt factory sent Sanford 20,000 rounds of caliber .44 ammunition for the 100 revolvers.[42] The serial numbers on these .44 caliber Colts appear to be in the low 40000 range. One of the Army Colt revolvers, with the serial number 40886, was stolen off the gunboat *Essex*.[43]

By July, all the ships in the Mississippi Flotilla were armed with the .44 caliber Colt revolvers. These ships included ironclads — *Cairo*, *Carondelet*, *Cincinnati*, *Louisville*, *Mound City*, *Pittsburg*, *St. Louis*, *Benton* and the *Essex*. As of July 12, only five Colts were still in storage at Cairo. Needing additional revolvers, Sanford placed an order for 150 more Colts. The Colts were unavailable, so the Navy had to settle for single-shot pistols instead.[44]

Remington Revolvers

In April, E. Remington & Sons contacted the Navy requesting a testing of their revolvers. The Navy agreed, and one of the Remington .36 caliber Beals revolvers was tested. The Beals was fired 600 times with good results. While the accuracy with the Remington was slightly better than the Colt, the Navy gave the overall superiority to the Colt revolver. A second firing occurred in September. This time, two Old Model 1861 Remingtons were tested. In Lieutenant Commander William Mitchell's September 8 report, he writes: "I am of the opinion that Beal's is fully equal to that of Colt's."[45] As a result of this test, a week later the Navy placed an order for 120 Beals revolvers plus ammunition and spare parts. Portsmouth Navy Yard received the Remington on September 19. In September, Portsmouth was outfitting the sloops *Ossipee* and *Sacramento* for sea. The Navy Yard issued each vessel 60 Remington revolvers. Both vessels were assigned to the Atlantic coastal areas on blockade duty. The *Ossipee* remained in the Navy's inventory until her decommission in November 1889, while the *Sacramento* was lost off the coast of India in June 1867. By the year's end, the Remington factory had forwarded 791 revolvers in eight deliveries.

Chapter 4 • The Clash of the Ironclads, 1862

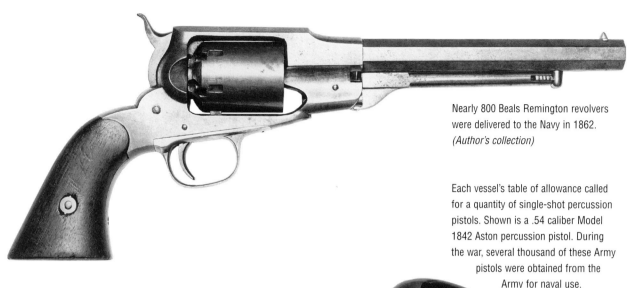

Nearly 800 Beals Remington revolvers were delivered to the Navy in 1862. *(Author's collection)*

Each vessel's table of allowance called for a quantity of single-shot percussion pistols. Shown is a .54 caliber Model 1842 Aston percussion pistol. During the war, several thousand of these Army pistols were obtained from the Army for naval use. *(Author's collection)*

Pistols at Sea

In 1862, the Army supplied the Navy with nearly 2,000 single-shot pistols. In April, the Mississippi Squadron obtained 300 pistols from the St. Louis Arsenal. In December, they received an additional 300 pistols. Twenty-seven of these pistols were delivered from the St. Louis Arsenal and the balance from the Washington Arsenal.[46] Fifty thousand cartridges were delivered to Cairo in May for the Army pistols. The largest order placed with the Ordnance Department in 1862 occurred in September. The request of September 5 called for the following quantities and delivery locations:

Pistol Deliveries[47]
September 1862

New York Navy Yard	300	Philadelphia Navy Yard	300
Boston Navy Yard	300	Fort Monroe	100

Deliveries were made the next day. Philadelphia sent 60 pistols to Lieutenant Commander Oscar C. Badger, Naval Ordnance Officer at Cincinnati, Ohio. In addition, Badger received from Philadelphia Sharps rifles, Ames cutlasses and Colt revolvers. Badger placed the small arms on board the river ironclad *Indianola*.

Small Arms Issued[48]
USS *Indianola*
September 1862

Ames Cutlasses	100	Colt Revolvers	25
Sharps Rifles	50	Pistols	60

The *Indianola* was to have a short life. On February 24, she ran aground and surrendered to Confederate forces and was destroyed by them eight days later.

Pistols aboard ship were usually kept loaded to repel boarders. After a period of time, they would be discharged at target practice and then reloaded. This practice kept the pistols in serviceable condition. The deck logs of the ironclad *Galena* show that on August 9 they discharged all their loaded pistols for cleaning and then reloaded them. Earlier, on May 15,

95

The ironclad *Galena* — a view of the port side looking forward. During the action at Drewry's Bluff, Corporal John F. Mackie, of the ship's Marine detachment was awarded the first Medal of Honor to a Marine. *(U.S. Historical Center)*

"This is the knot sailors use to ornament the lanyards they hang their knives from, when they wear them round their necks."
Caulfield and Saward:
Dictionary of Needlework, 1882.

FROM THE
ASHLEY BOOK OF KNOTS

within eight miles of the Confederate capital, the Navy had been stopped by the batteries at Drewry's Bluff. In this engagement, the *Galena* took the brunt of the battle with Confederate batteries located on the 200-foot bluffs. The *Galena*, one of three experimental ironclads authorized in 1861 and commissioned at New York on April 21, was seeing her first major combat action at Drewry's Bluff. A small detachment of Marines was on board

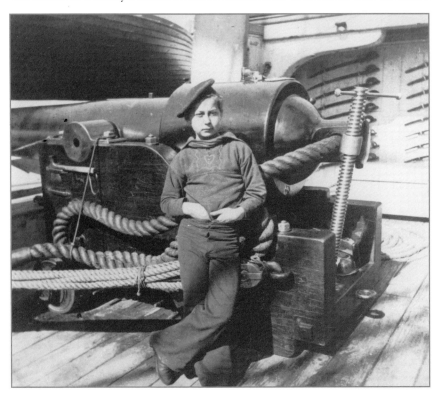

A "powder monkey" on deck of the USS *New Hampshire*. Note the Ames cutlasses in the background. *(MOLLUS - USAMHI)*

the *Galena*. The Marines' task was to keep at bay the Confederate sharpshooters' fire from the rifle pits on shore. In the action, the Marines were armed with the .58 caliber rifle muskets. When a shell struck a powder monkey killing several of the crew, Corporal John F. Mackie rallied the men and got three of the guns back in action. For his actions, Corporal Mackie, a 26-year-old native of New York City, was awarded the first Medal of Honor received by the Marine Corps by General Order #17 of the Navy Department dated July 10, 1863. The *Galena* was heavily damaged, having been struck 28 times by the shore batteries. Thirteen men were killed and eleven wounded. Of those killed, one was a Marine, Joseph Johnson. The *Galena* armor, found to be unacceptable, was removed in 1863. She remained in naval service until being decommissioned on June 17, 1865.

The sloop *Constellation* was assigned to the Mediterranean in 1862. She had been outfitted in February at the Portsmouth Navy Yard. When the *Constellation* left for sea, her crew consisted of 77 seamen, 68 ordinary seamen, 42 landsmen, 17 boys and 21 officers under the command of Commander Henry K. Thatcher. The Marine guard was made up of 36 privates, three corporals, two sergeants and two musicians. At pistol practice on September 19, the *Constellation's* first and fifth divisions fired three rounds each at a target with their pistols.[49] After returning from the Mediterranean in 1864, she was a receiving ship for the next 63 years and decommissioned on February 4, 1955. The *Constellation* is currently on display in the Baltimore harbor.

Reconnaissance near shore required the sending out of launches. These launches were perfect targets for Confederate troops on shore. The problem

The sloop *Constellation* ship's logs indicate the regular exercise by the crew with their single-shot pistols and the Marines with their Model 1855 rifle muskets.
(U.S. Naval Historical Center)

CIVIL WAR Small Arms of the U.S. Navy and Marine Corps

is readily seen in an incident near Corpus Christi, Texas, on December 7. On this date, the *Sachem* sent out two launches with 18 men to investigate a Confederate schooner nearby. As the sailors rounded a bend in the river, they were fired upon by volleys of musketry. The first volley killed three sailors and wounded three more. In their retreat, the sailors left behind four percussion muskets, three holster pistols, four cutlasses, one bayonet, three cartridge boxes and three pistol cases.[50]

EDGED WEAPONS

Marine Corps Swords and Accouterments

On January 13, Major Slack requested that the firm of Bent & Bush of Boston deliver 50 sergeant and 25 musician swords. The swords were obtained by April. Later in August, the firm was directed to send 12 musician swords with 24-inch blades. The accouterments contracts for 1862 were given to:

1862 Accouterments Procurements

Henry A. Dingee	600 Cartridge Boxes
	600 Bayonet Scabbards
J. Logowitz	600 Knapsacks
	600 Musket Slings
	300 Canteens
	300 Haversacks

Boarding Pikes

In January, the New York Navy Yard received 300 pikes from Richard M. Nichols at a cost of $685.50. In September, Miles Greenwood sent 60 pikes at a cost of $2.00 each to the Navy.[51] In November, Lieutenant Commander Badger, while in St. Louis, learned that the Army had 1,500 pikes in storage at the arsenal. The pikes had been purchased by Major General

(Above) In February, the Army sent to the Mississippi Squadron 300 Model 1832 foot artillery swords for the use of the fleet. *(Steve Selenfriend collection)*

(Right) The sloop *Hartford* shown in 1871 with a complete spar deck. In April, when the *Hartford* passed the forts on the way to capture New Orleans, 12 Joslyn rifles were damaged from fire from the forts. See page 100 for more details. *(U.S. Naval Historical Center)*

Chapter 4 • The Clash of the Ironclads, 1862

Officers of the gunboat *Miami* shown after a hunting trip on shore.
(MOLLUS - USAMHI)

John C. Fremont when he was in command. Since his departure, the pikes had been in storage. Since the Army had no use for the pikes, Badger requested and received approval to requisition them for naval use. These pikes were to take the place of muskets since there was a shortage of muskets on hand. On November 30, the arsenal received orders to turn the pikes over to the Navy.[52]

Model 1861 Ames Cutlasses

The Ames factory continued to send forward cutlasses as fast as they could be manufactured. On February 26, Captain Wise wrote Ames: "…you will please continue the manufacturing of Navy cutlasses until the aggregate number reaches twenty thousand (20,000)."[53] By July 3, Ames had 4,000 remaining to deliver on their contract. Two days later, the Navy increased the contract an additional 5,000 for a total of 25,000 cutlasses. The inspector on the Ames contracts was Daniel Reynolds. For the three-month period ending September 30, he inspected 7,869 cutlasses which passed inspection.[54] By December 1, Reynolds had finished the inspection of the 25,000 cutlasses. In the last two months, an additional 1,491 had been accepted.[55] Reynolds also inspected a few gilt swords that were obtained for officers' use. These officers' swords cost the Navy $10.15 each.

By early 1862, the Ames M1861 cutlass was the standard cutlass issued to ships being outfitted for sea on the East coast. Two of many vessels to receive the Ames cutlass were the *Paul Jones* and the *Stepping Stone*, which were both outfitted at the Washington Navy Yard.

A sailor armed with cutlass and pistol.
(Jerry Rinker collection)

USS *Paul Jones* June 1862	USS *Stepping Stone* September 1862
45 Boarding Pikes	6 S&H Rifles w/Saber Bayonets plus 600 Cartridges
25 Colt Revolvers	
60 Ames Cutlasses	6 Colt Revolvers plus 480 Cartridges
100 Muskets	12 Ames Cutlasses
30 Rifled Muskets	

99

In June, the Marine Corps enlisted strength stood at 2,355. One of these wartime Marines was Private Richard W. Drenning. *(Rance Hulshort collection, USAMHI)*

The gunboat *Paul Jones* saw service in both the South Atlantic and East Gulf Blockading Squadrons during the war, while the *Stepping Stone* was assigned to the Potomac Flotilla.

Besides the Ames cutlass, the Navy also received from the Army the Model 1832 Foot Artillery sword for the Mississippi Squadron. In February, the squadron received 300 of these artillery swords. Two hundred swords were issued to the fleet and the balance went to the two ammunition boats. The first 300 Ames cutlasses were delivered to the Mississippi Squadron in November.

The *Wabash*, the flagship of the South Atlantic Blockading Squadron, received 20 Colts and 30 Ames cutlasses in October. Earlier, in April, the *Wabash* obtained 150 single sticks. The single sticks were used in fencing drills aboard ship. Fencing drills were held on a regular basis. The deck logs of the *Minnesota* show that on August 11, the first division exercised with single sticks and there is a like entry from the *Constellation* dated May 9.[56]

When the Sloop *Hartford* passed the two forts in April to capture New Orleans, the amount of equipment damaged was:

USS *Hartford*[57]
Small Arms Damaged
April 24–25, 1862

12 Joslyn Rifles
7 Revolvers (Colts and Starr)
5 Rifle Muskets
6 Ames Cutlasses
6 Single Sticks
4 Battle Axes
1 Pistol

In the two-day engagement, Farragut's fleet suffered casualties of 37 killed and 147 wounded. By year's end, the Confederate stronghold of Vicksburg still held out. The Mississippi River was, therefore, not totally open for commercial traffic.

Chapter 5
Opening the Mississippi, 1863

Small Arms for the Mississippi Squadron

One of the major goals for the Navy at the beginning of 1863 was to cooperate with Grant's Army in capturing the Mississippi River stronghold of Vicksburg. With the capture of Vicksburg, the Confederacy would be cut in two.

Lacking the additional sailors needed to man the Mississippi Squadron, Acting Rear Admiral David Porter requested and received from Grant 800 soldiers for the vessels. By March, the Army had supplied the 58th Ohio Infantry for the *Mound City, Signal, Carondelet, Baron deKalb, Benton, Pittsburg, Linden* and the *Louisville*. Companies from the 101st Illinois, 39th Illinois and the 20th Illinois Infantry were also assigned to Porter's vessels. These infantrymen, armed with their Enfield rifles, were used in place of Marines for sharpshooters and to help man the guns.[1]

With the threat of attack a constant problem, Porter gave strict orders for the night watch aboard ship assigned to the Yazoo River. No lights were to be shown. No bells struck and no "All's Well." A rowboat would be kept 400 yards forward of the fleet to give the alarm by firing their muskets if a ship should approach them. In addition, each vessel was to post six lookouts

Rear Admiral David Porter in 1863 held the Spencer rifle in high regard. By the following year, over 250 Spencers were in the Mississippi Squadron.

CIVIL WAR Small Arms of the U.S. Navy and Marine Corps

THE SUNSET GUN IN THE YAZOO.—Sketched by Mr. Theodore R. Davis.—[See Page 215.]

on the upper deck with loaded muskets to guard against possible boarding parties.[2] The arms issued to the lookouts included Enfield rifles, Spencer rifles and Sharps & Hankins carbines.

By early January, the Mississippi Squadron had received 1,000 Enfield rifles from back East. One of the Mississippi stern wheeler steamers, the USS *Champion*, was issued a quantity of them. The rifles were stored for an extended length of time without being fired. On July 4, Quartermaster W. Angus Miller made his escape, while in double irons, by taking one of the boats on the stern of the vessel. The sentry, quartermaster on watch, and the officer of the deck all attempted to fire at the escaping sailor, but because the rifles failed to go off, Miller made his escape to the Kentucky shore.[3]

In late February, 200 single-shot pistols were obtained from the St. Louis Arsenal.[4] Three hundred Ames cutlasses, and like quantities of Remington and Whitney revolvers, were also provided early in the year.

An 1863 naval recruiting poster.
(National Archives)

MEN WANTED FOR THE NAVY!

All able-bodied men not in the employment of the Army, will be enlisted into the Navy upon application at the Naval Rendezvous, on Craven Street, next door to the Printing Office.

H. K. DAVENPORT,
Com'r. & Senior Naval Officer.

New Berne, N. C.,
Nov. 2d, 1863.

Small Arms Issued[5]

	USS *Osage*	USS *Neosho*	USS *Ozark*	USS *Fawn*
Sharps & Hankins Carbines	30	30	30	—
Whitney Revolvers	13	13	—	—
Remington Revolvers	—	—	14	40
Ames Cutlasses	50	50	20	40
Carbine Cartridge Boxes	30	30	30	—
Revolver Ammunition	1,300	1,300	1,400	4,000
Carbine Ammunition	5,000	5,000	4,000	—
Percussion Caps Revolvers	2,500	2,500	3,000	—
Enfield Rifles w/Bayonets	—	—	—	40

In July 1863, the river monitor *Osage* was issued Sharps & Hankins carbines, Whitney revolvers, and Ames cutlasses. *(U.S. Naval Historical Center)*

The Remington revolvers for the *Ozark* arrived at St. Louis on May 18, while the Whitney revolvers were received April 24. The Sharps & Hankins carbines came from the Philadelphia Navy Yard in late March. They were marked "Naval Ordnance" for the gunboats *Neosho* and *Osage* and were addressed to Lieutenant Commander Oscar Badger.[6]

Spencer Rifles for the Mississippi Squadron

When the 600 Spencer rifles arrived at Boston in early January, 100 Spencer rifles were sent forward on the 10th of the month and arrived at their destination of Cairo, Illinois, on February 11.[7]

Spencer Rifles Received at Cairo
February 11, 1863

Spencer Rifles	100	Wiping Rods	10
Sword Bayonets	100	Cartridge Boxes	100
Screwdrivers	100	Metallic Cartridges	20,000

Ninety-one of these Spencer rifles were quickly placed on board ship by early April. Their distribution was as follows: 30 issued to both the *Louisville* and *Cincinnati*, 11 to the *Benton*, 10 each to the *General Price* and the *Tuscumbia*.[8] On May 19, Philadelphia sent their 100 Spencer rifles forward to the Mississippi fleet.[9] Later in the year, Spencers were issued to the *Pittsburg, Mound City, Lafayette, Conestoga, Choctaw* and the *Forest Rose*. The *Forest Rose* obtained 10 Spencers on October 8, *Mound City* received 20 Spencer rifles on November 18, and ten days later, *Conestoga* also received 20 Spencers. The *Benton* obtained 20 additional Spencers on December 20.[10] Fifty additional Army Model Spencer rifles were sent from

In the spring of 1863, the gunboat *General Price* had on board Spencer rifles, short Enfield rifles and Remington revolvers. *General Price* took part in the Vicksburg bombardment. *(U.S. Naval Historical Center) (Library of Congress)*

the Washington Navy Yard to this squadron in early 1864. The *Cincinnati* Spencers were lost in May when the ship was sunk by enemy batteries. The vessel was raised in August, and her Spencers were returned to the factory for repairs. After new stocks and barrel bands plus some mainsprings were replaced, they were returned to the Navy at a cost of $6.50 each.

The Spencer rifles were well received by the squadron. Porter wrote Dahlgren on June 12 from the flagship *Black Hawk* about his impressions of the Spencer. He states: "I have tested the Spencer Repeating Rifle in every way. I find that it is the best gun in use in every respect, and should be glad to receive any number of them."[11]

In early April, Grant made up his mind to attack Vicksburg from the south. On the night of April 16, Porter passed the Vicksburg batteries with little damage. In action on April 29, at Grand Gulf, Mississippi, three of Porter's ships with Spencer rifles were heavily damaged. The *Benton*, *Pittsburg* and *Tuscumbia* suffered casualties of 24 killed and 56 wounded. The *Benton* was struck 47 times by Confederate fire, while the *Tuscumbia* took 81 hits. After this attack, the Navy settled into a general bombardment of Vicksburg. The bombardment caused great suffering on the local population and finally, on July 4, the city surrendered to Grant. Five days later, Port Hudson also fell to the Northern armies. The Mississippi River was now firmly in Union hands. The Confederacy had been cut in two. With the Mississippi in Union hands, the Army troops assigned to the fleet were reassigned to the Army.

During the summer months of 1863, the quantities of small arms on hand at Cairo for fleet issue are shown in the following chart:

Small Arms Inventory — 1863[12]
Cairo, Illinois

	July 1st	August 1st	September 1st
Boarding Pikes	848	816	835
Lances	487	487	487
3-Band Enfield Rifles	110	345	332
2-Band Enfield Rifles	40	104	104
Springfield Rifle Muskets	64	64	64
Springfield Smoothbore Muskets	138	138	138
Army Boarding Pistols	—	35	65
Remington Revolvers	1	319	307
Whitney Revolvers	55	—	—
Spencer Rifles	—	18	18
Navy Swords and Scabbards	243	255	252
Single Sticks	110	98	98
.44 caliber Colt Revolvers	—	—	9

Ammunition Inventory July 1, 1863[13]
Cairo, Illinois

Cartridges		Cartridges	
Buck & Ball cal. .69	97,680	Colt Revolver cal. .36	18,820
Enfield cal. .577	8,500	Colt Revolver cal. .44	11,076
Rifle Musket cal. .58	13,000	Boarding Pistols cal. .54	23,000
Spencer Rifle	7,000	Round Ball cal. .69	21,000
Sharps Rifle cal. .52	29,000	Percussion Caps Musket	64,750
Remington Revolver cal. .36	126,642	Percussion Caps Revolver	174,600

Capture of the USS Satellite and CSS Atlanta

Back East, at the mouth of the Rappahannock River in Virginia, the USS *Satellite* and the *Reliance* were anchored for the night. The date was Thursday, August 22. At about 12:20 a.m. on the morning of August 23, both steamers were boarded by 60 Confederate sailors led by Lieutenant J. Taylor Wood, C.S. Navy. Before either of the Union ships could slip their cables, they had been overpowered by the boarders. In the action on the *Satellite*, Acting Ensign Rudolph Sommers grabbed his cutlass and pistol, but he was wounded before he could use his side arms. Two of the other officers reached for the boarding pikes but were also quickly overcome. By the time the ship surrendered, one was dead and five wounded out of a crew of 32. No shots were fired by the *Satellite* crew because their small arms were loaded but not capped.[14] The *Satellite* was in Confederate service for only a few days before it was destroyed to prevent its recapture. Earlier in the year, the *Satellite* showed the following small arms on board:

USS *Satellite*[15]
Small Arms on Board
January 1863

Boarding Pikes	9	Muskets	15
Colt Revolvers	4	Ames Cutlasses	15
Sharps Rifles	5	Roman Swords	2

The *Satellite* was a small prize for the Confederates compared to the capture of the ironclad CSS *Atlanta* by the Union Navy. On June 17, at Wassaw Sound, Georgia, the *Atlanta* was attacked by the two Union monitors *Weehawken* and *Nahant*. The Confederate ironclad went aground and was unable to bring her guns to bear on the Union monitors. After being struck six times by the 400-pound shots from the 15-inch Dahlgren from the *Weehawken*, she surrendered. The *Atlanta* surrendered a crew of 21 officers and 124 men, of which 28 were C.S. Marines. Sixteen of the *Atlanta* crew were wounded in the engagement.

The CSS *Atlanta* shown after her capture in June 1863. When captured, the *Atlanta* had on board Enfield rifles, .69 caliber muskets, Maynard carbines, cutlasses and pikes. *(U.S. Naval Historical Center)*

These small arms were captured from the *Atlanta*:

CSS *Atlanta*[16]
Small Arms Captured
June 17, 1863

Enfield Rifles	23	AMMUNITION:	
U.S. Muskets cal. .69	11	Revolver Cartridges	500
Maynard Carbines	30	Maynard Cartridges	200
Cutlasses	3	Rifle Cartridges	500
Pikes	20	Musket Cartridges	255

Note that the captured items included revolver ammunition. While no revolvers are listed among the captures, the *Atlanta* in May showed in inventory 32 Colts and three LeMat revolvers plus 16 battle axes.

The *Atlanta* was sent North to the Philadelphia Navy Yard for repairs and refitting. On February 5, 1864, the Navy Yard sent forward one of the captured Maynard carbines to the Ordnance Bureau for their inspection. When the now USS *Atlanta* left Philadelphia for duty in the James River fleet, she was armed with Enfield rifles and Whitney revolvers plus Ames cutlasses. The Confederate Maynard carbines were in storage at Philadelphia as late as December 1, 1866, when 27 were accounted for.[17] The *Atlanta* remained in naval service until May 4, 1866, when she was sold to Haiti. Later in the year, she was lost at sea.[18]

Mare Island

Mare Island Navy Yard on San Francisco Bay was founded in the 1850s as the repair and outfitting location for the Pacific Fleet. The first deliveries of Remington and Whitney revolvers arrived in 1863. During that year, the Boston Navy Yard forwarded to Mare Island 50 Remingtons and 40 Whitneys. The Whitney revolvers were issued in November to the steamer *Saranac*. Earlier in the year, the yard issued to the *Saranac* and the *Cyane* the following small arms:

Small Arms Issued Mare Island[19]

	USS *Cyane*	USS *Saranac*
Battle Axes	32	10
Muskets	84	54
Navy Pistols	85	58
Colt Revolvers	56	—
Remington Revolvers	—	20
Boarding Pikes	50	48
Navy Swords	83	127
Sharps Carbines	—	60

The Marines aboard the *Cyane* obtained for their use 90 cutlasses from the navy yard. While the type of swords issued are not stated, they are believed to have been the Ames M1861 cutlass. In addition, the Marines were issued 3,900 musket cartridges caliber .58. The navy yard had large quantities of small arms that were obsolete and unserviceable and were sent back to Boston for disposal. The items included:[20]

Pikes	108	Rifled Muskets	2
Cutlasses	28	Navy Pistols	11
Jenks Carbines	21	Army Pistols	7
Hall Carbines	2	Flintlock Pistols	11
Colt Revolvers	1	Smoothbore Muskets	20
U.S. Rifles	3		

The first deliveries of Plymouth rifles and Sharps & Hankins did not arrive on the West Coast until the following March.

1863 Procurements and Field Service

The small arms ammunition used by the Navy was manufactured at the Washington Navy Yard. As the small arms ammunition requisitions came in from the various naval locations, the Washington Navy Yard was directed to fill these requests. In March, they supplied over a quarter million musket cartridges for naval service as follows:

Musket Ammunition Issued[21]
Washington Navy Yard, March 1863

	.58 Cartridges	.69 Cartridges	Musket Percussion Caps
Boston Navy Yard	—	50,000	50,000
New York Navy Yard	100,000	50,000	50,000
Portsmouth Navy Yard	—	25,000	25,000
Philadelphia Navy Yard	—	25,000	25,000
Ordnance Ship *Dale*	20,000	10,000	100,000
Baltimore	5,000	8,000	15,000

MUZZLELOADERS

Marine Corps

On January 7, Ripley notified the Marines that the 500 rifle muskets requested in December would be delivered along with 10,000 cartridges. The first 300 rifle muskets were finally delivered on April 1, from Springfield Armory. The balance of the order came from the Washington Arsenal. While most of the rifle muskets were probably the Model 1861, some deliveries were of the Model 1863. This weapon differed from the 1861 in that it had a casehardened lockplate and hammer. The hammer was straight and not curved, as found on the early models. It had the flat bolster and not the clean-out screw as found on the M1855 and 1861. The barrel bands were of the oval type, being retained by a clamp screw. In September, Springfield Armory forwarded to the Marines in Boston, by way of the New York Navy Yard, the following items: 11 caliber .58 Springfield rifle muskets, 11 cartridge boxes and percussion cap pouches, one drum and fife plus five swords.

One of the two Medals of Honor awarded to the Corps in 1863 was issued to Orderly Sergeant Christopher Nugent of the USS *Fort Henry*. On June 15, while on reconnaissance up the Crystal River in Florida, Nugent noticed a rebel breastwork fortification manned by eleven Confederate soldiers. He landed his party of four Marines and charged the position with fixed bayonets. In the attack, Sergeant Nugent had his men hold their fire to prevent harm to a woman among the fugitives. The attack drove the rebels into the swamps with the capture of all their small arms and camp equipment. The only shot fired, which hit the waist pouch of the sergeant, was fired by the commanding officer of the rebels. For this action and the capture of a rebel boat, Orderly Sergeant Nugent was to receive the Medal of Honor. The schooner *Alabama*, attached to the South Atlantic Blockading Squadron, was assigned a Marine detachment aboard the ship. On August 22, at St. Andrews Sound, Georgia, the Marine guard went ashore to drill and take target practice with rifle muskets.

Plymouth Rifles

Nine days into the new year, Dahlgren wrote Whitney the following letter, which reads, in part:

Bureau in need of 100 muskets of .69 caliber which you are manufacturing for the department. If you can not deliver these at an early date, the department will have to purchase them elsewhere and the number will be deducted from your contract.[22]

This brought a rapid response from Whitney that the rifles would be ready shortly. Therefore, on January 14, Lieutenant Commander Richard L. May, Assistant Inspector of Ordnance at Boston, was notified to proceed to the Whitney factory to inspect the Plymouth rifles. May was informed that John Griffith would be his assistant in the inspection of the 100 rifles. By February 5, the rifles were on their way to the New York Navy Yard. May returned to Boston and turned over the inspection of the rifles to Griffith.[23] In April, 13,000 cartridges were sent to Whitney for proving the Plymouth rifles. On June 4, the next delivery of rifles to Boston was serial numbered 81, 86, 88 and 104 through 200.[24] The new inspector on the Plymouth contract, Franklin Warner, wrote weekly inspection reports, of which the following was submitted for the week ending June 13:

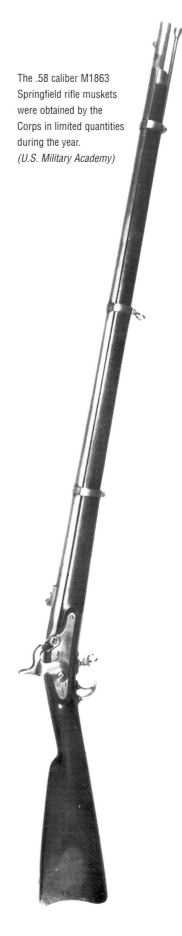

The .58 caliber M1863 Springfield rifle muskets were obtained by the Corps in limited quantities during the year.
(U.S. Military Academy)

Inspection of Plymouth Rifles[25]
For the Week Ending
June 13, 1863

Finish Barrels	500	Sword Bayonets	115
Guard Plates and Bows	500	Lock Plates	300
Swivel Plates	500	Mainsprings	100
Bands	1,000	Hammers	300
Band Springs	1,000	Tumblers	200
Guard Plate Screws	1,000	Bridles	200
Swivel Plate Screws	1,000	Sears	200
Ramrods	220	Sear Springs	200
Cones	500	Finish Locks	400

(Inset) The ungraduated single-leaf rear sight on Plymouth rifle serial number 637. Most of these rear sights were returned to the factory to have the sights corrected to up to 1,000 yards.

The next delivery of June 22, was sent to the Philadelphia Navy Yard. All Plymouth rifles delivered up to this time did not have the rear sights graduated. Whitney's reason for not graduating the sights was because the sample arm sent to him was not graduated. He was agreeable to graduate the sights if he was provided with a sample by the Navy Department. The pattern rear sight was sent to Whitney from the Washington Navy Yard.[26] The rear sights for the Plymouth rifles sent to Boston were sent back to the factory to be graduated after they had been numbered. The sights were received back at Boston by August 8.

The side-wheel steamer *Nansemond* was one of the first vessels to be issued Plymouth rifles. The *Nansemond* was commissioned at Baltimore on August 19.

USS *Nansemond* Issues[27]
August 1863

Plymouth Rifles	25	Pistols	10
S&H Carbines	50	Battle Axes	20
Ames Cutlasses	70		

Of the 100 Plymouth rifles sent to the Washington Navy Yard in September, the schooner *William Bacon* obtained about 30 Plymouths and the gunboat *Eutaw* acquired 60. All three of these vessels were assigned to the North Atlantic Blockading Squadron in 1863. In September, a major fire occurred at the Philadelphia Navy Yard which caused damage to a large quantity of small arms. Included in the arms damaged were 392 Plymouth rifles. In December, Philadelphia forwarded to Mound City 400 Plymouth rifles and 300 Ames cutlasses. Eighty thousand rounds of .69 caliber ammunition for the Plymouth rifles were sent from Washington Navy Yard to Mound City.[28] The December delivery was the first Plymouths received at Mound City.

The nine pound, ten ounce .69 caliber Plymouth rifle delivered in this year was usually stamped on the lockplate with the large spread eagle and panoply of flags forward of the hammer. The lockplate is marked either "1862" or "1863" and is stamped "U.S./WHITNEY-VILLE". The rear sights were graduated to 1,000 yards. The saber bayonets were supplied by Collins & Co. of Hartford, Connecticut. Deliveries for 1863 totaled 5,300 Plymouth rifles.

An early Plymouth rifle serial numbered 637. The lockplate is dated 1862, while the barrel is unmarked except for the number "15" and the letter "W". The rear sight single leaf is unmarked. The early deliveries were of this pattern. *(Author's collection. Photo by Mike O'Donnell)*

Deliveries 1863[29]
Plymouth Rifles

February	100	September	1,100
June	600	October	500
July	1,000	November	1,000
August	500	December	500

BREECHLOADERS

First Model Maynard Carbines

The Maynard carbines saw limited naval service throughout the war. In January, Captain Dahlgren wrote to Commander Nicholson at the New York Navy Yard. Dahlgren directed Nicholson to issue the Maynard carbines only to officers that requested them. He felt that the Maynard was too delicate for general use of the sailors and should be issued to them only in special instances. One of the vessels being outfitted for sea from the Brooklyn Navy Yard was the sloop *Ticonderoga*. When she left for sea in June, her small arms included Spencer rifles, Whitney revolvers, Ames cutlasses and two Maynard carbines for the use of the officers aboard ship.[30] The *Ticonderoga* remained in naval service until September 1882, and during the period 1877–1880, she made a cruise around the world.

Sharps Rifles and Carbines

The 1855 Sharps were still in active duty in 1863. The sloop *St. Louis*, which patrolled the transatlantic area between 1862–1864, had in their

During the war, the Navy issued the Maynard carbines to naval officers only upon their request. *(Author's collection)*

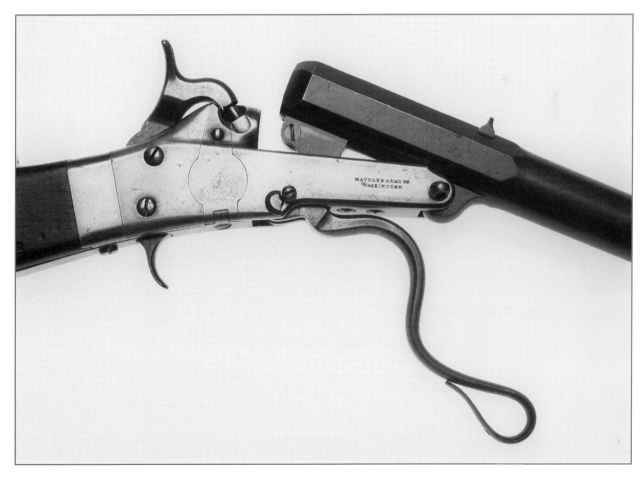

inventory 17 Model 1855 Sharps. The problem with these Sharps carbines and rifles was that, due to the weakness of the mainspring, only four of them would explode a percussion cap.³¹ The *St. Louis* also had in inventory smoothbore muskets, Ames cutlasses, and single-shot pistols. She remained on station until late in 1864, when she arrived back in American waters.

The NM1859 Sharps rifles were now in extensive use. When she went to sea in December, the *Hendrick Hudson* was to receive 24 Sharps rifles with bayonets and cartridge boxes plus 25 three-band Enfield rifles, five Remington revolvers and 20 cutlasses. The Sharps rifle was the weapon of choice for night picket duty. The port regulations for Port Royal, South Carolina, called for the night boat watch in the harbor to be issued Sharps rifles when possible and a revolver. If the Sharps were not available, the Enfield rifle was to be issued.³² The Sharps were also used by the night watch on the vessels on the inland rivers.

At 2:00 a.m. on April 13, the steamer *Mount Washington* was fired on by Confederates from shore while on station on the Nansemond River in Virginia. The night watch returned the fire with their Sharps. The vessel was struck several times by the Confederate musket fire, but no one was injured. The ship's logs of the gunboat *Owasco* dated November 3 and 4 stated that two of their boats were sent to help land troops from the transport steamer near Monongahela, Texas. In the process of crossing the bar in heavy seas, one of their boats capsized, drowning two sailors and several soldiers. The sailors lost five Sharps rifles and their bayonets and the revolver belonging to Assistant Acting Master Sears.

The tinclad gunboat *Lexington's* small arms included the .52 caliber NM1859 Sharps rifles. On one of the crew's trips ashore to kill beef for the vessel, one of the ship's Sharps rifles was lost. (U.S. Naval Historical Center)

Sharps & Hankins Carbines

By June 25, the first 1,000 S&H carbines had been delivered. On July 1, the factory sent to the Navy a sample carbine for Dahlgren's inspection. This carbine was equipped with a shorter leather cover and a ring on the side of the frame. These carbines were probably the shorter 19-inch barrel model carbine. The Navy placed an order for 1,000 of the pervious model carbine. By year's end, the Navy had placed orders for 2,898 carbines of which 2,350 were received. Included in these deliveries were 500 of the 19-inch barrel carbines delivered to the New York Navy Yard in November.³³

Sharps & Hankins
Carbine Deliveries
1863

Delivery	Quantity	Navy Yard
March	250	Philadelphia (60 carbines to St. Louis and 40 to USS *Dale*)
June	250	Philadelphia
	250	New York
September	150	Philadelphia
	50	Washington (Issued to the USS *Roanoke*)
	300	Boston
October	50	Portsmouth
	300	New York (Sent to New Orleans)
November	250	Boston
	500	New York (the 19-inch barrel carbines)
Total	**2,350**	

The Sharps & Hankins rifles were issued in January from the New York Navy Yard to the monitor *Catskill* and the sloop *Lackawanna*. The deck log of the *Catskill* reads that, while the ship was being repaired at Port Royal on November 10, the gun crew was drilled with their Sharps & Hankins rifles. While stationed off Morris Island near Fort Sumter on October 23, the *Catskill* noticed a large, low object floating toward the fleet. They fired their rifles at it and sent a boat to investigate. The object turned out to be only a raft and not something more sinister.[34] The *Lackawanna* was assigned to Farragut's West Gulf Blockading Squadron located off of Mobile. Standard orders for the squadron called for picket duty on every even day. A picket boat would be sent after dark to be on the lookout for vessels that may be attempting to either enter or leave Mobile harbor. On May 9, while on picket duty, the *Lackawanna* guard boat crew lost two saber bayonets for the Sharps & Hankins rifles. They had been also issued with Colt revolvers and Ames cutlasses.[35]

On May 3, the bark *William G. Anderson,* on station at St. Joseph's Island, Texas, sent three launches to tow a sloop that had gone aground. Just as one of the launches landed on shore, the sailors were attacked by 28 men of "D" Company, 8th Texas Volunteer Infantry. The five sailors had little choice but to surrender and hand over their Sharps & Hankins rifles, cartridge boxes and ammunition. The story does not end there. One prisoner, Landsman James Ceder, escaped from his imprisonment near Houston on August 16. He traveled nearly 600 miles to get back to his ship. By the time he reached his ship, Cedar's service had expired. He requested and was granted his discharge from service on October 15, 1863, at New Orleans.[36]

The most powerful ship in the U.S. Navy inventory during the war was the *New Ironsides*. The detachment of Marines aboard the *New Ironsides* was under the command of 2nd Lieutenant Jas B. Young. The Marines were armed with the M1861 Springfield rifle muskets while the sailors had Sharps rifles and Sharps & Hankins carbines. After dark, on October 5, the CSS torpedo boat *David* attacked the *New Ironsides*. As she neared the Union ship, the watch called for her to identify herself. When she would not respond, the sailors and Marines poured an intense fire into the *David*. The *David* managed to return to Charleston while the *New Ironsides* suffered only slight damage from the torpedo attack. The Marine guard remained on board

(Above, right) The majority of the Sharps & Hankins carbines delivered to the Navy were equipped with the 24-inch, leather-covered barrel.
(Steve Selenfriend collection)

(Left) The New York Navy Yard in November received 500 Sharps & Hankins Cavalry Model carbines with the 19-inch barrel.
(Steve Selenfriend collection)

The deck of the monitor *Catskill*. The Sharps & Hankins rifles were issued to the night watch while the *Catskill* was stationed at Charleston, South Carolina. *(Library of Congress)*

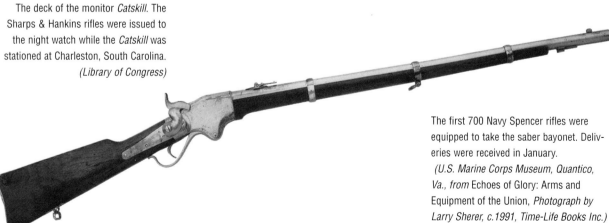

The first 700 Navy Spencer rifles were equipped to take the saber bayonet. Deliveries were received in January.
(U.S. Marine Corps Museum, Quantico, Va., from Echoes of Glory: Arms and Equipment of the Union, *Photograph by Larry Sherer, c.1991, Time-Life Books Inc.)*

for the duration of the war. On the morning of April 6, 1865, the *New Ironsides* was decommissioned at the Philadelphia Navy Yard. The Marines left the ship at 6:30 a.m. A year and a half later, on December 16, 1866, she was destroyed by fire.[37]

Spencer Rifles

The payment for the 703 Spencer Navy rifles was sent to the Spencer Repeating Rifle Company on February 3. The actual deliveries were made in January. The Washington Navy Yard was notified on January 4 that they were to receive 50 Spencer rifles from Boston. On February 10, one Spencer rifle was sent to the Bureau for Gustavas Fox, Assistant Secretary of the Navy. He received an additional Spencer plus a supply of ammunition for his use aboard the supply ship *Baltimore*.[38] The Spencers were quickly placed in service. The USS *Primrose*, being outfitted at Washington on February 25, received the Spencer as shown in the following chart:

Small Arms Issued[39]
USS *Primrose*
February 25, 1863

Spencer Rifles	8	Ames Cutlasses	8
Navy Pistols	8	Boarding Pikes	10
Colt Revolvers	4		

The *Primrose* departed the Navy Yard on March 15 to join the Potomac Flotilla. Six days later, while on shore at Pope's Creek, Virginia, the crew fired their Spencers 56 rounds in practice and, four days later, an additional 75 Spencer rifle cartridges were expended in practice. On May 30, the *Primrose*, along with three other vessels, sent launches on shore. Their target was to destroy the Confederate stores at Rappahannock, Virginia. The crew from the *Primrose* with their Spencers and the other sailors with Sharps rifles kept at bay a company of Confederate cavalry. The sailors destroyed 20,000 bushels of grain before returning to their ships. No casualties were suffered in the engagement.[40]

The Marines received their first Spencer Navy rifles while aboard the frigate *Minnesota*. The *Minnesota* received their supply of Spencers on April 30. The Marines were issued Spencers for night watch. In the morning, at the end of the watch, the Marines guards would fire a blank cartridge from their .58 caliber rifle muskets.[41] It appears that when the Navy attacked Fort Fisher in 1865, the Marines from the *Minnesota* were armed with their Springfield rifle muskets and not the ship's Spencer rifles. The *Minnesota* remained in service until January 1868 and was sold in January 1901.

The second naval request for Spencer rifles occurred in August 1863. On the 13th of the month, the Washington Navy Yard requested that the Bureau

The screw frigate *Minnesota* in 1871. In April of 1863, the *Minnesota* received on board an allotment of Spencer rifles which were issued to the Marines for night watch duties. *(National Archives)*

The August and September deliveries of 300 Spencer rifles were of the Army model to take the angular bayonet. They were received without the bayonets. These Spencers were originally manufactured for the State of Massachusetts but were turned over to the Navy instead. The majority of the rifles were issued to the Potomac Flotilla.

obtain for their use 100 Spencer rifles and a like quantity of Whitney revolvers. These small arms were scheduled for issue to the gunboat *Eutaw*, then being outfitted for service. The next day, the orders were sent forward to be filled. The Spencer factory responded that they could provide 100 Spencer rifles with the Springfield bayonet (triangular) which had had Army inspection.[42] The Bureau accepted the Army Spencer rifles but declined the angular bayonets for them. The navy yard issued 60 Spencers to the *Eutaw*, and a few were received by the schooner *William Bacon*, which was also being fitted out for sea at Washington.

The previous ordnance chief and now commander of the Potomac Flotilla, Commodore Andrew A. Harwood, placed an order through the Washington Navy Yard for 200 Spencer rifles and 20,000 cartridges. The request was forwarded to Spencer on September 5, not for rifles, but for the Spencer carbine. The factory responded that they could not supply the arms since they were supplying orders for the War Department and the State of Massachusetts. The only way the last 100 rifles were available was to take them from the Massachusetts order. On the 7th of the month, the factory wrote back that they could supply 200 rifles if the Navy was willing to take second-quality barrels. The barrels had been laid aside for slight exterior blemishes but they had all passed ordnance inspection.[43] The Navy requested that ten rifles be sent forward for inspection and, if found satisfactory, they would take the rest of the Army Spencer rifles. The ten Spencer rifles were inspected at the Washington Navy Yard on the 11th. Each rifle was fired 14 times and found to be in complete working order. The balance of the order was sent to Washington.

Spencer Army Rifle Inspection Report

When the 190 Army Spencer rifles arrived at Washington, they were inspected by Lieutenant Commander Mitchell. Mitchell's report of October 10 found nine rifles that were unacceptable and had to be replaced by the factory. His report reads in part:

The one hundred and ninety (190) rifles received from the Spencer Repeating Rifle Company have been examined, fired, and then reexamined.

No. 10,121   *The breech piece is cracked in four places not fit for service*
     9,925   *Cracked in the corner of breech piece next to the end of barrel*
   10,108   *The hammer has a flaw nearly the whole length — not serviceable*
     9,893   *Has a small flaw in the hammer*
   10,132   *Has a crack in the corner of breech piece*
   10,009   *Works very stiff and the breech piece is full of veins 9,929 -9,930-*
              9,939- 9,898- 10,000- 10,142 and 10,184 The breech pieces are
              full of veins and scaled
   10, 070   *Shows a leakage of gas on the right side*

In nearly all of them, the finger for disengaging the empty cooper cylinder failed to performed.[44]

As in previous orders, a cartridge box at $1.25 each was ordered with each rifle. The last deliveries of cartridge boxes were obtained without the belts. The Spencer rifles delivered at Washington were issued to the following ships of the Potomac Flotilla: *Primrose, Commodore Read, Dragon, Ella, Fuchsia, William Bacon, Coeur de Lion, Teaser* and *Yankee*. The *Yankee* received 10 Spencer rifles with cartridge boxes and belts plus 1,008 Spencer cartridges and 100 Joslyn revolver cartridges on November 17.[45] Ten days later, the gunboat *Dragon* received 10 Spencer rifles and cartridge boxes plus 1,000 rounds of metallic cartridges. A month later, the gunboat *Currituck* received eight Spencer rifles plus 15 frogs and cartridge boxes for their Colt revolvers. Fifty of the last 200 Army Spencer rifles were sent to the Mississippi Squadron in early 1864.

EDGED WEAPONS

Bowie Knives and Ames Cutlasses

In early August, the Bureau inquired if the Washington Navy Yard had any Bowie knives on hand. The answer back was that all the Bowies had been sent to Dahlgren. Therefore, at 12:45 p.m. on August 3, Captain Henry A. Wise, Chief of Naval Ordnance, sent a telegram to James T. Ames for 500 Bowie knives for delivery at the New York Navy Yard. Five hundred more Bowies were requested from Ames nine days later. The last 500 were to be delivered to Washington. All 1,000 Bowie knives were received before the end of the year with a portion being forwarded to Dahlgren. Dahlgren's picket order for the fleet called for the picket boats to be armed with rifles, revolvers and Bowie knives. His orders of December 3 also stated that hot coffee was to be served to the boat crews going on duty and returning from guard duty. It also allowed the pickets to be supplied with a ration of tobacco to smoke or to chew.[46] Ames was to supply the Navy with only a few cutlasses during the year, since most of their energy was spent on manufacturing howitzers. Less than eighty cutlasses were ordered.

Marine Corps Accouterments and Swords

In January, Major Slack placed his yearly orders with his contractors for supplies and equipment for the Corps. Each of the vendors was instructed to send their deliveries to Captain Maddox at the Marine Corps depot in Philadelphia. The items of interest to this study are:

Bent & Bush[47]
Boston, Massachusetts

75 Sergeant Swords (NCO)
18 Musician Swords (24-inch),
and 10 of Large Size

A Marine corporal with white buff leather waist belt. The waist plate is unmarked. Note that the Marines wore their chevrons pointed up, which is the opposite of how the Army wore theirs during the war.

A wartime photo of a detachment of Marines at Annapolis, Maryland, commanded by Captain McLane Tilton. *(Collection of Michael J. Winey, USAMHI)*

Thomas Peddie supplied the Corps with 700 knapsacks and 350 canteens during the year. *(Jim Stamatelos collection, from Echoes of Glory: Arms and Equipment of the Union, photograph by Larry Sherer, c.1991, Time-Life Books, Inc.)*

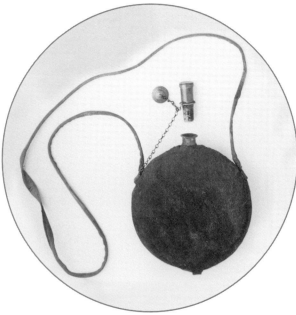

Thomas B. Peddie
New York

- 700 Knapsacks
- 300 Haversacks
- 350 Canteens
- 150 Musket Slings

C.S. Storms
New York

- 600 Bayonet Belts
- 600 Waist Belts
- 600 Waist Plates
- 600 Breast Plates
- 600 Cartridge Boxes
- 600 Bayonet Scabbards
- 600 Cap Pouches
- 600 Cartridge Box Plates
- 100 Sword Frogs

In July, Storms received a second request for 350 additional cartridge boxes.

(Above) The bayonet scabbards, breast plates and white buff leather bayonet belts purchased by the Marine Corps in 1863 came from the New York firm of C.S. Storms. *(Jim Stamatelos collection. Photo by Mike O'Donnell)*

(Right) The Marine Corps depot in Philadelphia received deliveries of 950 cartridge boxes during 1863. *(Jim Stamatelos collection. Photo by Mike O'Donnell)*

REVOLVERS

Colts

One order was placed by the Navy for Colt revolvers. In August, they requested that the Colt factory supply 100 Colt revolvers plus spare parts. The spare parts were delivered but not the revolvers. The reason for not delivering the revolvers is unclear. The Colt factory did sell the Navy 287,000 caliber .36 paper cartridges for the Colt Navies.[48]

The largest land action for the Navy and the Marines in 1863 was the attack on Fort Sumter on the night of September 8. The general assault plan called for the Marines to let the sailors land in front of the fort and to keep up a steady musket fire on the defenders in the fort from their boats. As soon as the sailors had landed, the Marines were to cease firing, land and use the bayonet. The combined force consisted of 400 sailors and Marines. The attack was a total failure. The few that made it to shore were unsupported and quickly defeated by the Confederate defenders that were waiting for them. The only Marine detachment to land was led by 1st Lieutenant Percival C. Pope of the frigate *Powhatan*. Out of 20 men in his detachment, Pope had two wounded and nine captured.[49] The total loss of the combined attack consisted of four killed, 19 wounded and 102 captured. One of the vessels involved in the fight was the steamer *Lodona*. They sent 20 sailors in two cutters on the attack and suffered one wounded and nine missing.

The monitor *Nahant* in 1898. As of February 14, 1863, the *Nahant*, while off Newport News, Virginia, exercised the crew at target practice with their Colt revolvers. *(Detroit Photographic Co. — Library of Congress)*

The USS *Miami* gun crew exercising with a nine-inch Dahlgren gun. Several sailors are shown equipped with Colt revolvers. Note the Marine with the white buff leather cross belts.
(U.S. Naval Historical Center)

The Remington factory delivered to the Navy during the year 1863 nearly 3,200 New Model .36 caliber revolvers. (Author's collection)

Included in their losses were four Colt revolvers, three Ames cutlasses and three pistols.[50] Fort Sumter remained in Confederate control until the last months of the war, when it fell on February 18, 1865.

Remington

The year of 1863 saw the Remington factory deliver to the Navy 4,019 revolvers. Nearly half of the total deliveries went to the New York Navy Yard. In March, the navy yard sent to the New Orleans depot for Farragut's fleet 100 Beals revolvers plus 20,000 revolver cartridges and 30,000 percussion caps. At least 20 of these Beals revolvers were issued to the gunboat *Tennessee*. Late in the year, New York requested that the Bureau requisition for the yard's use 500 Sharps & Hankins carbines and a like number of pistols. The 500 revolvers were supplied by Remington. Deliveries were made in November. By the end of the year, the yard had obtained 1,955 Remington revolvers.

On June 17, the Washington Navy Yard requested 100 revolvers for general use of the Potomac Flotilla. The need was urgent since the yard had in inventory only 18 Joslyns and a like number Savages.[51] The next day, the order was placed for 100 Remington revolvers. Deliveries were received a few days later. In October, the Naval Academy requested 30 Remington revolvers and 98 Sharps & Hankins carbines for issue to the cadets' practice ship *Macedonian*.[52]

The cartridges supplied for the Remington revolvers were manufactured by Johnson and Dow. In December, the Remington factory was notified that the cartridges being supplied were too large for the cylinder. The cartridges would be returned to them and their account adjusted for the returns. During the month, a total of 220,757 cartridges was sent to Remington at a cost to the company of $3,652.60.

Johnson and Dow Cartridges Returned[53]
December 1863

Locations	Cartridges Turned In
Portsmouth	1,194
Boston	11,437
Philadelphia	32,000
Baltimore	7,000
Fort Monroe	44,274
Mound City	125,852
Total	**221,757**

The New York and Washington Navy Yards turned in their cartridges in early 1864.

One of the vessels armed with Remington revolvers from the Boston Navy Yard in April was the gunboat *Niphon*. She was assigned to the North Atlantic Blockading Squadron. On the morning of August 18, near Ft. Fisher, the steamer *Hebe* attempted to run the blockade but went aground. Her cargo consisted of drugs, coffee, clothing and provisions. Because of the heavy seas, two of the cutters from the *Niphon* swamped when they went to investigate the *Hebe*. The crew swam to shore and was captured by Confederate cavalry. The Confederates captured from the 15 sailors five revolvers, six rifles, nine pistols, ten cutlasses and one battle ax. Before the sailors had surrendered, they had

expended 95 rifle cartridges, 50 revolver cartridges and 10 musket cartridges.[54] In December, the *Niphon* reflected the following small arms on board:

Late in 1863, the Naval Academy practice ship, the sloop *Macedonian*, received on board for cadet use 30 Remington revolvers and 98 Sharps & Hankins carbines. *(U.S. Naval Academy)*

Small Arms Inventory[55]
USS *Niphon*
December 11, 1863

4 Remington Revolvers	23 Boarding Pikes	26 Spencer Rifles
3 Battle Axes	30 Rifle Muskets	23 Army Pistols
38 Army Cutlasses		

Whitney

The Navy placed their first wartime request for Whitney revolvers on February 4. Dahlgren's letter to Eli Whitney states:

Bureau of Ordnance
Navy Department
Washington City

Feb. 4th, 1863
Sir:
The Bureau wishes you to send with the utmost dispatch to Cairo, Ill., addressed to Lieutenant Sanford, U.S.N. and marked "Navy Ordnance".
100 revolvers same pattern, with 120 rounds of ammunition for each pistol.
Also sent to the New York Navy Yard marked "For Ordnance Depot Western Gulf Squadron". 100 revolvers same pattern with 120 rounds of ammunition for each pistol.
I am very respectfully your obst. Servt.

J.A. Dahlgren
Chief of Bureau[56]

Eli Whitney
Whitneyville, Conn.

Deliveries were made in February. In April, New York sent 30 Whitney revolvers to Port Royal to the *Wabash* for issue to the gunboat *Ottawa*. In August, the Washington Navy Yard ordered 100 Whitney revolvers. Seventy of the revolvers were issued to the *Eutaw* along with 7,000 cartridges. From the same location in October, the converted frigate *Roanoke*, now a three-turret ironclad, was issued 50 Whitney revolvers plus an equal quantity of Sharps & Hankins carbines. By year's end, Whitney had provided the Navy with over 2,400 revolvers.

The next year would bring the war to the Gulf and establish Farragut as one of the war's great naval commanders.

Eli Whitney sent forward over 2,400 Whitney .36 caliber revolvers to the Navy in 1863. *(Author's collection)*

Chapter 6
Mobile Bay, 1864

August 5th Action, Mobile Bay

As long as Mobile Bay was open to blockade traffic, the Confederacy had one major port left open on the Gulf coast. Finally, in the summer of 1864, Farragut had sufficient Army support to attack the forts leading into Mobile Bay. Farragut's task would not be an easy mission. He would first have to pass the batteries of Fort Morgan, stay clear of the minefield laid out by the Confederates, and be on the lookout for the Confederate ironclad *Tennessee*.

On the morning of August 5, at 6:47 a.m., the first shots of the battle for Mobile Bay were fired. The shots came from the 15-inch guns of the monitor *Tecumseh* leading the fleet past Fort Morgan. Soon the battle was in full force. To get a better view, Farragut climbed up the rigging of the *Hartford*. A crew member was sent up to tie a rope around the admiral so that he would not fall in the event of a sudden motion of the ship. At about 8 o'clock, the *Tecumseh* moved west of the line marked by red buoys and hit a mine. The monitor sank within minutes taking down with her 93 of the crew. Only about eight survived. Having lost the *Tecumseh*, Farragut took the lead with the *Hartford* with these immortal words: "Damn the torpedoes! Full speed ahead!" The fleet passed over the minefield without further damage. After passing the fort, the fleet came to anchor. It was at about 8:45 that the *Tennessee* came on to attack the Union fleet. The fight with the *Tennessee* lasted until 10 o'clock when she lowered her colors. During the action, the *Tennessee* was attacked by most of the fleet including the sloop *Lackawanna*. The Marines and the sailors aboard the *Lackawanna* fired their .58 caliber rifle muskets and Colt and Whitney revolvers into the gun ports to prevent the crew of the *Tennessee* from reloading her guns.[1] In the day's battle, Farragut's losses consisted of 150 killed and 170 wounded. The last Confederate port on the Gulf coast was now closed.

Rear Admiral Farragut's flagship *Hartford*, shown at Mobile Bay in 1864. *(U.S. Naval Historical Center)*

Rear Admiral Farragut.

The August 5, 1864, deck logs of the *Hartford* on the day of the battle at Mobile Bay. *(National Archives)*

When the *Tecumseh* sank, she had been in service just over three months. As of April, when the *Tecumseh* was outfitted at New York Navy Yard, she was issued:

Small Arms Issued[2]
USS *Tecumseh*
April 20, 1864

Battle Axes	24
Whitney Revolvers	35
S&H Carbines	25
Boarding Pikes	20
Spencer Rifles	1
Single Sticks	20
Ames Cutlasses	30
Metallic Cartridges	2,600
Revolver Cartridges	3,500
Revolver Percussion Caps	5,000

When she struck her colors, the *Tennessee* became the property of the U.S. Navy. A strict inspection by the order of Admiral Farragut revealed that the following small arms were on board at the time of her capture:

Small Arms Captured
CSS *Tennessee*
August 5, 1864

Rifled Muskets w/Bayonets	40
Waist Belts (leather)	90
Springfield Muskets w/Bayonets	41
Waist Belts (canvas)	25
Cartridge Boxes	87
Cutlass Frogs	27
Cap Boxes	47
Boarding Pikes	47
Cutlasses	22

The value of the small arms captured from the *Tennessee* was placed at $1,629.35.[3] The *Tennessee* was commissioned into the United States Navy on August 19, and remained in service for one year to the day of its commission. A second gunboat captured in the battle was the CSS *Selma*. The day after the battle, the sloop *Richmond* was directed to send ten Marines with their knapsacks and two-day rations to take over the *Selma*. Lieutenant Sherman and his detachment of ten Marines from the *Richmond* complied with the admiral's orders.[4]

The CSS ironclad *Tennessee* shown after her capture at Mobile Bay. Small arms taken from the captured ironclad included 81 muskets, 22 cutlasses and 47 boarding pikes. *(U.S. Naval Historical Center)*

Albemarle Raid

The Federal Navy was stopped before Plymouth, North Carolina, in the summer and fall of 1864. The Navy's path was blocked to the Union's wooden ships by the Confederate ironclad ram CSS *Albemarle*. As long as the Confederate ship blocked the way, the city could not be taken.

Enter the story of one of the true naval heroes of the war, Lieutenant William Barker Cushing. Cushing was born on November 4, 1842. On September 25, 1857, at the age of 14, he entered the Naval Academy. Shortly before graduation in 1861, he was dismissed from the Academy for deficiency in Spanish. With the outbreak of the war coming within a month of his resignation, Cushing was granted a commission in the Navy. By the summer of 1864, he was already well known for his bravery. Earlier that summer, Cushing,

Lieutenant William B. Cushing — one of the true naval heroes of the war. On the night of October 27, he lead a raiding party which resulted in the sinking of the Confederate ironclad *Albemarle*. For his action, Cushing was given the thanks of Congress and promoted to lieutenant commander. *(Library of Congress)*

with two officers and 15 men, made a reconnaissance up the Cape Fear River towards Wilmington and Fort Fisher. Cushing's men were armed with Colt revolvers, pistols and Sharps rifles. After the two-day trip, he came back with an excellent knowledge of the city land and water defenses, which he turned over to his superiors. For their actions, three of Cushing's men (with his recommendation) were awarded the Medal of Honor.[5]

Cushing's plan for the *Albemarle* raid called for a surprise night attack to sink the Confederate ironclad with a torpedo. His task would not be easy. The Confederates had placed pickets on both shores expecting such an attack. He would have to travel eight miles upstream to get to his objective. He would also pass the Union wreck *Southfield*, which had Confederate guards on it. On the night of October 27, he and 14 men made their way upriver in Picket Boat No. 1. The sailors assigned to the boat were armed with short Enfield rifles, and the rest of the men with Sharps & Hankins carbines. The boat was equipped with a 12-pound howitzer. When they neared the *Southfield,* four men went aboard and captured the guard. The rest of the crew proceeded on. They were not challenged until they were within 20 yards of the *Albemarle*. The sentry opened fire, and soon a storm of musket fire was directed at Cushing and his men. Cushing managed to bring the boat in contact with the *Albemarle*, lower the torpedo and set it off. Within minutes, the Confederate ironclad was on the bottom of the river. With his boat also destroyed, Cushing told his men to save themselves. He and seaman William Hoftman managed to swim to shore and make their way back to the fleet. The balance of his crew was either killed or captured. Hoftman, with Cushing's recommendation, was awarded the Medal of Honor, while Cushing received the thanks of Congress and a promotion to lieutenant commander.[6] With the *Albemarle* no longer a threat, Plymouth surrendered to Union forces five days later. Cushing remained in the Navy after the war and rose to the rank of commander. His last assignment was as executive officer at the Washington Navy Yards in 1874. He became ill after Thanksgiving and died on December 17, 1874. He is buried at the Naval Academy.[7]

Issues of Small Arms to Vessels

During the period March to early May, the navy yards were reporting to the Bureau of Ordnance on a standard form the quantity and types of ordnance being issued to the ships being outfitted for sea.

Small Arms Issued[8]

	Onondaga	Nereus	Cornubia	Proteus	Hydrangea	Agawam	Canonicus
Battle Axes	15	30	—	30	6	30	—
S&H Carbines	63	50	—	50	—	35	—
Spencer Rifles	1	1	—	1	1	—	20
Ames Cutlasses	45	64	40	64	25	70	50
Remington Revolvers	55	30	—	30	10	—	—
Whitney Revolvers	—	—	—	—	—	40	45
Single Sticks	25	30	—	40	15	50	—
Plymouth Rifles	—	50	—	50	25	50	30
Boarding Pikes	—	40	—	40	15	45	8
Army Pistols	—	30	20	30	—	35	—
Colt Revolvers	—	1 (M1849)	17	—	—	—	—
.69 cal. Rifled Muskets	—	3	—	—	—	—	—
.577 cal. Enfield-Long	—	—	30	—	—	—	—

In addition to the small arms issued to the steamer *Agawam* from the Portsmouth Navy Yard, the vessel received for the Marine guard aboard ship 1,500 musket ball cartridges and 300 musket blank cartridges. The detachment was led by Orderly Sergeant Thomas Clifford and consisted of two corporals and twelve privates.

Small Arms Continued

	Massasoit	*Pontoosuc*	*Mattabesett*
Spencer Rifles	—	—	1
Plymouth Rifles	70	20	68
Whitney Revolvers	90	8	—
Remington Revolvers	—	—	70
M1849 Colt Revolvers	—	—	1
Ames Cutlasses	90	20	50
S&H Carbines	70	—	27
Army Pistols	—	—	—
Navy Pistols	—	20	—
Battle Axes	—	—	20
Boarding Pikes	—	—	35
Single Sticks	—	—	30

(Below, top) The double-turret monitor *Onondaga* on the James River in 1864–1865. *The Onondaga was commissioned at New York on March 24, 1864.* (Library of Congress)

(Below, bottom) The gunboat *Agawam* on the James River, 1864–1865. The *Agawam* was commissioned on March 9, 1864, at the Portsmouth Navy Yard. (U.S. Naval Historical Center)

Table of Allowance, Changes For 1864[9]

In 1864, the Navy revised the table of allowance for the allocation of small arms to be issued to the sizes of vessels in naval service. The new allowance is shown in the following chart:

	Single Sticks	Rifles or Carbines	Muskets	Pistols or Cutlasses	Revolvers
Ships of the Line	70	124	270	290	185
Frigates	60	100	120	170	110
Sloops of War					
1st Razees	50	80	80	125	76
2nd Razees	50	80	80	110	76
1st	40	70	70	90	60
2nd	40	60	60	80	50
3nd	30	50	50	60	40
Brigs	20	20	20	30	20
Steamers					
1st Class Screw	60	100	120	20	120
2nd Class Screw	50	80	80	130	80
3nd Class Screw	40	50	50	70	40
4th Class Screw	20	20	20	30	20
1st Class Side-Wheel	50	80	80	110	76
2nd Class Side-Wheel	40	70	70	100	60
3nd Class Side-Wheel	30	30	30	40	25
4th Class Side-Wheel	20	20	20	30	20

Accouterments

Navy

The accouterments used with small arms by the sailors were manufactured at the various navy yards with the exception being the cartridge boxes purchased from the Spencer Repeating Rifle Co. for the Spencer rifle. It was the practice of the Navy for the sailors to wear the cartridge box on the waist belt. In January, the Boston Navy Yard took up the task of manufacturing over 12,000 various types of accouterments. With 50 workers on the project, it took ten weeks to complete. The items manufactured were:

Accouterments Manufactured[10]
Boston Navy Yard
February–April 1864

Musket Cartridge Boxes	2,800	Waist Belts	4,568
Revolver Cartridge Boxes	1,100	Battle Axe Frogs	495
Revolver Frogs	1,425	Pistol Frogs	500
Sword Frogs	965	Primer Boxes	168

The Boston Navy Yard sent 500 of the waist belts to Mound City for the Plymouth rifles previously sent there. One thousand musket and revolver cartridge boxes were sent to New York. The musket cartridge boxes manufactured at Boston are stamped on the inside flap "U.S.N.Y./BOSTON". When the Navy used the term frog, it meant a holster. The pistol frogs were made of different sizes to fit the types of revolvers intended for their use.

Chapter 6 • Mobile Bay, 1864

Cannon drills on board the gunboat *Mendota*. Note that the fourth sailor on the rope with his back to the camera has a musket cartridge box and a scabbard for a Plymouth rifle saber bayonet which is missing. *(Library of Congress)*

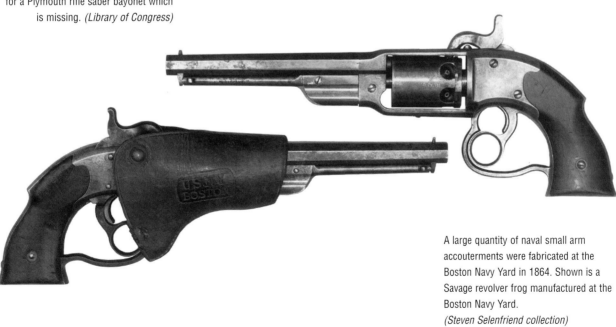

A large quantity of naval small arm accouterments were fabricated at the Boston Navy Yard in 1864. Shown is a Savage revolver frog manufactured at the Boston Navy Yard.
(Steven Selenfriend collection)

Marine Corps

In 1864, the Marines placed their accouterment requirements with the New York firm of C.S. Storms. The March 26 and 27 contract with Storms called for the firm to send to Philadelphia:

C.S. Storms[11]
New York
March 1864
1,200 cartridge boxes with Higgens adjustable magazines
1,200 bayonet scabbards with frogs
1,200 percussion cap pouches
1,200 cartridge box belts and waist belts
200 sword frogs
1,400 knapsacks
600 haversacks
600 canteens
400 musket slings
1,500 bayonet frogs at a cost of 18 cents each

In September, Captain Maddox at Philadelphia was directed to distribute the bayonet scabbards with frogs as follows: Portsmouth 125, Boston 150, Brooklyn 175, Philadelphia 150, Norfolk 100, Pensacola 125, Cairo 75, and 200 to Mare Island. After the distribution, only 100 bayonet scabbards with frogs remained in storage.

Small Arms Inspections

Only a small portion of the small arms received by the Navy were stamped by the inspectors prior to 1864. In August, Captain Henry A. Wise, Chief of the Bureau of Ordnance, put out the following guidance for the inspection of small arms. It states:

(CIRCULAR.)[12]

BUREAU OF ORDNANCE
Navy DEPARTMENT
WASHINGTON CITY, Aug. 29, 1864

The Bureau directs that hereafter all small arms, when passed by the inspector, be stamped in the following manner:

MUSKETS, CARBINES, and PISTOLS.
On top of the barrel near the breech, with an anchor; and, on the lock-plate, the letter P over the initials of the Inspector, thus: P/A.B.

The 1864 Bureau of Ordnance circular called for the top of the revolver barrel to be stamped with an anchor. Shown is a Whitney revolver stamped with an anchor on the top of the barrel.
(Author's collection)

REVOLVERS.

On the top of the barrel, near the cylinder, with an anchor, and on the face of the cylinder, the letter P over the initials of the inspector, as above.

CUTLASSES.

On the blade, immediately below the guard, with an anchor, and the letter P over the initials of the Inspector, as above. The Bureau will furnish to each Inspector two sizes of stamps. MUSKET CARBINES and CUTLASSES are to be marked with the larger, (.15-in.,) and PISTOLS and REVOLVERS with the smaller (.1-in.,) size of stamps.

H.A. WISE,
Chief of Bureau.

Note. — To be pasted into the Book of Ordnance Circular

1864 Procurements and Field Service

MUZZLELOADERS

Navy

On March 28, the Navy requested from the Ordnance Department 150 cadet rifles for the Naval Academy. Only 144 were available. Ninety-eight were delivered from the St. Louis Arsenal, 42 from Springfield and 4 from Frankford Arsenal.[13] The cadet rifle muskets delivered were the M1855 with the date "1859" on the lock, .58 caliber, and 53 inches in length.[14]

Later in October, the Army supplied the Navy with 200 of the 1864-dated .58 caliber Springfield rifle muskets at Boston and 500 to the New York Navy Yard. The New York deliveries were slated for shipment to Mare Island. In November, the Navy ordered 500 caliber .69 rifled muskets for issue to the Mississippi Squadron. The rifled muskets were issued from the Allegheny Arsenal and the bayonets and scabbards from St. Louis. In addition, one Lindsay M1863 double rifle musket was sent to the Navy from the Washington Arsenal. The Navy wanted the Lindsay for their museum and for test trials.

The Enfield and the Plymouth rifles were the major muskets issued in 1864, but a few vessels did obtain the .58 and .69 caliber muskets. In July, the ironclad *Pittsburg* received on board 20 smoothbore muskets with bayonets plus cartridge boxes. In May, the *Winnebago* obtained 40 rifle muskets plus 30 Whitney revolvers.[15] The *Pittsburg* took part in the Red River campaign while the *Winnebago* was at Mobile Bay. In December, Rear Admiral Dahlgren's flag ship the *Harvest Moon* received 30 muskets with bayonets, cartridge boxes, and 1,800 rounds of .69 caliber buckshot cartridges. In Lake Erie, the gunboat *Michigan* was on guard off Sandusky, Ohio, at Johnson's Island. On Johnson's Island were several thousand Confederate prisoners of war. In September, the Confederates made an attempt to free the prisoners but failed. In March, the Michigan was showing the following small arms in inventory:

USS *Michigan*[16]
Small Arms on Board
March 1864

30 Muskets, Smoothbore and Rifled Marked on Barrel "V/P 1832", on lock "Harpers Ferry 1853"
37 Boarding Pikes
35 Flintlock Pistols (unserviceable)
25 Carbines — J.H. Merrill, Baltimore 1856
22 Colt Revolvers
58 Cutlasses

In the spring, while the *Michigan* was stationed at Erie, Pennsylvania, the night watch was issued muskets and Colt revolvers. At the end of the watch, at 6:00 a.m., the arms would be turned back in and then reissued the next night. In addition to watching for possible Confederate attacks on Johnson's Island, the *Michigan* patrolled the Great Lakes. In June, at Marquette, Michigan, the crew expended 120 musket cartridges and 75 Jenks-Merrill carbine cartridges in target practice. Interestingly, while at Marquette the crew fired one of the Parrott guns at a target a mile

The gunboat *Michigan* as of September 17, 1868. In March 1864, the *Michigan* was listing among its small arms inventory 30 muskets, both smoothbore and rifled, the barrels dated 1832 and the locks marked Harpers Ferry 1853.
(U.S. Naval Historical Center)

away with the shots striking just over the target. The old .69 caliber muskets on the *Michigan* remained on board throughout the war. Two vessels to replace their old muskets for Plymouth rifles were the tug *Yankee* and gunboat *Currituck*.

Turn In[17]

	USS *Yankee* May 3	USS *Currituck* April 29
Spencer Rifles	10	8
Colt Revolving Rifles	5	—
Muskets .69 caliber	16	30
Sharps Rifles .56 caliber	—	8
.69 Caliber Ball Cartridges	541	1,230
Spencer Ball Cartridges	630	573
Sharps Ball Cartridges	—	3,413
Colt Ball Cartridges	600	—

Capture of CSA Muzzleloaders

During the war years, the Navy captured quantities of muskets from the Confederates. One of the lesser-known models was the Mendenhall, Jones and Gardner .58 caliber rifle. On August 24, the USS *Niphon* off New Inlet, North Carolina, noticed 60 to 80 rebel infantry throwing up breastworks at the entrance to Masonboro inlet. As the Confederates had no artillery support, the ship sent three launches to try to capture them. The sailors were well armed with Spencer and Sharps rifles. As they neared the beach, the Confederates flew into the marshes and escaped by boats. The rebels left behind nine rifles and 160 rounds of ammunition. The captured rifles were marked "C.S. 1863. N.C."[18] These markings are found on the Mendenhall, Jones and Gardner rifles.

Marine Corps Muzzleloaders

The year saw no deliveries of rifle muskets to the Corps, but large quantities of spare parts were requested from the Ordnance Department. A small order was placed in February and a larger order was requisitioned in October.

The October order reads:

Head-Quarters, Marine Corps[19]
QUARTERMASTERS OFFICE
Washington, Oct. 20, 1864

There is required for the use of the U.S. Marine Corps the following ordnance stores,

3,000	three thousand wipers	for Springfield Rifle Muskets Cal. .58
500	five hundred tumbler screws	do do do do do
100	one hundred main springs	do do do do do
50	fifty ramrods	do do do do do
100	one hundred main spring swivels	do do do do do
200	two hundred ball screws	do do do do do
150	one hundred fifty bayonets	do do do do do
200	two hundred spring vices	do do do do do
150	one hundred fifty tumblers	do do do do do

W.M. Slack
QMMC

Approved
J. Zeilin
Col. Commandant

(Above) A Marine detachment with the Marine band. *(Library of Congress)*
(Below) Marines from the Washington Navy Yard in April 1864, armed with the Model 1842 muskets. *(Library of Congress)*

Jacob Zeilin, the seventh commandant of the Marine Corps, took command of the Corps with the death of John Harris in May 1864.

The spare parts were supplied by Springfield Armory in November. During this period, Captain D.M. Cohen commanding the Marine guard aboard the *Lancaster* at the Bay of Panama requested delivery of 5,500 caliber .58 cartridges and 11,000 percussion caps that were supplied from the New York Navy Yard. In the fall of the year, Major Slack forwarded to the Marine barracks at Philadelphia and Brooklyn 100 rifle muskets with bayonets while Washington obtained 20 and Boston 40.[20] In addition to the rifle muskets carried by the Marines, at least one officer, 2nd Lieutenant Frank Church of the *Black Hawk*, carried a Henry rifle during the Red River campaign of 1864.

A sad day fell on the Corps on May 12, when its commandant, Colonel John Harris, died after five years in office. To take his place, the Secretary of the Navy selected the 33-year veteran of the Corps, Major Jacob Zeilin, as seventh commandant. Zeilin had been a company commander at Bull Run where he was wounded. He held the position until his retirement on November 1, 1876.[21]

Enfield Rifles

In June, the Philadelphia Navy Yard was in the process of outfitting the six picket boats that were to be assigned to the James River. The following equipment was to be issued to each of the vessels:

Small Arms Issued[22]
U.S. Picket Boats #1–6

Short Enfield Rifles	8	Waist Belts	16
Saber Bayonets	8	Ball Cartridges	800
M1841 Cutlasses	8	Percussion Caps	1,750
Rifle Cartridge Boxes	8		

Picket boat #2 was captured by the Virginia Home Guard on October 8 at Wicomico Bay, Virginia. The picket boat had gone into the bay to repair the engines. The Home Guard under the command of Captain Covington attacked the Union vessel while in the act of repair. After expending all its rifle ammunition and having gone aground, the Union picket boat surrendered.[23]

Act of Treason

Money can turn the loyalty of an individual. This is what happened in 1864 with the near capture of the gunboat *Rattler* on the Mississippi River. The plan called for Acting Master Daniel W. Glenney, Commander of the *Rattler*, to send a large portion of his crew on shore and have them captured. The Confederates would then row back to the Union vessel and capture it. For his part in the plan, Glenney was to receive $2,000 and 100 bales of cotton. It appears that Glenney received the cash but not the cotton. On the night of September 4, Glenney sent 22 men ashore who were quickly captured by the waiting Confederates. Among the small arms captured were 17 Enfield rifles and three Colt revolvers. The plan fell apart when the lookout on the *Rattler* spotted the Confederates rowing toward the ship. Because of his questionable answers to this affair, Glenney was placed under close arrest on the *Rattler*. With the help of one of the crew, he made his escape on the night of November 4. He was not captured, and therefore, was dismissed from naval service.[24] The *Rattler* would survive only until the end of the year when she sank near Grand Gulf, Mississippi, after going aground in a gale.

Plymouth Rifles

The first delivery of Plymouth rifles occurred on January 2, 1864, when 500 were sent to New York. One hundred of these rifles were forwarded to Mare Island and an additional 50 went to the ordnance ship *Dale* at Key West, Florida. Included in this delivery were the first 100 Plymouths manufactured in early 1863. These rifles had iron barrels without proof marks or inspection cartouche and were dated 1862. The rear sights were not graduated. While the navy yard kept the Plymouths, they were not satisfied with them.[25] In January, New York received an additional 500 rifles, which were then sent to Mound City. Five hundred rifles were delivered to Washington

in March. All rifles delivered up to this time were equipped with a saber bayonet serial number to the rifle. Since the bayonets were not interchangeable, the yard saw this as a major defect. To correct the problem, the yard repaired the bayonets to make them interchangeable. By April 19, two hundred bayonets had been repaired.[26] In May, the last of the 1861 contract were delivered. The total number of Plymouth rifles delivered in 1864 came to 4,695.

Plymouth Rifle Deliveries[27]
1864

January	1,000	February	500	March	1,500
April	1,000	May	695		

The lockplate on the 1864 deliveries are marked with the date to the rear of the hammer. Forward of the hammer is stamped a small spread eagle over "U.S." and "WHITNEY-VILLE". The small spread-eagle markings will also be found on some 1863 locks.

Large numbers of Plymouth rifles were sent out to the fleet. By September, Boston notified the Bureau that they had no more Plymouths for issue. The following is a partial list of vessels issued the Plymouth during the year, besides the ones already listed:

Mingoe	*Pawnee*	*Ascutney*	*Jacob Bell*	*Fuchsia*	*Harvest Moon*
Pontiac	*Saranac*	*Iroquois*	*Vindicator*	*Ella*	*Conemaugh*
Saratoga	*Farrallones*	*Mendota*	*Sibyl*	*Avenger*	*Saco*
Memphis	*Unadilla*	*Mercury*	*Flambeau*	*Wissahickon*	*Teaser*
St. Louis	*Don*	*Otsego*	*Winona*	*Sonoma*	*Niad*

It is interesting to note that the Potomac Flotilla became so disenchanted with their Spencer Army rifles that they turned them in for the Plymouth rifle. This story is found in the Spencer section. Less than a month after

The tinclad *Rattler*. On the evening of September 4, 22 sailors from the *Rattler* were captured on shore. Among the weapons captured were 17 Enfield rifles and three Colt revolvers. When the Confederates tried to row out to the ship, they were spotted and were unable to seize the *Rattler*. (U.S. Naval Historical Center)

The six picket boats outfitted at the Philadelphia Navy Yard were each to receive eight short Enfield rifles with saber bayonets. These boats were scheduled for duty on the James River. (U.S. Military Academy)

The monitor *Canonicus* at Hampton Roads in 1907. When commissioned on April 16, 1864, at Boston, the *Canonicus'* small arms included 30 Plymouth rifles. The ship deck logs reflect several occasions when the turret and port watch crews were exercised with Plymouth rifles.
(Detroit Publishing Co. Library of Congress)

going to sea, *Mattabesett* was one of the wooden Union ships attacked by the Confederate ironclad *Albemarle*. The attack occurred on May 5. In the action, the Union ships had little effect on the Confederate ironclad. One of the six-inch shells from the *Albemarle* struck the *Mattabesett* killing two of the crew and destroying eight Plymouth rifles in the small arms locker. In the attack on Plymouth, North Carolina, the *Otsego* expended 300 rounds of Plymouth rifle ammunition, 230 S&H carbine cartridges, and 248 Remington revolver cartridges.[28]

Tulifinny Crossroads, December 9

In late November, a combined Army-Navy force attempted to cut the Charleston and Savannah Railroad. For the Navy's part, Rear Admiral Dahlgren supplied three battalions — two batallions of sailors and one battalion of Marines — totaling about 500 men. The 182-man Marine battalion was led by 1st Lieutenant George Stoddard. The Marines had come from 12 ships in the fleet. While the Marines were armed with their .58 caliber rifle muskets, the sailors not assigned to the howitzers were issued Plymouth rifles.

One of the largest skirmishes with Confederate forces during this six-week campaign occurred on December 9 at Tulifinny Crossroads. At a little after 9:00 a.m., the Union skirmish line, with a force of 600 including Marines, moved toward the Confederate position. The skirmishers advanced through a dense swamp that was from knee to waist deep. The swamp was so thick that a man could not be seen three or four paces away. The column advanced under a heavy Confederate fire to within 50 yards of the rebel works. The Marines did not receive the word to fall back and were nearly captured by the Confederates. The Marines made their way back to their lines by following the river. After the retirement of the Union force, the rebels attacked the Union positions which were protected by the sailors with their howitzers. In these rebel attacks, one of the sailors shot the color bearer of the 5th Georgia Infantry with his Plymouth rifle. In the day-long action, the sailors suffered 15 men wounded while the Marine casualties included one killed, seven wounded and three missing.[29]

Breechloaders

Sharps Carbines and Rifles

In 1864, the M1855 Sharps carbines were still assigned to the *New London*. She was assigned to the West Gulf Blockading Squadron. At Calcasieu Pass, Louisiana, on May 10, a launch from the *New London* was sent to investigate why the *Granite City* was not returning their signals. Unknown to the launch, the *Granite City* had been captured. Seeing the Confederate flag flying from the ship, the launch mistook it as a practical joke being played by the crew and fired on the flag. The officer firing the shot at the flag was shot dead by fire from the captured vessel. The remaining six members of the launch crew were taken prisoners. Among the items captured by the Confederates were seven Sharps carbines with 120 rounds of ammunition plus 200 percussion caps for the Sharps. Other items captured included four Navy pistols, four Colt revolvers, five Navy swords and one Navy cutlass.[30]

Small Arms of the USS *Kearsarge*

The most famous sea battle of the war outside of U.S. waters occurred between the CSS *Alabama* and the Union sloop *Kearsarge*. In twenty-two months of raiding Union commercial shipping, the *Alabama*, under the command of Raphael Semmes, had destroyed over $7 million of cargo. The battle of these two ships occurred off Cherbourg, France, on Sunday, June 19. Thousands of the local citizens lined the shore to witness the famous battle. The Union sloop was under the command of Captain John Winslow. In the battle, the shots of the gunners of the *Alabama* struck the *Kearsarge* several times but caused little damage. The *Alabama* was, in turn, hit several times at the waterline. Being disabled and sinking, the *Alabama* surrendered. The loses in the battle for the *Kearsarge* consisted of three wounded while the *Alabama* sustained 19 dead and 21 wounded.

Two years prior, in February 1862, the *Kearsarge* had been outfitted for her duty in the European waters at the Portsmouth Navy Yard. Issued to the *Kearsarge* were Ames cutlasses, boarding pikes, M1861 Colt revolvers and NM1859 Mitchell-contracted Sharps rifles. The deck logs of April 14, 1864, has this entry: "…exercise first division for 30 minutes (Sharps rifles)."[31] In November, the *Kearsarge* returned to the U.S., to the Boston Navy Yard. She remained in naval service until February 2, 1894, when she was wrecked on the Roncador Reef, in Central America.[32]

Sharps & Hankins

In 1864, the Navy placed orders for 2,550 S&H carbines. With previous orders, the naval small arms inspectors inspected over 3,600 carbines at the factory. The company also supplied the Navy with over a half million metallic cartridges during the year.[33] One of the inspectors, John M. Coffman, billed the Navy $1,399.56 for his work at the S&H factory.[34]

In September, Mare Island received their second delivery of S&H carbines. This delivery from New York also included:

The screw sloop *Kearsarge* in New York Harbor about 1890. At the time of her victory over the CSS *Alabama* in June 1864, the *Kearsarge's* small arms included the .52 caliber NM1859 Sharps rifles delivered on the Mitchell contract in 1861. *(U.S. Naval Historical Center)*

Mare Island Deliveries[35]
September 1864

400 Plymouth Rifles w/Cartridge Boxes	350 S&H Carbines w/Cartridge Boxes
200 Battle Axes	100 Whitney Revolvers w/200 Cartridge Boxes
200 Boarding Pikes	50,000 Cartridges for the Plymouth
49,000 Cartridges cal. .58 for Rifle Muskets	5,000 Cartridges for Pistols
35,000 Cartridges for S&H Carbines	15,000 Cartridges for the Whitney Revolvers

Earlier in the year, 1,000 cartridge boxes for the S&H carbines had been sent from Boston to New York.

Rear Admiral S.P. Lee commanding the North Atlantic Blockading Squadron, had a high regard for the S&H carbines. In May, he requested 20 of the S&H carbines plus 2,000 cartridges be delivered to the flag ship *Malvern*. On May 20, the *Malvern* received 28 S&H carbines plus a detachment of Marines. The Marine guard consisted of a lieutenant, two sergeants and 21 privates.[36] Lee also directed that 50 men recently transferred from

Officers of the gunboat *Mendota*. The Sharps & Hankins carbines can be seen stored on the side of the ship between the two officers nearest the cannon. *(National Archives)*

the Army to the Navy be issued the improved short Sharps rifle (actually S&H carbines). The men were to perform picket duty on the James River. On June 12, the steamer *Meteor* at New Orleans was issued from the ordnance depot 30 S&H rifles and a like quantity of muskets. Later in the year, from the same location, the steamer *Elk* was issued 20 S&H rifles, while the *Octorara* obtained 15. In June, the sloop *Dacotah*, attached to Lee's command, lost 14 S&H rifles and 12 cartridge boxes when one of its cutters was swamped. In December, the gunboat *Tacony* lost three S&H rifles when one of its cutters was struck and sunk by enemy batteries at New Inlet, North Carolina.[37]

On the last day of November, while at Erie, the gunboat *Michigan* received on board 40 S&H carbines with ammunition and the needed accouterments. Three days later, the ship sent to New York their 25 Jenks-Merrill carbines, 23 cartridge boxes plus 2,250 rounds of ball cartridges.

On the night of February 26, a picket boat was sent out from the *Nipsic* for duty off of Charleston. The crew consisted of an officer and five sailors. Each man was armed with a cutlass, revolver and a S&H carbine. Nearing Fort Sumter and Moultrie, they were hailed by a Confederate picket craft. Unable to escape, the Union crew attempted to fight it out with the other side. After several volleys were fired, and being greatly outnumbered, the *Nipsic* crew surrendered after tossing their small arms overboard. The officer was exchanged in November. However, his crew was sent to Andersonville where they died. Many a sailor and Marine found their way to Andersonville after their capture.[38]

Smith Carbines

No records have been found concerning any purchases of Smith carbines by the Navy, but at least one Artillery Model Smith was used by Rear Admiral David Porter. Porter felt the Smith carbine a superior arm to the Spencer rifle. He wrote this interesting letter to the Bureau of Ordnance requesting their purchase:

An Artillery Model Smith carbine. Rear Admiral David Porter considered the Smith carbine superior to the Spencer rifle. He requested that the Navy obtain it for naval service, but no orders were forthcoming. (U.S. Military Academy)

NO. 11
Mississippi Squadron[39]
Flag Ship "Black Hawk"
Mound City, June 25, 1864

Sir:

I have had in use now two years a gun invented by "Smith."
This gun has not been cleaned in all that time, nor does it need it — I have kept it under constant trial by firing and pronounced it the best gun for Naval purposes, that has ever been made — In accuracy and range it is superior to the "Spencer Rifle", which I consider one of the best guns, and I Imagine it cost much less (or should cost less) than any gun now made.
I strongly recommend it for Naval use.
There has been a new "Patent Metallic Cartridge" made for the gun by "Poultney" which I consider a very good one.

Very Respectfully Your Obst Servant
David D. Porter
Rear Admiral

Commander H.A. Wise
Chief of Bureau of Ordnance
Washington DC

At the time of Porter's letter, the Army was purchasing Spencer rifles at $35 while the Smith carbines cost $23.50 under contract. Dahlgren had tested a Smith carbine in February 1858 and recommended it for naval service but none were delivered.

Spencer Rifles

One order was placed for Spencer rifles in 1864. On April 13, the Navy requested delivery of 300 Spencer rifles and 100 cartridges per rifle. The rifles were intended for the Mississippi Squadron. The factory wrote back that they could only supply the cartridges. The Navy also inquired of the Army whether they could provide the rifles, and they also were unable to help the Navy. Wise had to tell the Mississippi Squadron that no Spencer rifles were available, and therefore, their request could not be honored.

The Spencer rifles issued to the *Mound City* in 1863 were still on board as of December 1864. On December 7, near Hurricane Island, Louisiana, the second cutter of the *Mound City* tipped over drowning Dr. Rice and five crew members. Lost in the accident were eight Spencer rifles and 165 rounds of ammunition. Three of the Spencers were recovered.[40] The *Ouachita* lost two of their Spencer rifles when one of their launches capsized. The boat crew of the *Hartford* during April and May were exercised on several occasions while off the Pensacola Naval Yard with their Spencer rifles.

Favorable Reports

Early on the morning of July 30, Acting Volunteer Lieutenant R.P. Swann, with two cutters from the *Potomska*, left on a trip up the Back River. The lieutenant's objective was to destroy an extensive salt works near Darien, Georgia. After destroying the Rebel salt works, the sailors were fired on when returning to their ship. The cutters were within ten yards of shore when the Confederates opened fire, wounding 5 of the 19 sailors. The water being very low, the men got behind the boats and used them as breastworks. The sailors armed with Spencer rifles poured such a massive fire into the Confederates' position that the rebel fire was ineffective. After 45 minutes, the Confederates broke off the engagement. The sailors had fired 200 rounds of ammunition in the fight. During part of the fight, the crew had been in mud up to their knees. Dahlgren was so impressed with the fighting qualities of Lieutenant Swann's men that he had a general order be read throughout the fleet.[41]

On July 4, at 2:20 p.m., the transport *Olive Branch* came upriver at Grand Gulf, Mississippi. The ironclad *Pittsburg* directed the transport to stop and pick up passengers. When the *Olive Branch* refused to stop, the *Pittsburg* fired a couple of shots from their Spencers at the transport. She then came to a stop and picked up two passengers. The *Lafayette* also on the Mississippi had two of its crew desert and take two Spencer rifles with them.[42]

Unfavorable Reports

Not everyone was sold on the Spencer rifles. The report from Lieutenant Commander Eastman of the picket boat *Ella* stated that any little jarring of the Spencer rifles would set them off. He was so dissatisfied with them that he requested permission to turn them in and replace them with Plymouth rifles.

USS Ella
June 22, 1864

Sir:

I would respectfully call your attention to the fact that the vessels armed with Spencer rifles, are continually having accidents with that description of small arms. The charge is so easily exploded that if a man jumps into a boat with a loaded Spencer rifle in his hand, and should strike the butt in any way, it is almost certain to explode the piece, unless he takes the precaution to first empty the bore, and in sudden emergencies that is practically impossible and in going through woods at night the men will occasionally fall and every fall renders the firing of one piece almost certain.

Another objective is that they have no bayonets which in my estimation reduces the strength of a crew against boarders, one half.

At present the accidents from the Spencer rifles have caused the death of two men and the wounding of two others, in this squadron. While there has been no accidents from the other rifles, and in consequence of these facts, I respectfully request that the Spencers may be turned in, and the Plymouth rifle supplied in their place.

This change will reduce the caliber's of rifles in the flotilla to <u>one</u> and greatly improve its efficiency, we can send parties from different vessels, ashore, from company, and known that all have the same arms, and can depend on each other for ammunition.

Respectfully
T.W. Eastman, Lt. Cdr.[43]

On July 10, the *Ella* received on board 51 Plymouth rifles, 5,000 rifle cartridges, and 9,000 percussion caps. Ten days later, they turned in 20 Spencer rifles, 20 belts and cartridge boxes, plus 834 cartridges. The *Fuchsia* turned in 26 Spencers for 25 Plymouth rifles while the *Coeur de Lion* turned in 8 Spencers and 13 muskets for 20 Plymouths. The tug *Yankee* turned in 29 Sharps and a like quantity of Spencers for 40 Plymouth rifles and 4,000 rounds of ammunition.[44] Three additional ships to exchange their Spencers for the Plymouth were the *Commodore Read*, *Currituck* and *Dragon*. It appears that the Plymouth rifle, and not the Spencer, was the arm of choice with the sailors in the Potomac flotilla.

(Above) On December 7, near Hurricane Island, Louisiana, the second cutter of the *Mound City* tipped over, drowning the ship's surgeon and five sailors. Lost in the accident were eight Spencer rifles and 165 rounds of ammunition. *(U.S. Naval Historical Center)*

Rear Admiral Farragut at the wheel of the *Hartford* with Captain Drayton at his right at Mobile Bay, 1864. Note the rack of Spencer rifles in the background. *(U.S. Naval Historical Center)*

The tug *Yankee*. On July 20, 1864, the *Yankee* turned in 29 Spencer rifles for 40 Plymouth rifles. The Yankee was also one of the few vessels to be issued Joslyn revolvers. *(Library of Congress)*

Revolvers

Remington

In June, the New York Navy Yard had 13 vessels undergoing repairs or taking on machinery. To meet this demand, orders were placed for 500 Remingtons and a like quantity of Whitney revolvers. The Remington revolvers were inspected, and 27 were found defective. The defects included broken half cock notch, no thread cut into the frame, broken cones, and broken mainsprings and hand springs.[45]

The next order was for 200 Remingtons to be sent to the Washington Navy Yard in July. This order was received by the navy yard in August. On August 15, they were test fired. During the testing of the Remington revolvers, one sailor was wounded when a ricocheting bullet hit the sailor. He was not seriously hurt. Later in the year, three of the revolvers serial numbered 28582, 28730 and 28713 were found to be slightly defective. The rammer would not enter the cylinder without force when empty. The problem did not occur when the cylinder was loaded.[46] The last order was placed in December for 250 for Mound City and delivered in 1865.

The *Niphon* Remington revolvers were in need of constant repairs. The mainsprings were poor and broken, making the revolvers worthless. On September 30, the ship sent to the Washington Navy Yard for repairs 10 Spencer rifles, 3 Remington revolvers, 5 boarding pistols and 3 Enfield rifles. The repairs were made and the arms sent back to the *Niphon* in November. Aboard ship the crews were drilled with small arms nearly every day. Accidents were bound to happen. At 10:00 a.m. on January 15, the crew of the *Choctaw* was in the midst of small arms drill when Charles Andrews' Remington revolver accidentally discharged mortally wounding Acting Master Mate Townsend Hopkins. Hopkins, age 28, of Pennsylvania, died of his wounds at 11:20 a.m. He was buried on shore the next day.[47]

Marine Corps Sentry Revolvers

While the officers obtained their own revolvers, sentries at the navy yards were issued revolvers for sentry duty. The numbers obtained from the Navy were very small.

Marine Corps Revolver Issues[48]
1864

	Boston October	Mare Island November
Remington Revolvers	—	3
Savage Revolvers	3	—
Cartridge Boxes	3	3 (holsters)
Waist Belts	3	—
Cartridges	300	36

The Marines at Mare Island also obtained from the navy yard 5,000 rifle musket .58 caliber cartridges and a like quantity of percussion caps.

Whitney

The July order for 500 Whitney revolvers for New York was received before the end of the month. On September 13, they were notified by the Bureau of Ordnance to transfer 300 of these revolvers to Mound City for the Mississippi Squadron. The Philadelphia Navy Yard in August placed an order for 300 Whitney revolvers. Deliveries were received in November, and a portion of them were issued to the *Midnight* and the *Unadilla*.[49] One ship to be issued Whitney revolvers was the monitor *Winnebago*. The vessel was commissioned on April 27, and on May 2 received on board 30 Whitney revolvers and 40 rifle muskets. Ship's logs of July 15 state that the 1st division exercised with revolvers and the 2nd with rifles.[50] The *Winnebago* was assigned to the West Gulf Blockading Squadron and took part in the Battle of Mobile Bay. She remained in

The ironclad *Choctaw* at Vicksburg, Mississippi. During small arms drills on January 15, one of the officers was mortally wounded by a Remington revolver which was accidentally discharged. *(Tim Brooks collection — USAMHI)*

Officers and crew of the gunboat *Agawam*. When outfitted for sea at Portsmouth on April 18, 1864, her small arms inventory included both Whitney revolvers and single-shot pistols. The officers are pictured with their M1852 Officer's swords. *(USAMHI)*

naval service until September 27, 1865, when decommissioned at Mound City.[51] The *Michigan* received on board 30 Whitney revolvers and 12 battle axes at Erie on December 13. The day before, the ship's 35 old flintlock pistols had been sent to Philadelphia. The monitor *Canonicus*' starboard watch crew was exercised at target practice with their Whitney revolvers on the morning of June 13.

In February, the Washington Navy Yard received 200 Whitney revolvers from the factory. On February 12, Commander William Jeffers inspected 42 of the Whitney revolvers. Each of the revolvers was test fired two times with Colt cartridges. The cartridges contained a 118 grain bullet with 14.4 grains of powder. The serial numbers of the revolvers tested were:

Whitney Revolvers Inspected[52]
February 12, 1864
Washington Navy Yard

23004	22086	22277	22294	22158	22287
22178	23035	22068	23045	22159	22279
23013	23021	22044	22024	22076	22037
22014	22184	22256	22015	22058	23031
23034	22096	23029	22045	22276	22251
23001	22178	23026	23375	22360	22381
23014	22267	22176	23025	22078	22021

Note that 22178 is listed twice. All 200 revolvers were sent to Commander Lynch at the Norfolk Navy Yard. In December, Washington received 100 more Whitneys. Each revolver was test fired 12 times and found to be serviceable. Serial number 26318's rammer was broken and was replaced by the factory. Though accepted for naval use, the Navy was not happy with them. Jeffers considered them inferior to all other revolvers then in service. The problem was with the check screw that retains the rammer. A cartridge could not be inserted into the cylinder without raising the rammer and partially tuning the cylinder. This motion doubled the time required to load the revolver. Washington sent the Whitney revolvers to the North Atlantic Blockading Squadron. The serial numbers were:

Whitney Revolver Inspection[53]
December 8, 1864
Washington Navy Yard

25371	25400	26001	26002	26904	26006
26007	26009	26017	26020	26023	26028
26035	26038	26040	26044	26045	26167
26191	26203	26210	26219	26222	26228
26233	26237	26318	26244	26246	26295
26301	26304	26240	26308	26309	26310
26320	26321	26307	26327	26328	26340
26341	26342	26323	26346	26349	26402
26404	26405	26344	26409	26411	26413
26414	26415	26408	26421	26423	26425
26427	26429	26419	26432	26436	26437
26439	26442	26430	26448	26503	26504
26518	26532	26444	26540	26549	26551
26553	26559	26536	26563	26569	26570
26576	26578	26560	26585	26586	26587
26590	26591	26584	26593	26594	26596
26600	25443	26592	25443		

In this chart, there are two 25443s. One of the numbers may actually be 26443.

Edged Weapons

Sailors at drill aboard the monitor *Lehigh*. Several of the sailors are armed with Ames cutlasses. *(Library of Congress)*

Ames Cutlasses and Bowie Knives

One thousand Ames cutlasses were delivered to the New York Navy Yard in January on a contract given in December of the previous year. An additional 993 were received in February, and 12 gilt cutlasses were sent to the Navy Academy in April.[54] New York sent 800 cutlasses to Mound City, and the balance was used at the yard for the outfitting of vessels. The last wartime order for the 1861 Ames naval cutlass was given on September 24, which called for 1,000 cutlasses at a cost of $5.25 each. Deliveries were made at New York.[55] During the year, Ames delivered 2,505 cutlasses to the Navy. In February, Boston was notified that all of the old Roman sword cutlasses (M1841) were to be sold as condemned stores.

On June 14, Rear Admiral Dahlgren wrote the Bureau requesting 1,000 Plymouth rifles and a similar quantity of Bowie knives for his squadron. To fill his request, on the 27th of the month 500 Bowie knives were ordered. The price paid was $6.75 for the Bowie knife and $1.75 for the belt, frog and holster complete.[56] Deliveries of 100 were made on August 26 and the balance forwarded on October 28. The Bowie knives were then forwarded to Dahlgren.

The sloop *Saratoga's* small arms included both the Plymouth rifle and Bowie knives. On picket duty one night, one of the *Saratoga* Bowie knives was lost overboard. The hook on the belt broke, and the cartridge box, belt and Bowie knife all went overboard together.[57] On June 25, the gunboat *Paul Jones* received on board 50 Bowie knives plus the following articles:

Ordnance Stores Received[58]
USS *Paul Jones*
June 25, 1864

- 49 Ames Cutlasses
- 30 Enfield Rifles
- 20 Remington Revolvers
- 8 Colt Revolvers
- 2 Whitney Revolvers
- 50 Bowie Knives
- 50 Frogs for the Bowie Knives
- 30 Musket Cartridge Boxes
- 30 Revolver Cartridge Boxes and Holsters
- 1,750 Revolver Percussion Caps
- 2,500 Musket Caps
- 2,000 Musket Cartridges

On August 29, the flag ship of the South Atlantic Blockading Squadron the *Harvest Moon* received on board 10 Bowie knives along with 10 Plymouth rifles and saber bayonets.

Marine Corps NCO and Musician Swords

Major Slack placed one order for swords for the Corps for 1864. As of the last day of the previous year, he contracted with Bent & Bush of Boston for the firm to deliver 100 swords for sergeants, 50 musician swords plus 40 drums.[59] The manufacture of the type of NCO swords and the musician swords delivered by Bent & Bush is not stated.

As the year came to a close, the naval blockade was nearly complete. Only Fort Fisher and Fort Sumter held out on the Atlantic Coast. These locations would be the main goals of the Navy as the fifth year of the war was about to start.

Chapter 7
Fort Fisher, January 15, 1865

Capture of Fort Fisher

With the dawn of the new year, Rear Admiral David Porter was determined that his naval forces would play a major role in the second attack on Fort Fisher. While the Army forces attacked Fort Fisher from the land side, Porter would send a naval landing force from the sea. The attack orders read:

GENERAL ORDERS   North Atlantic SQUADRON
NO. 81 *Flagship Malvern, January 4, 1865*

Before going into action, the commander of each vessel will detail as many of his men as he can spare from the guns as a landing party.

That we may have a share in the assault when it takes place, the boats will be kept ready, lowered near the water on the off side of the vessels. The sailors will be armed with cutlasses, well sharpened, and with revolvers, When the signal is made to man the boats, the men will get in, but not show themselves. When signal is made to assault, the boats will pull around the stern of the monitors and land right abreast of them, and board the fort on the run in a seaman-like way.

The Marines will form in the rear and cover the sailors. While the soldiers are going over the parapets in front, the sailors will take the sea face of Fort Fisher.

We can land 2,000 men from the fleet and not feel it. Two thousand active men from the fleet will carry the day.

Two boat keepers will be kept in each boat.
     David D. Porter
     Rear Admiral, Commanding North Atlantic Squadron[1]

The gunboat *Vanderbilt*. In the attack on Fort Fisher on January 15, 1865, the *Vanderbilt* suffered in the land attack one killed and 14 wounded of which four were Marines. In the land attack, the sailors from the *Vanderbilt* lost 12 Remington revolvers.
(U.S. Naval Historical Center)

The attack was made on Sunday, January 15. The first order of business called for a detachment of sailors under Lieutenant Samuel W. Preston to dig rifle pits for use of the Marines. These positions would be constructed as close as possible to the fort and occupied by the Marines in covering the attack of the sailors. The Marine and Navy assault parties started landing after ten in the morning and formed four lines. The Marines were commanded by Captain L.L. Dawson while the overall assault forces were directed by fleet captain Lieutenant Commander Kidder R. Breese. His force consisted of 1,600 sailors and about 400 Marines.[2] Lieutenant Preston and his men, armed with shovels and picks, threw up rifle pits to within 200 yards of the fort. These advance positions were quickly occupied by 1st Lieutenant Lewis Fagan from the frigate *Wabash*.[3] Fagan's Marine detachment of three sergeants, three corporals, and thirty-eight privates was armed with the .58 caliber rifle musket. Also sent forward to these positions were Marines commanded by 1st Lieutenant Charles F. Williams of the sloop *Ticonderoga* with their seven-shot Spencer Navy repeating rifles. Four days prior to the attack, Williams' twenty-five-man detachment had practiced with their Spencers aboard ship.[4] Several of the 190 sailors from the frigate *Minnesota* were equipped with Sharps rifles in addition to their revolvers and cutlasses. Records indicate that 18 of *Minnesota's* Sharps rifles, along with 17 saber bayonets, were lost in the attack.[5] See the chart that follows later in the chapter for additional lost equipment in the attack.

The plans called for the Army to make the main attack. After the Army was engaged, the sailors would attack the fort from the seaward approach. At near 3 p.m., the command was given for the sailors to advance. Arriving before the Army, the sailors took the brunt of the fire from the defenders in the fort. The sailors proceeded until they reached the palisades of the fort where the attack fell apart. Here the lines broke, and the sailors retreated with only a few holding their position until nightfall. While the naval attack was underway, the Army approached the fort from the land side and was able to fight their way into the fort. The battle lasted into the night when the fort finally fell to the attackers. Later in the evening, 200 Marines were sent to Army headquarters for duty in the trenches. The Marines were relieved the next morning.

The major controversy surrounding the attack was the part played by the Marines. Both Porter and Breese claimed, in their official reports, that the Marines did not sufficiently man the rifle pits, and therefore, caused the attack to fail. In Captain Dawson's defense, he stated that he had only about 350 Marines armed with rifle muskets and 40 rounds of ammunition per man. He was in the process of placing his men in position when ordered to proceed with the

The attack by the sailors and Marines on Fort Fisher. *(Library of Congress)*

Chapter 7 • Capture of Fort Fisher, January 15, 1865

Photograph of the screw sloop *Ticonderoga* taken in Venice, Italy, in the late 1860s. While at Fort Fisher, her complement of Marine guard, were issued the Navy Spencer rifles from the ship's inventory. In the attack the Marines lost four Spencers and had one Marine killed. *(National Archives)*

sailors in the attack from the beach.[6] As late as 1895, Captain Rodney R. Evans, commanding the battleship *Indiana*, was outspoken in his beliefs on the effectiveness of Marines. As a young ensign at Fort Fisher, he was twice wounded and blamed the Marines for the failure of the attack.

Porter's casualty report for the assault on Fort Fisher consisted of six officers killed and 26 wounded. The enlisted losses were given as 82 killed and 245 wounded with 34 missing. The total of Marines included in these figures consisted of two officers wounded, plus seven enlisted men killed, 47 wounded and five missing.[7] Among the naval officers killed were Lieutenants Samuel W. Preston and Benjamin H. Porter. Both officers had been captured at Fort Sumter in 1863 and had only recently been exchanged as prisoners of war.[8] As previously noted, the sailors were armed with more than their revolvers and cutlasses. The following chart shows the quantity of small arms lost or destroyed in the action of January 15:

Lieutenant Benjamin H. Porter was one of the six naval officers killed in the attack on the fort. He had only recently been paroled after being captured at Fort Sumter in September 1863. *(Library of Congress)*

Fort Fisher
January 15, 1865
Small Arms Lost or Destroyed[9]

Vessels	Breech and Muzzleloaders	Revolvers	Cutlasses
Ticonderoga	4 Spencer Rifles	6 Whitney	8
Shenandoah	1 Sharps Rifle	10 Colts	7
Cherokee	—	2 type not stated	—
Osceola	—	10 Whitney	2
Powhatan	7 Sharps Rifles	28 Colts	—
Kansas	1 S&H Carbine	—	—
Minnesota	1 Spencer and 18 Sharps Rifles	21 Colts	—
Seneca	2 S&H Carbines	1 Remington	—
Tuscarora	—	12 Colts	6
Iosco	—	24 Whitney	12
Tacony	—	12 Whitney	11
Fort Jackson	3 Spencer and 5 Sharps Rifles	—	—
Chippewa	5 S&H Carbines	7 Colts	—
Yantic	1 Enfield Rifle	1 Remington and 4 Pistols	—
Pontoosuc	—	8 Whitney	7
Huron	1 Smoothbore Musket	4 Whitney	1
Mackinaw	—	11 Remingtons and 4 Pistols	10
Vanderbilt	—	12 Remington	—
Susquehanna	—	17 Whitney	4

Other small arms lost and not reported by the above vessels included Springfield rifle muskets and S&H rifles.

1865 Procurement and Sea Service

The gunboat *General Bragg* attached to the Mississippi Squadron. On February 5, 1865, her ship's logs stated the receipt on board of 35 rifled muskets caliber .69, 35 bayonets and scabbards, 35 cartridge boxes, 2,000 rifle musket cartridges and 25 Roman swords with scabbards.
(U.S. Naval Historical Center)

MUZZLELOADERS

The 500 caliber .69 altered rifled muskets sent to Mound City in November of the previous year were issued to the Mississippi Squadron in the early months of 1865.

Rifled Muskets Issued[10]
Caliber .69
Mississippi Squadron
1865

Vessel	Rifled Muskets	Bayonets and Scabbards	Cartridges
General Bragg	35	35	2,000
Chillocothe	20	20	2,000
Little Rebel	10	10	1,500
Oriole	40	40	4,000
Colossus	40	40	4,000
Gamage	40	40	4,000
Niad	10	10	1,000

As late as the last year of the war, some old flintlock muskets were still on board ship. In January, at Ship Island, Mississippi, a board of survey on the sloop *Vincennes* found 56 Springfield muskets pattern 1824 flintlocks to be condemned because of age and defects. The board concluded that they were liable to burst at any time. The ship's log of the tinclad riverboat #28 *Silver Cloud* reads that on February 3 all of their muskets were fired and then cleaned and reloaded. In this process, 30 musket cartridges were fired and 100 percussion caps. It was the practice of the gunboat *Octorara* to discharge their smoothbore Model 1842 muskets each morning at the completion of the night watch. Five sailors deserted the double-turret monitor *Kickapoo* on January 13, taking with them 5 muskets of .58 and .69 caliber plus 5 Remington revolvers.[11] The day before, at Clarendon, Arkansas, the tinclad *Exchange* had five of its crew desert while on picket duty. The deserters took their Enfield rifles with them.

Marine Corps Muzzleloaders and Accouterments

On the 28th of January, Captain Wise contacted the Army requesting that 500 rifle muskets be sent to the Marine Corps Headquarters in Washington. Two days later they received the following response:

Ordnance Office
Washington Jan. 30th, 1865

Captain W.A. Wise
Chief of Bureau of Ordnance
Navy Department

Sir:

I have to acknowledge the receipt of your requisition of the 28th inst., and in answer would say 500 Springfield Rifle Muskets Cal. 58 complete have been ordered today to be sent from the Washington Arsenal to Quarter Master W.B. Slank at the headquarters of the Marine Corps in the city.

Respectively
Your Obedient Servant
A.B. Dyer
Brig. Gen. Chief of Ordnance[12]

The .58 caliber Springfield rifle muskets delivered were the pattern 1864 rifle musket. The major difference between this model and the prior 1863

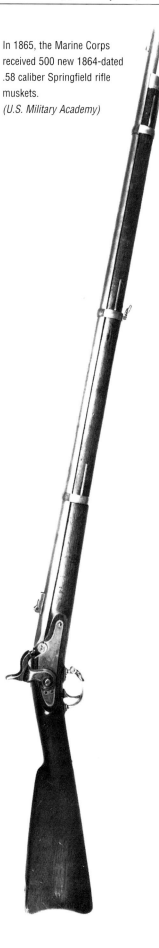

In 1865, the Marine Corps received 500 new 1864-dated .58 caliber Springfield rifle muskets. *(U.S. Military Academy)*

The ship-of-the-line *Ohio* as a receiving ship at the Boston Navy Yard in 1870s. In 1865 the Marine detachment aboard the *Ohio* received an issue of the new 1864-dated .58 caliber Springfield rifle muskets in exchange for their old altered .69 caliber muskets. *(U.S. Naval Historical Center)*

Springfield is that the 1864 rifle muskets are equipped with oval and solid barrel bands with the conventional band springs forward of the bands. Many of the 1864s are found with the knurled-type ramrod. Some of the 1864 rifle muskets may have been issued to the Marine guard aboard the gunboat *Chenango* in March. The detachment on the *Chenango* consisted of one sergeant, one corporal, and 12 privates. The Marine guard aboard the *Ohio*, a ship of the line that was being used at Boston as a receiving vessel, requested new muskets. As of early 1865, they were still using the old altered muskets. Their request was filled with 42 of the new 1864 Springfields. Five of the old altered muskets were kept for night watch.[13]

The last of the war procurements for accouterments occurred on January 19 with the firms of C.S. Storms and T.B. Peddie, both of New York City. The Peddie contract called for the delivery of 1,400 knapsacks, 600 haversacks, 600 canteens and 500 musket slings. Storms's contract called for 1,200 cartridge boxes with the magazines being of tin. They were also to deliver bayonet scabbards with frog attachments, percussion cap pouches, cartridge boxes belts, waist belts, and waist plates each in the quantity of 1,200 plus 150 sword frogs.[14]

Late in the war, some of the Marines started to wear their cap pouch, cartridge box and bayonet scabbard on a white buff leather waist belt.
(James Stamatelos collection. Photo by Mike O'Donnell)

At Fort Fisher, the Marines were armed with the .58 caliber rifle musket, probably the Model 1861. In this engagement, three Medals of Honor were awarded to the Marines. One went to 20-year-old Corporal Andrew Tomlin of Goshen, New Jersey. Tomlin was assigned to the frigate *Wabash*. He had been recommended for the medal by his commanding officer, Lieutenant Fagan. While under a withering fire, Tomlin crossed an open plain to move a wounded Marine to a place of safety near the fort.[15]

c.1865 Marine detachment at the Brooklyn Navy Yard. Note the cannonballs stacked in the background.
(Jack McCormick collection, USAMHI)

Chapter 7 • Capture of Fort Fisher, January 15, 1865

A Marine armed with a Model 1861 Springfield rifle musket, guarding Lewis Payne, an assassination conspirator. *(Library of Congress)*

Breechloaders

Sharps & Hankins

The last wartime procurement for the S&H occurred on January 23. The order called for the S&H factory to deliver 200 carbines and 20,000 metallic cartridges. Deliveries were received at the Philadelphia Navy Yard and then forwarded to Commander Lynch at Norfolk.

From the Naval Ordnance Depot at New Orleans on January 6th came a requisition for 200 S&H carbines and 50 battle axes. The battle axes were supplied from New York and the carbines from Philadelphia. The Philadelphia order consisted of the 200 S&H carbines, 200 cartridge boxes, and 20,000 carbine cartridges.[16] By February 19, 20 of these S&H carbines, 20 waist belts and a like number of cartridge boxes, plus 4,000 metallic cartridges, were issued to the ironclad *Chillicothe*.[17] Out West at Mare Island, the steamer *Saginaw* was being outfitted with 20 S&H carbines and Colt revolvers.

The gunboat *Malvern* was Porter's flagship at Fort Fisher. When Richmond fell to Union forces, Admiral Porter and President Lincoln entered the city with an escort of ten sailors each armed with a Sharps & Hankins carbine. *(U.S. Naval Historical Center)*

Three vessels armed with S&H carbines were to lose them for a variety of causes. The most serious loss occurred on the March 18 on the Blakely River when the double-turret monitor *Milwaukee* struck a torpedo and sank. She took to the bottom a quantity of S&H carbines and Springfield rifled muskets. A small quantity of her small arms were able to be salvaged; therefore, she was not a total loss. On the March 6, the sloop *Juniata* had her number one cutter capsized upon the bar at Georgetown, South Carolina. Lost when the cutter sank were 10 S&H carbines, 80 cartridges, 4 cartridge boxes with belts, and one Colt revolver. One of the launches from the gunboat *Pontiac* sank on the Savannah River on March 14, drowning one sailor

The double-turret monitor *Milwaukee* sank in the Blakely River on March 18 after hitting a mine. Among the small arms lost were .69 caliber Springfield rifled muskets and Sharps & Hankins carbines. *(U.S. Naval Historical Center)*

Officers of the gunboat *Mendota*. The officer in the center is holding a Sharps & Hankins carbine. *(USAMHI)*

and losing 8 S&H carbines and cartridge boxes. Earlier in the year the *Pontiac* lost 17 of her S&H carbines by capture to the Confederates.[18] In June, while at Detroit and later at Mackinaw and on Lake St. Clair the crew of the gunboat *Michigan* was drilled on the use of their S&H carbines. The *Michigan* ship's logs show a regular use of the carbine.

Lincoln in Richmond

President Lincoln arrived at Hampton Roads, Virginia, on March 28 to confer with Grant, Sherman and Porter on ending the war in Virginia. Afterward, Lincoln stayed on as a guest of Porter on his flagship *Malvern*. On the third day of April, the Confederate capital of Richmond was evacuated. The next day, Lincoln and Porter entered the city. Admiral Porter placed ten of his sailors armed with S&H carbines as an honor guard for the president. Six sailors marched in front of Lincoln and the remaining four in back of the president. After his day-long visit to Richmond, Lincoln stayed the night with Porter and returned to Washington the next day.[19] In less than two weeks, he would be dead, having been shot by John Wilkes Booth. On hearing the news of Lincoln's death, the fleet lowered their flags to half staff.

Marine Corps Sharps & Hankins

It was the practice for the Marine guard to provide their own arms aboard ship. From late November 1862, the Marines aboard the sloop *Lancaster* stationed with the Pacific Squadron had been armed by the Corps with the Model 1861 Springfield rifle musket. In June 1865, from Mare Island Depot, the Navy issued to the Marines on the *Lancaster* 80 Sharps & Hankins carbines with cartridge boxes.[20] As late as 1868, the Marine guard aboard the gun-boat *Wateree* was having target practice off the coast of Peru with the S&H rifles.

Sharps & Hankins Cartridges

Of note to the S&H cartridge collector is the difference in size of the rifle and carbine cartridge. The rifle cartridge is longer than the carbine cartridges. The carbine ammunition will fit into the rifle but not the other way around. The characteristics of the two cartridges is shown below:

S&H Cartridges[21]

	S&H Rifle	S&H Carbine
Caliber between the lands	.53 inches	.52 inches
Caliber between the grooves	.555 inches	.53 inches
Caliber chamber inner end	.58 inches	.56 inches
Caliber chamber at junction with bore	.56 inches	.55 inches
Length of chamber	1.3 inches	1.3 inches

Spencer Rifles

A portion of the 50 Army Spencer rifles delivered to Mound City from the Washington Navy Yard was issued to the river ram *Vindicator*. In February, seaman George F. Williams, attached to *Vindicator*, deserted his post on shore while on picket duty. He took with him his Spencer rifle serial numbered 9977.[22] The *Vindicator* was assigned to the Mississippi Squadron. Also armed with Spencers in the squadron was the ironclad *Choctaw*. On April 20, she engaged a party of 30 Confederates at Bayon Gara, Louisiana. Firing at the party on shore, the *Choctaw* expended 25 Enfield rifle cartridges, 22 Spencer rounds, and 18 Remington revolver cartridges.[23] No casualties were reported. The gunboat *Eutaw*, located on the James River in February, was sending seven sailors armed with the Army Spencer rifles on picket duty nearly every night.

=== *Revolvers* ===

Remington and Whitney

During the first three months of 1865, the factories of Remington and Whitney supplied the Navy with over 1,700 revolvers as shown below:

Revolver Deliveries[24]
1865

	Remington	Whitney
January	450	850
February	—	—
March	—	450
April	—	20
Total	**450**	**1,320**

In addition to the revolver procurements, the Navy took delivery of 28,000 Whitney revolver cartridges plus 50,000 Colt .36 caliber revolver ammunition from the Colt factory.

In February, the New York Navy Yard sent to Mound City 47 battle axes, 250 Whitneys and 244 Remington revolvers. On March 10, the Philadelphia

In 1865, the side-wheel gunboat *Paul Jones'* small arms included Colts, Remington and Whitney revolvers. (U.S. Naval Historical Center)

In 1865, the frigate *Sabine* received from the Ames Mfg. Co. two hundred fencing swords. During this period, the *Sabine* was being used as a training ship at Philadelphia. *(Library of Congress)*

Navy Yard sent to Baltimore for issue on the sloop *Wyoming* 40 Whitney revolvers plus 100 rounds of ammunition per revolver.[25] Revolvers were easily lost or stolen. The steamer *Thomas Freeborn* had one of their Remington revolvers lost overboard. On March 1, the tug *Yankee* had a Joslyn revolver stolen by John Powers. During this same timeframe, a Colt Model 1861 revolver serial number 2408 was stolen from the monitor *Casco*.[26]

On March 4, Lieutenant Commander George W. Young and three sailors of the gunboat *Nyack* left Wilmington, North Carolina. Young and his men, armed with Sharps rifles and Remington revolvers, were carrying a coded message from Brigadier General John Schofield to Major General William T. Sherman. Young's journey took him over land to the sea. For two days of the trip, he and his men hid out in a Negro hut to evade capture. Later, he captured and paroled pickets of Company A, 51st North Carolina Infantry. He and his party finally arrived at Sherman's headquarters at Fayetteville, North Carolina, at 1:00 p.m. on March 12. Sherman was greatly surprised at receiving the coded message from Navy personnel and also the route they took to reach his location.[27]

At war's end, the single-shot .54 caliber percussion pistol was still in active sea service. When the sloop *Brooklyn* left for station in South American waters in October, she was armed with 78 single-shot pistols plus a quantity of carbines, muskets, revolvers and 129 cutlasses.[28] In September, the New York Navy Yard requested from the Army spare parts for both the Johnson and Aston pistols.

Edged Weapons

The last 500 Model 1861 cutlasses arrived at New York in January. This delivery finished the order of the previous September. In early 1865, Ames was requested to deliver 200 fencing swords. The fencing swords were intended for use aboard the practice ship *Sabine* at Philadelphia. The swords arrived sometime in May, but payment was not forthcoming to Ames until October 10. One final postwar delivery of 18 gilt-mounted swords at a cost of $25 each, plus sword belts at $5.50 each, was sent to the Navy in February 1866.[29] The cutlasses were still being received by vessels in the last few months of the war. On February 24, the steamer *Banshee* received on board 20 cutlasses and 40 Plymouth rifles with 4,000 rounds of ammunition. Fifty

Ames cutlasses were received by the gunboat *Michigan* on March 15. The *Oriole*, *Gamage* and the *Colossus* were being outfitted at Cairo, Illinois, in March. Each vessel was issued 40 Roman swords, since the yard had no Ames cutlasses to issue. Two months later, the *Oriole* turned in their old swords and received 41 Ames M1861 cutlasses and 16 single sticks. The other two vessels maintained their Roman swords throughout their short naval service.

Small Arms Issued[30]
Cairo, Illinois
March 1865

	Oriole	*Colossus*	*Gamage*
Roman Swords	40	40	40
Single Sticks	30	—	—
Altered .69 cal. Muskets	40	40	40
Boarding Pikes	20	20	—
Whitney Revolvers	40	40	40

The Marines placed their last wartime contract for swords on January 27 with Bent & Bush. The Boston firm made deliveries of 100 NCO swords and 50 musician swords.[31]

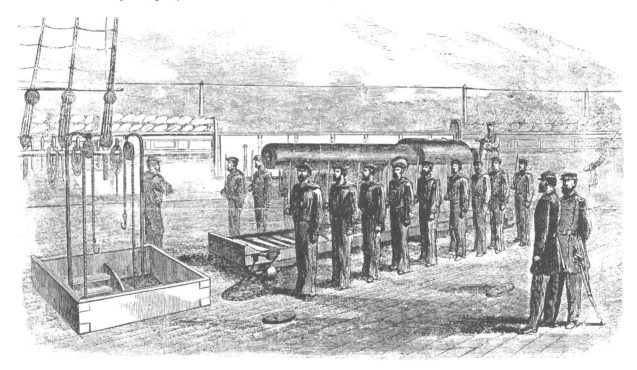

Sunday morning inspection on board the gunboat *Metacomet*. Each sailor is armed with an Ames cutlass. *(Sketched by George Watters. Library of Congress)*

Decommissioning of Vessels

With the fall of Fort Fisher and Fort Sumter, Rear Admiral Dahlgren commanding the South Atlantic Blockading Squadron was directed by the Secretary of the Navy on February 24 to start reducing the size of his fleet. Reducing the size of the squadron would reduce the Navy operational expenses. By the end of July, Dahlgren's fleet had gone from about 90 vessels at the start of the year to 44 of all types. By June 14, the East Gulf Blockading Squadron was down to 13 vessels, and the Mississippi Squadron was at 25 vessels as of May 18.[32]

Chapter 7 • Capture of Fort Fisher, January 15, 1865

Lieutenant Commander Edward Barrett and Lieutenant Cornelius Schoomaker of the monitor *Catskill* at Battery Bee, Sullivan Island, Charleston Harbor, 1865. Both officers are shown with their M1852 Officer's swords. *(Library of Congress)*

Two sailors from the *Pensacola* fencing with cutlasses about 1888. *(U.S. Naval Historical Center)*

Types of small arms turned in were:

Small Arms Turned In[33]
1865

	DeSoto	Augusta	Chenango	Benton	J.P. Jackson	Wissahickon	Octorara
Battle Axes	14	30	20	1	—	13	11
Cutlasses	40	114	50	—	44	31	80
.69 cal. Muskets	60	—	40	170	—	19	37
Pikes	30	40	35	60	40	31	41
Single Sticks	40	68	22	—	—	10	12
Navy Pistols	25	—	—	—	—	—	3
Army Pistols	—	—	—	—	48	28	39
Savage Revolvers	25	—	—	—	—	—	—
S&H Carbines	—	70	—	—	—	12	14 rifles
Plymouth Rifles	—	50	—	—	—	6	—
Remington Revolvers	—	30	—	27	—	—	—
Whitney Revolvers	—	30	—	—	—	—	—
Colt Revolvers	—	—	64	42	4	6	57
Sharps Rifles	—	—	24	—	14	20	—
Spencer Rifles	—	—	—	20	—	—	—
Enfield Rifles	—	—	—	—	58	—	—

When the *Wissahickon* was decommissioned at the New York Navy Yard on July 1, she turned in 24 Bowie knives.

As the South Atlantic Blockading Squadron was being reduced in size, the ordnance depot at Port Royal, South Carolina, shipped north to Portsmouth on June 26 the following small arms:[34]

25 Enfield Rifles (short)	20 Enfield Rifles (long)	4 Plymouth Rifles
7 Enfield Carbines	15 S&H Rifles	16 S&H Carbines
42 Sharps Rifles cal. .56	63 Saber Bayonets	20 Common Bayonets

In August, the ordnance depot at Bay Point, Florida, sent to Philadelphia:[35]

179 Plymouth Rifles w/Bayonets	10 Sharps Rifles w/Bayonets	19 Springfield Muskets w/Bayonets
5 Spencer Rifles	108 Harpers Ferry Muskets w/Bayonets	3 Colt Revolvers
5 Prussian Muskets w/Bayonets	46 Remington Revolvers	129 Short Enfield rifles w/Bayonets
178 Bowie Knives	67 Long Enfield Rifles w/Bayonets	135 Ames Cutlasses
10 S&H Carbines	13 Roman Swords	

With the war over, the Mississippi Squadron had to find a permanent location for the ordnance stores at Mound City, Illinois, which, being unsuited for long-term storage, had part of their stores sent to New Orleans in July. By September, the balance of the ordnance had arrived at Jefferson Barracks, Missouri. The following small arms and ammunition was sent to New Orleans in July:

Ordnance Stores Delivered[36]
To New Orleans In
July 1865

Ammunition

Plymouth Rifle	7,467	Gallager Carbine	8,570	Rifle Musket .58 cal.	12,406
Colt Revolver .44 cal.	24,088	Spencer Rifle	20,000	Remington Revolver	14,168
Sharps Rifle .52 cal.	38,930	Boarding Pistols .54 cal.	40,310		

Note ammunition for the Gallager carbines. These cartridges may have been for Ellet Marine Brigade.

Chapter 7 • Capture of Fort Fisher, January 15, 1865

Small Arms

Hall Carbines	1	Colt Revolvers .44 cal.	23	Army Cutlasses	38
Ames Cutlasses	65	Starr Revolver	1	Navy Pistols	121
Roman Cutlasses	239	Whitney Revolvers	250	Altered Rifle Muskets	55
Plymouth Rifles	1	Pikes	310	Smoothbore Muskets	203
Enfield Rifles	300	Army Lances	28		

In addition, the following damaged arms were also sent to New Orleans: 15 Kentucky rifles, 17 double-barrel shotguns, and 105 single-barrel shotguns.

When the ironclad *Benton* was decommissioned in July 1865 at Cairo, Illinois, the *Benton* turned in 170 muskets, 60 pikes, one battle ax, 42 Colt revolvers, 27 Remington revolvers and 20 Spencer rifles. *(Library of Congress)*

In the years just after the war, the Marines remained armed with their old .58 caliber muzzle-loading rifle muskets. In December of 1865, they did exchange with the Ordnance Department 1,300 of their old caliber .69 muskets for a like quantity of .58 caliber muskets.[37] On March 13, 1870, Captain McLane Tilton, commanding the Marine guard aboard the frigate *Colorado*, complained to the commandant that his men were still armed with the old Springfield muzzleloaders and wanted to obtain 50 of the new .50/.70 Springfield centerfire rifles.[38] The year before, he had been the Marine Corps representative to the Navy Board that recommended the Remington Rolling Block .50/.70 rifle for naval use. Tilton made the Corps his profession, retiring in February 1897 as a lieutenant colonel.[39] When the Marines went into Korea in 1871, they still had their muzzleloaders. The first 3,000 centerfire .50/.70 Springfield rifles were received by the Marine shore units in September 1870, but the fleet Marines were not armed with these rifles until a later date.

A year and a half after the close of the war, the House of Representatives adopted a resolution on December 6, 1866, calling on the Secretary of the Navy to provide data on the quantity of ordnance stores then in the Navy's possession. In response, the weekly returns of all ordnance and ordnance stores as of December 1st was submitted to Congress. The following list is a schedule of the class "V" small arms totals at the various locations:

157

Brevet Capt. William Wallace and 2nd Lt. George C. Reid standing, with Capt. McLane Tilton seated c.1865. As late as 1870, Tilton's Marine detachment on the frigate *Colorado* were armed with .58 caliber rifle muskets. Tilton retired from the Corps in February 1897, with the rank of lieutenant colonel. *(National Archives)*

Weekly Returns of Ordnance Stores[40]
Naval Stations
December 1, 1866

Edged Weapons		Saber Bayonets		Angular Bayonets	
Ames Cutlasses	17,451	NM1859 Sharps .56 cal.	72	.58 cal. Rifle Musket	184
Old Navy Cutlasses	861	NM1859 Sharps .52 cal.	319	.69 Altered R/Musket	513
Old Roman Swords	1,399	Plymouth Rifle	1,713	.69 Smoothbore Musket	446
Boarding Pikes	10,759	Sharps & Hankins Rifle	223	Enfield (long) Rifle	461
Battle Axes	3,509	Spencer Rifle	122		
Bowie Knives	1,445	Enfield (short) Rifle	211		

Muzzleloaders

.69 cal. Altered Rifle Musket	3,534	.69 cal. Plymouth Rifle	7,264
.577 cal. Enfield (long) Rifle	5,138	.577 cal. Enfield (short) Rifle	1,713
.69 cal. Smoothbore Musket — Army	4,021	.58 cal. Rifle Muskets	1,316
.54 cal. 1855 Rifle Carbine	4	Enfield Artillery Carbines	433
Muskets Flintlocks	20		

Chapter 7 • Capture of Fort Fisher, January 15, 1865

The M1861 Ames cutlass remained on board ship throughout the balance of the 19th century. Shown here are fencing drills aboard the *Lancaster* about 1883. *(U.S. Naval Historical Center)*

Sharps .56 cal.	821	**Breechloaders**			
Sharps .56 cal.	821	Sharps .52 cal.	1,530	S&H Rifles	214
S&H Carbines	3,004	Colts Rifles	47	Spencer Rifles	847
Jenks Carbines	107	Maynard Carbines	68	Halls	15
Joslyn Rifles	6	Perry Carbines	6		

Revolvers and Pistols

Whitney Revolvers	3,923	Army Pistols	2,527	Savage Revolvers	317
Navy Pistols	907	Remington Revolvers	3,590	Various types of Pistols	1,350
Colt .36 cal. Revolvers	1,956	Colt .44 cal. Revolvers	997	Kerr Revolvers	98
Army Pistols Flintlock	35	Starr Revolvers	27	Colt Pocket Revolvers	5
Revolvers, Ames Mass.	5				

Cartridge Boxes

Plymouth Rifle	3,063	Spencer Rifle	283	S&H Rifle	2,773
Remington Revolver	647	Whitney Revolver	401	Enfield (long) Rifle	440
Colt Revolver	5,461	.69 cal. Musket	4,605	.58 cal. Rifle Musket	2,683
.56 cal. NM Sharps Rifle	157				

Waist Belts

.58 cal. Rifle Musket	5,187	Remington Revolver	405	Sharps & Hankins	7,211
Assorted Muskets	2,976	Plymouth Rifle	2,639	Carbine	10,210

The wartime small arms remained in naval service throughout the balance of the 1860s. Finally, in 1871, the Navy took delivery of 12,000 of the new .50/.70 centerfire Remington Rolling Block Rifles. The use of the old Civil War small arms in active sea service was coming to an end. One arm that remained in active service throughout the balance of the 19th century was the Ames Model 1861 Cutlass. It would be the last of the Civil War arms to see military use with the Navy.

During the war, approximately 16,000 African-American sailors served in the U.S. Navy. The young sailor here, named Johnson, is most likely posing with his father. *(Jerry Rinker collection)*

Chapter 8
Small Arms Inventories, 1861–1865

Ship Inventory for Nearly 400 Vessels

Many types of vessels were purchased during the war for naval use. Shown is the *Commodore Morris,* a converted New York ferryboat. After the war, it returned to New York and operated on ferry service until 1931. *(Library of Congress)*

When the research for this book was originally begun, it was hoped that standard reports similar to the Army's quarterly reports would be uncovered. No such reports were found. So where did the partial listing of small arms for nearly 400 vessels in this section come from? The answer is from three major sources. They are Record Groups 24 and 74 from the National Archives and the Official Records of the Union and Confederate Navies in the War of the Rebellion.

Record Group #24 "List of Logbooks of U.S. Navy Ships and Miscellaneous Units, 1801–1947"

In this series of records are approximately 73,000 logbooks of United States Navy ships and miscellaneous units for the 147-year period 1801–1947. In the Civil War period, the logbooks were kept on a daily basis with one page for each day and entries being made in the log every four hours. If a vessel was in active service for a full three-year period, such as the frigate *Wabash*, she would have over 1,000 pages of log entries.

Reference to small arms entries in the logs are very uneven. A typical entry when the vessel was first being outfitted for sea would read: "Received ordnance stores from the Navy yard." Therefore, the types of small arms were not stated. In rare cases, the officer of the deck did enter the quantities of small arms brought on board, as in the September 29, 1862, log reading of the gunboat *Stepping Stone*. See Chapter 4, "Clash of the Ironclads," for the

On board the monitor *Nahant*, a wartime photo. *(Tim Brooks collection — USAMHI)*

The double-turret monitor *Onondaga* on the James River in 1864–1865. After the war, the *Onondaga* was sold to France in 1867 and remained in the French navy until 1903. *(U.S. Naval Historical Center)*

actual arms issued that Monday the 29th. The same pattern occurred when the ship was being decommissioned in the summer of 1865. The entry would state that the ordnance stores were sent to the yard. Again, very few gave an accounting of their disposals. One of the few vessels that did give the breakdown was the river ironclad *Benton*, right down to the serial numbers of the cannon on board. Some ship's logs for this time period were not on file in the Archives. Two examples of missing logs were for the *Cumberland* and the *Congress*, both of which were destroyed by the *Merrimack* in the March 8, 1862, engagement. The ship's logs of these two vessels probably went to the bottom with the ships when they sank.

At sea, the general entry would typically follow the pattern of the following August 11, 1862, entry from the frigate *Minnesota*: "First division exercise with single sticks and 5th division with small arms." This type of entry was found on nearly all vessels. Some vessels would give the small arms in use. The river ironclad *Choctaw's* log entry of March 3, 1865, reads: "Co. A, B, C and D at target firing expending 70 Enfield Rifle cartridges, 128 percussion caps and 20 Spencer cartridges." A second source of data on the small arms on board ship was from when they were resupplied. Two examples of such reissue involve the *Little Rebel* and *Pittsburg*. The *Little Rebel* on November 11, 1864, received on board 20 cutlasses with scabbards, 10 Remington revolvers, and 20 Remington revolver frogs. The *Pittsburg's* log of July 5, 1864, reads: "The receipt of 20 smoothbore muskets with bayonets and cartridge boxes, 4,000 ball cartridges .69 caliber, 100 Spencer rifle cartridges and 2,000 revolver cartridges (Whitney)."

Record Group #74 "Preliminary Inventory of the Records of the Bureau of Ordnance"

The Bureau of Ordnance records covers the period of 1842 to 1951. This record contains about 6,900 cubic feet of records. The records of major interest for this study of small arms inventory aboard ship are found in Entries 18 and 19.

Entry #18 — Letters Received from Naval Officers 1842–1884

This entry was of great help in finding information for a large number of the vessels in this section. In 1865, it appears that the ships involved in the attack on Fort Fisher were required to report the quantities of small arms lost in the attack of January 15, 1865. The *Iosco, Tacony, Vanderbilt, Fort Jackson, Chippewa, Yantic, Kansas* and *Minnesota* reported their loss to the Navy Department. The *Minnesota* stated that, in addition to the arms they lost, after the attack, the crew picked up 7 Springfield muskets, 10 Austrian rifles, 1 Enfield rifle, 1 Sharps improved rifle, 4 Sharps carbines pattern 1859, and 2 Remington revolvers on the beach. Large numbers of letters were received stating the types of small arms. On April 29, 1863, the officer on the *Young Rover* wrote stating that 20 Remington revolvers were received to replace their Savage revolvers. In May 1863, the steamer *Putnam* had on board 11 Colt revolvers. A month later, on June 22, 1863, the *Gem of the Sea* turned in 6 Harpers Ferry rifled muskets .69 caliber, 11 caliber .58 Springfield rifle muskets, plus one small Colt revolver.

Entry #19 — Letters Received from Navy Yard and Stations 1842–1884

This entry is broken down by navy yard. In the early months of 1864, the Navy yards at Portsmouth, Boston and New York reported their issuance of small arms to the vessels being outfitted at their locations. The vessels' reports can be reviewed in Chapter 6, "Mobile Bay" which covers 1864. The reporting was only done for about three months. The serial numbers of the Whitney revolvers and the Sharps & Hankins rifles reported in the text came from the Washington Navy Yard. From the Washington Navy Yard in April 1861, there were issued 120 Sharps rifles to the *Anacostia*. The *Anacostia* was in the process of being one of several vessels sent to help protect the Norfolk Navy Yard from Confederate capture. On September 22, 1864, the Philadelphia Navy Yard sent the *Fort Jackson* 50 sword bayonets for the .52 caliber Sharps rifle.

Official Records of the Union and Confederate Navies in the War of the Rebellion

Series 1, which consists of 27 volumes and over 21,000 pages, was reviewed for entries on small arms usage. These volumes contain the reports, orders and correspondences from all naval commands. The reports often did not give a clear clue to the types of small arms they actually had. For example, in May 1862, the sloop *Wachusett* had pistols and swords, while the *Seminole* also had the same arms. In this case, the items are too general in nature to tell which actual arms that the reports were discussing. In other reports, like the one dated November 6, 1861, the gunboat *Cambridge* sent out a party of 30 sailors armed with Sharps rifles. Their mission was to destroy the schooner *Ada* five miles up the Corrotoman Creek in Virginia. The sailors destroyed the schooner and returned to their ship after engaging the Confederates on the way back to the ship.

The screw sloop *Richmond* saw action at New Orleans, Vicksburg and later at Mobile Bay. The *Richmond* stayed in naval service until 1919 with its last duty as the receiving ship at the Norfolk Navy Yard between 1903 and 1919. *(U.S. Naval Historical Center)*

The side-wheel gunboat *Suwanee* was assigned to the Pacific Squadron between 1865 and 1868. It was wrecked in Queen Charlotte Sound, British Columbia, Canada on July 9, 1868. *(Civil War Library and Museum MOLLUS, Philadelphia, Pa.)*

No casualties were sustained (Vol. 6, pg. 408). Among the sailors involved in this action was William B. Cushing who, in 1864, would sink the Confederate ironclad *Albemarle*. The ORNs and the other two entries were the source of nearly all of the ship inventories that follow.

The schedule that is shown includes muzzleloaders and breechloaders, plus single-shot pistols and revolvers. Cutlasses are not shown since, after late 1861, nearly all cutlasses issued to the fleet were the Model 1861 Ames cutlass. The reader should keep in mind that the cutlass at the beginning of the war, the Model 1841 (also called the old roman sword) was standard issue but was replaced with the Model 1861. The ships' small arms inventory starts in early 1861 just prior to the outbreak of hostilities and goes up to the end of 1865. The muskets shown are both the .69 caliber muskets (less the Plymouth) and the .58 caliber Springfield rifle muskets. The pistols are the .54 caliber Army and Navy pistol. The Sharps and Enfield rifles are the three-band rifles unless shown as short (s). Army pistols are followed by (a); Navy pistols are followed by (n). The Colt revolvers are .36 caliber unless stated as .44 caliber. Remington, Savage, Starr, and Whitney are .36 caliber revolvers. Sharps & Hankins (S&H) are carbines unless stated as rifles.

Chapter 8 • Small Arms Inventories, 1861–1865

The Navy built the tug *Pinta* shown in Juneau Harbor, Alaska, in 1889.
(U.S. Naval Historical Center)

Name of Vessel	Small Arms
Abeona	Enfield Rifles
Acacia	Enfield Rifle, Remington
Adirondack	Enfield Rifle
Agamenticus	Muskets, Whitney
Agawam	Whitney, Pistols (a), Plymouth Rifle, S&H
A.M. Lancaster	Muskets, S&H
Anacostia	Sharps
Alabama (U.S.)	Colts, Sharps
Ariel	Sharps
Aries	Remington
Arletta	Colts, Enfield Rifle
Aroostook	Muskets
Arthur	Colts, Enfield Rifle
Ascutney	Muskets, Remington, Plymouth Rifle,
Atlanta	Enfield Rifle, Whitney
Augusta	Muskets, Enfield Rifle(s), Whitney, Remington, Pistol (a), Plymouth Rifle, S&H
Avenger	Spencer rifles, Remington, Plymouth Rifle
Baltimore	Colts
Banshee	Plymouth Rifle
Baron deKalb	Colts (44)
Bat	Muskets
Beauregard	Savage
Benton	Colts (44), Spencer Rifle, Remington, Muskets
Beta	Enfield Rifle (s)
Blenville	Enfield Rifle
Black Hawk	Spencer Rifle, Colts
Bohio	Muskets, Jenks, Sharps
Boxer	Colts (44), Muskets
Brandywine	Muskets, Pistols (n)
Brilliant	Plymouth Rifles
Brooklyn	Joslyn Rifle, Enfield Rifle, S&H
Cairo	Colts (44)

The screw gunboat *Kansas* on the James River 1864. Note the white painted funnel. She remained in naval service until August 10, 1875.
(Library of Congress)

165

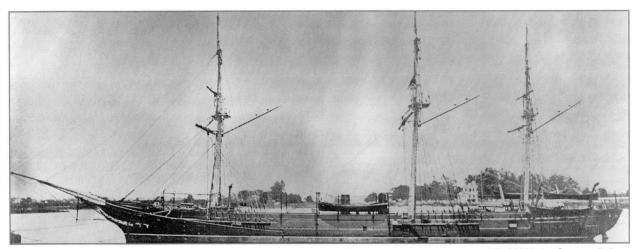

In 1864, the screw gunboat *Saco* was assigned to search the North Atlantic for Confederate raiders. As late as the fall of 1871, the *Saco* was listing 21 Plymouth rifles and 3 Colt revolvers. The *Saco* was decommission in July 1876. *(U.S. Naval Historical Center)*

Name of Vessel	Small Arms	Name of Vessel	Small Arms
Calypso	Colts	*Cherokee*	Plymouth Rifle
Cambridge	Colts, Sharps	*Cimarron*	Sharps
Canonicus	Spencer Rifle, Whitney, Plymouth Rifle	*Chimo*	Remington
Carondelet	Colts (44), Muskets, Enfield Rifle	*Choctaw*	Spencer rifle, Enfield Rifle (s), Remington, Pistols (a)
Carrabasset	Sharps	*Chocura*	Muskets
Casco	Colts	*Chickasaw*	Muskets
Catskill	Enfield Rifle, S&H Rifle	*Chicopee*	Whitney
Cayuga	Colts, Pistols (a)	*Chillicothe*	Muskets, S&H
Champion	Enfield Rifle, Remington	*Chippewa*	Colts, Spencer Rifle, S&H
Chenango	Colts, Plymouth Rifle, Sharps	*Cincinnati*	Colts (44), Spencer Rifle, S&H Rifle

Eads ironclad *Cairo*. The *Cairo* was assigned to the Mississippi River Squadron. While operating on the Yazoo River on December 12, 1862, she struck two mines and sank within twelve minutes. No casualties were incurred. *(U.S. Naval Historical Center)*

Chapter 8 • Small Arms Inventories, 1861–1865

Name of Vessel	Small Arms	Name of Vessel	Small Arms
Circassian	Colts	Elk	Whitney, Muskets, S&H Rifle
Clyde	Enfield Rifle	Ella	Spencer Rifle, Plymouth Rifle
Coeur de Lion	Colts, Muskets, Spencer Rifle, Plymouth Rifle	Ellen	Muskets
Collier	Enfield Rifles	Ellis	Muskets
Colorado	Sharps, Whitney	Essex	Colt (44)
Colossus	Muskets, Whitney	Ethan Allen	Muskets, Remington, Sharps Enfield Rifle
Columbine	Enfield Rifle	Eureka	Colts, Sharps
Commodore Hull	Muskets	Eutaw	Spencer Rifle, Whitney, Plymouth Rifle
Commodore McDonough	Plymouth Rifle		
Commodore Morris	Enfield Rifle, Colts	Exchange	Enfield Rifles
Commodore Perry	Muskets, Pistols (a), Colts	Fairplay	Plymouth Rifles
		Fairy	Plymouth Rifles
Commodore Read	Muskets, Spencer Rifle, Plymouth Rifle	Farrallones	Plymouth Rifle, S&H
Conestoga	Muskets, Sharps, Spencer Rifle, Colts 44	Fawn	Enfield Rifles, Remington
Conemaugh	Colts, Whitney, S&H, Pistols, Enfield and Plymouth Rifles	Fernandina	Muskets
		Flag	Sharps
		Flambeau	Enfield Rifle, Plymouth Rifle
Connecticut	Enfield Rifle, Sharps		
Congress	Colts	Forest Rose	Spencer Rifle, Enfield Rifle, Colts
Constellation	Muskets		
Cornubia	Colts, Enfield Rifle, Pistols (a)	Freeborn	Colts, Remington, Sharps
Corwin	Sharps	Fort Henry	Colts, Enfield Rifle (5), Pistols (n)
C.P. Williams	Colts, Muskets, Pistols (a)		
		Fort Hindman	Enfield Rifle
Cricket	Muskets	Fort Jackson	Spencer Rifle, Sharps
Crusader	Colts	Florida	Remington
Currituck	Colts, Muskets, Sharps, Plymouth Rifles	Fuchsia	Spencer Rifle, Plymouth Rifle
Cyane	Colts, Muskets, Pistols (n)	Galatea	Remington, Sharps
		Galena	Muskets, Pistols
Dacotah	S&H Rifle	Gamage	Muskets, Whitney
Dai-Ching	Muskets	Gamma	Enfield Rifle(s)
Dale	Muskets	Gem of the Sea	Colts, Muskets, Enfield Rifle, Remington
Dan Smith	Colts, Muskets, Enfield Rifle, Pistols (a-n)		
		General Bragg	Muskets, Colts
Dart	Muskets	General Lyon	Remington
Dawn	Colts, Musketoon	General Price	Spencer Rifle, Enfield Rifle (s), Remington
Daylight	Colts, Enfield Rifle		
Delta (Linda)	Enfield Rifle (s)	General Sherman	Muskets
DeSoto	Muskets, Savage, Pistols (n)	Genesee	Enfield Rifle
		George Mangham	Colts, Muskets, Enfield Rifle, Pistol (n)
Dictator	Colts, Sharps		
Don	Enfield Rifle, Plymouth Rifle	George Washington	Colts, Enfield Rifle
		Gettysburg	Colts, Spencer Rifle, Plymouth Rifle, S&H
Dragon	Spencer Rifle, Plymouth Rifle		
Eastport	Muskets	Glasgow	Colts
E.B. Hale	Colts	Glide	Remington
		Governor Buckingham	Remington
		Grand Gulf	Colts

167

Name of Vessel	Small Arms	Name of Vessel	Small Arms
Great Western	Remington	Kenwood	Enfield Rifle
Harcourt	Muskets, Colts	Kensington	Remington
Harriet Lane	Muskets, Maynard Carbine	Keystone State	Enfield Rifle
		Kickapoo	Muskets, Remington
Hartford	Colts, Muskets, Joslyn Rifle, Starr, Plymouth Rifle Enfield Rifle, Spencer Rifles	Kingfisher	Enfield Rifle
		Lackawanna	Colts, Whitney, Pistols (n), S&H Rifle
		Lafayette	Muskets, Spencer Rifle
		Lancaster	Muskets, Jenks
Harvest Moon	Plymouth Rifle, Muskets, Remington	Lehigh	Enfield Rifle
		Lexington	Sharps, Colt 44
Hastings	Enfield Rifles	Linden	Enfield Rifle, Remington, Pistols (a)
Hatteras	Pistols (a)		
Hendrick Hudson	Enfield Rifle, Remington, Pistols (n), Sharps	Little Rebel	Remington, Muskets
		Lodona	Colts, Pistols (n)
Henry Janes	Muskets, Enfield Rifle	Louisiana	Sharps
Honduras	Whitney	Louisville	Spencer Rifle, Colts (44)
Horace Beals	Colts, Enfield Rifle, Pistols (a)	Macedonian	Enfield Rifle, Remington, S&H, Sharps Rifle and Carbine
Hunchback	Colts, Muskets		
Huron	Muskets, Whitney, Pistols (a)	Mackinaw	Enfield Rifle, Remington, Sharps
Hetzel	Colts, Muskets	Mahaska	Enfield Rifle (s)
Hydrangea	Spencer Rifle, Remington, Plymouth Rifle	Malvern	Pistols (a), S&H
		Manhattan	Spencer Rifle
Ice Boat	Muskets, Jenks	Maratanza	Muskets
Indianola	Colts, Pistols (a), Sharps	Marblehead	Muskets
Iosco	Whitney	Maria A. Wood	Colts
Iroquois	Colts, Enfield Rifle, Remington, Plymouth Rifle, S&H Rifle, Sharps	Maria J. Carlton	Colts, Enfield Rifle
		Marmora	Spencer Rifle, Enfield Rifle, Remington, Pistols (a)
Itasca	Colts, Pistols (n)		
Iuka	S&H	Massasoit	Whitney, Plymouth Rifle, S&H
Jacob Bell	Plymouth Rifle		
James Alger	Muskets, Savage, Remington, Sharps	Mattabesett	Spencer Rifle, Remington, Plymouth Rifle, S&H
J.C. Kuhn	Savage, Pistols (a-n)		
John Adams	Colts, Enfield Rifle	Matthew Vassar	Colts, Spencer Rifle, Enfield Rifle, Plymouth Rifle
John Griffith	Colts, Enfield Rifle		
John P. Jackson	Colts, Enfield Rifle, Pistols (a), Sharps		
		Memphis	Plymouth Rifle
John Lockwood	Muskets, S&H	Mendota	Remington, Plymouth Rifle, S&H
Jamestown	Colts, Prewar Plymouth Rifle, Pistols (n), Sharps		
		Mercury	Plymouth Rifle
Juliet	Remington	Meteor	S&H Rifle
Juniata	S&H	Miami	Colts
Kineo	Colts, Muskets	Michigan	Colts, Muskets, Jenks/Merrill, Whitney, S&H
Kanawha	Colts, Pistols (a), Sharps		
		Midnight	Whitney
Kansas	S&H	Milwaukee	Muskets, S&H
Katahdin	Muskets	Mingoe	Remington, Plymouth Rifle, S&H
Kearsarge	Colts, Sharps		
Kennebec	Spencer Rifle, Enfield Rifle	Minnesota	Colts, Muskets, Spencer Rifle, Sharps

Chapter 8 • Small Arms Inventories, 1861–1865

Name of Vessel	Small Arms
Mississippi	Colts, Jenks, Sharps
Mist	Enfield Rifles, Spencer Rifles
Mohican	Muskets
Monadnock	Sharps
Monitor	Either had Enfield or Sharps Rifles
Monongahela	Enfield Rifle
Montgomery	Colts
Monticello	Jenks, Sharps
Moose	Sharps
Morcteniga	Enfield Rifle (s), Pistols (n)
Mound City	Colts (44), Spencer Rifle, Enfield Rifle
Mount Vernon	Colts, Sharps
Niad	Plymouth Rifle, Muskets, Remington
Nahant	Sharps, Remington, Plymouth Rifles
Nansemond	Pistols (a-n), Plymouth Rifle, S&H
Nantucket	S&H Rifles
Narragansett	Colts, Remington, Sharps
Naubuc	Remington
Naumkeag	Enfield Rifles
Neosho	Whitney, S&H
Nereus	Colts, Muskets, Spencer Rifle, Remington, Pistols (a) Plymouth Rifle, S&H
New Era	Colts, Enfield Rifle
New Hampshire	Colts
New Ironsides	Colts, S&H, Sharps
New London	Sharps
Niagara	Colts

The double-ended *Maratanza*. This design allowed the vessel to proceed forward or backwards with a rudder at each end. The wind-sails were rigged for ventilation. After the war, the *Maratanza* was sold in 1868 to the Haitian Navy and used by them as a gunboat. *(Library of Congress)*

Engraving of "USS New Ironsides" with her masts and rigging removed for action. One of three experimental ironclads ordered by the Navy in 1861, she saw action at Charleston in 1863 and the attacks on Fort Fisher. She was decommissioned in April 1865 and destroyed by fire in December 1866. *(U.S. Naval Historical Center)*

Name of Vessel	Small Arms	Name of Vessel	Small Arms
Nina	S&H	Philadelphia	Muskets
Niphon	Muskets, Spencer Rifle, Enfield Rifle, Remington, Pistols (a)	Phlox	Muskets, Enfield Rifle, Enfield Rifle (s)
		Picket Boat #1	Enfield Rifle (s)
		Picket Boat #5	Enfield Rifle (s)
Nipsic	S&H	Pinola	Colts
Nita	Sharps	Pinta	S&H
Norfolk Packet	Colts, Muskets, Pistols (a)	Pittsburg	Colts (44), Muskets, Spencer Rifle, Enfield Rifle, Whitney
Norwich	Enfield Rifle		
Nyack	Remington, Sharps	Pocahontas	Whitney, Sharps
Nymph	Plymouth Rifles	Pontiac	Colts, Plymouth Rifle, S&H
Ouachita	Spencer Rifle		
Octorara	S&H Rifles, Colts, Pistols (a-n), Muskets	Pontoosuc	Whitney, Pistols (a), Plymouth Rifle
Oliver H. Lee	Colts, Enfield Rifle	Port Royal	Muskets
Oneida	Colts (44), Muskets, Pistols (a), Sharps	Portsmouth	Colts, Sharps
		Potomac	Colts, Muskets, Pistols (a)
Onondaga	Spencer rifle, Remington, S&H		
		Potomska	Spencer Rifle
Oriole	Muskets, Whitney	Powhatan	Colts, Jenks, Enfield Rifle, S&H, Sharps
Orvetta	Colts Enfield Rifle		
Osage	Whitney, S&H	Prairie Bird	Spencer Rifle
Osceola	Whitney, S&H Rifle	Preble	Sharps
Ossipee	Remington, Sharps	Primrose	Spencer Rifle, Pistols (n)
Otsego	Remington, Plymouth Rifle, S&H	Princess Royal	Enfield Rifle
		Princeton	Pistols (n)
Ottawa	Whitney	Proteus	Spencer Rifle, Remington, Pistols (a), Plymouth Rifle, S&H
Owasco	Remington, S&H, Sharps		
Ozark	Remington, S&H	Pursuit	Muskets
Para	Colts, Muskets, Enfield Rifle	Quaker City	Hall Carbines, Musketoon, Savage, Pistols (a), Sharps
Passaic	Colts, Enfield Rifles, Muskets		
		Racer	Colts, Enfield Rifle
Patapsco	Colts	Rattler	Colts, Enfield Rifle
Patroon	Muskets	Reindeer	Plymouth Rifles
Paul Jones	Colts, Muskets, Enfield Rifle, Whitney, Remington	Restless	Enfield Rifle, S&H
		Resolute	Pistols (n), Plymouth Rifle
Paw Paw	Enfield Rifle, Remington	Rhode Island	Whitney, Remington
		Richmond	Jenks/Merrill, Enfield Rifle, Sharps, S&H
Pawnee	Colts, Muskets, Pistols (n), Plymouth Rifle, Sharps		
		Roanoke	Colts, Muskets, Enfield Rifle, Whitney, Pistols (a), S&H
Pawtuxet	Colts, Pistols (a), Sharps		
		Romeo	Colts, Enfield Rifle
Pembina	Muskets, Pistols	Sabine	Jenks, Enfield Rifle
Pennsylvania	Jenks	Sachem	Muskets, Pistols (a)
Penobscot	Colts	Saco	Plymouth Rifle, Muskets
Pensocola	Muskets, Sharps	Sacramento	Remington
Peosta	Enfield Rifle	Sagamore	Colts, Muskets
Perry	Whitney, Colts, Muskets, Pistols	Saginaw	Colts, S&H
		Sangamon	Colts
Pequot	Plymouth Rifle, S&H	Samuel Rotan	Colts, Muskets

Chapter 8 • Small Arms Inventories, 1861–1865

The tinclad *Nymph* on the western rivers during 1864–1865. *(U.S. Naval Historical Center)*

Name of Vessel	Small Arms
San Jacinto	Colts, Muskets, Pistols (n), Sharps
Santee	Colts, Muskets
Santiago de Cuba	Muskets
Sarah Bruen	Muskets, Enfield Rifle, Whitney
Saranac	Colts, Muskets, Jenks, Pistols (n), Plymouth Rifle, S&H
Saratoga	Colts, Muskets, Plymouth Rifle, Maynard Carbines
Sassacus	S&H
Satellite	Colts, Muskets, Sharps
Saugus	S&H
Savannah	Colts, Muskets, Pistols (a)
Sciota	Colts, Muskets, Sharps
Sea Foam	Colts, Enfield Rifle
Sebago	Enfield Rifles
Selma	Enfield Rifles, Muskets, either Remington or Whitney Revolvers
Seminole	Hall Carbines, Pistols (a)
Seneca	Remington, Pistols (a), S&H
Shenandoah	Colts, Enfield Rifle, Sharps
Sibyl	Spencer Rifle, Plymouth Rifle
Sidney C. Jones	Colts, Enfield Rifle
Signal	Enfield Rifle
Silver Cloud	Muskets
Silver Lake	Enfield Rifle
Shamokin	Enfield Rifle, S&H
Shamrock	S&H
Shawsheen	Pistols
Shark	Muskets, Pistols
Somerset	Colts, Muskets, Whitney, Pistols (a), Sharps
Sonoma	Plymouth Rifle
Sophronia	Colts, Muskets, Enfield Rifle, Plymouth Rifle
South Carolina	Jenks, Pistols, Muskets, Enfield Rifle, Savage
Stars & Stripes	Savage
Stepping Stone	Colts, Enfield Rifle, Pistols (n), S&H rifles
St. Lawrence	Jenks, Savage, Sharps
St. Louis	Plymouth Rifle, Sharps Carbines
St. Mary's	Colts, Jenks
Sumter	Colts
Susquehanna	Jenks, Whitney
Suwanee	S&H
T.A. Ward	Enfield Rifle
Tacony	Whitney, Remington, Pistols (n), S&H
Tahoma	Muskets, Enfield Rifle, Sharps
Teaser	Spencer Rifle, Remington, Plymouth Rifle
Tecumseh	Spencer Rifle, Whitney, S&H
Tennessee	Enfield Rifle, Whitney, Remington

CIVIL WAR Small Arms of the U.S. Navy and Marine Corps

Several of the monitors were recommissioned for harbor defense during the Spanish-American War in 1898. The Civil War monitor *Sangamon* was recommissioned as the USS *Jason*, pictured here on May 27, 1898, at New York harbor. *(U.S. Naval Historical Center)*

Name of Vessel	Small Arms	Name of Vessel	Small Arms
Ticonderoga	Spencer Rifle, Whitney, Maynard Carbines	*Wateree*	Spencer Rifle
Trefoil	Whitney, Plymouth Rifle	*Water Witch*	Colts, Muskets, Pistols (a)
Tristram Shandy	Whitney	*Winnebago*	Whitney, Sharps
Tulip	Spencer Rifle, Plymouth Rifle	*Wild Cat*	Enfield Rifle
Tuscarora	Colts, Pistols (n), Sharps	*Wilderness*	Colts
Tuscumbia	Spencer Rifle	*William G. Anderson*	Savage, S&H Rifle
Tyler	Sharps, Colts, Enfield Rifles	*William Bacon*	Colts, Spencer Rifle, Enfield Rifle, Plymouth Rifle, Whitney
Unadilla	Whitney, Savage, Plymouth Rifle	*William Putnam*	Colts
Underwriter	Joslyn Revolvers, Sharps	*Winona*	Colts, Remington, Plymouth Rifle, Sharps
Union	Colts, Muskets, Remington	*Wissahickon*	Colts, Muskets, Pistols (a), Plymouth Rifle, S&H, Sharps
Valley City	Muskets, Whitney, Savage	*Wyalusing*	Plymouth Rifle, S&H
Vanderblit	Remington	*Wyandank*	Spencer Rifle
Vermont	Remington	*Wyandotte*	Enfield Rifle
Vicksburg	Enfield Rifle	*Wyoming*	Colts, Pistols (n)
Victoria	Whitney	*Yankee*	Spencer, Joslyn Revolvers, Plymouth, Colt Revolving, Rifle, Sharps, Pistol, Muskets
Victory	Sharps		
Vincennes	Colts, Muskets, Sharps		
Vindicator	Whitney, Plymouth Rifle, Spencer Rifle	*Yantic*	Muskets, Enfield Rifle, Remington, Pistols (n)
Wabash	Colts, Muskets, Pistols (a), S&H Rifle, Sharps	*Yazoo*	S&H
		Young Rover	Savage, Remington
Wachusett	Muskets	*Yucca*	Whitney
Wando	Whitney	*Zeta*	Enfield Rifle(s)

172

Endnotes

Chapter 1

1. NARG 74-18, letter from Perry April 19, 1852.
2. NARG 156-3.
3. NARG 74-5.
4. NARG 24, deck logs dated April 6, 1853, of the *Saratoga* and *Plymouth* stating Perry's arrival at Hong Kong.
5. *Ibid.*, deck logs of *Susquehanna* dated April 9, 15, 18 and 20 and *Powhatan* dated August 23, 1854.
6. *Ibid.*, deck log dated April 24, July 26, and August 24 and September 5, 1853.
7. *Ibid.*, deck logs of *Mississippi*.
8. *Ibid.*, from the deck logs of the *Mississippi, Plymouth, Saratoga* and *Susquehanna*.
9. *Ibid.*, *Susquehanna*, July 14, 1853.
10. *Ibid.*, September 26, 1853.
11. *Ibid.*, March 3, 1854, and *Powhatan* same date.
12. Kimbrough, Robert E., *Gun Collector Magazine*, Volume 33, September 1950, p. 461, and NARG 24, deck logs of *Powhatan* March 12, 1854.
13. NARG 24, deck logs of *Plymouth* dated April 3 and 4, 1854.
14. NARG 74-19, New York Navy Yard.
15. *Ibid.*
16. *Ibid.*, Norfolk Navy Yard letters dated October 1, 1852 and 1854.
17. *Ibid.*, Washington Navy Yard.
18. NARG 74-18, Ringgold to Morris dated October 11, 1852.
19. NARG 24, deck logs of *Vincennes* dated March 24 and April 9, 1853. Note the pistols were from a firm called E&B Company.
20. *Ibid.*, dated May 7 and June 7, 1853 and August 22, 1854.
21. NARG 127-4.
22. NARG 24, *Vincennes* dated December 12, 1854.
23. NARG 74-19, Norfolk Navy Yard letters dated March 11, 1851 and February 2, 1852.
24. *Ibid.*
25. NARG 74-19, Boston Navy Yard.
26. NARG 74-5, letter of November 4, 1852.
27. NARG 74-5, and 156-3 plus 1853 Senate Executive Document #3, 33rd Congress, 1st Session, Volume 3, p. 287.
28. NARG 156-3, letter of April 8, 1852, Craig to Morris.
29. NARG 74-18.
30. NARG 24, deck logs of *Powhatan*, August 5, 8 and 11, 1855.
31. NARG 127-4, General returns of officers, NCO, musicians, privates in USMC as of September 1852.
32. NARG 127-4 and RG 24, deck logs of USS *Constitution* various dates.
33. NARG 156-3, dated April 7, 1851 and October 12, 1853.
34. NARG 74-18, letter dated September 3, 1853.
35. NARG 24, deck logs of *Powhatan* March 31–April 2, 1855 and August 6, 1855, on the *Congress*.
36. Schmidt, Peter A., *Hall's Military Breechloaders*, Andrew Mowbray Publishers, Lincoln, RI, 1996, p. 152.
37. NARG 74-19, and 22.
38. NARG 74-19, June 22, 1852, letter from Washington Navy Yard.
39. Schmidt, Peter A., *op. cit.*, pp. 152–153.
40. NARG 74-19, Norfolk Navy Yard letter dated January 27, 1853.
41. NARG 74-19, New York Navy Yard letter dated July 15, 1853.
42. *Ibid.*, Boston dated February 9, 1854.
43. NARG 156-3, letter of October 26, 1854.
44. NARG 74-5, letter dated October 24, 1854 to Craig.
45. NARG 24, deck logs of the frigates *Constitution* and *Congress* — various dates.
46. NARG 74-18, and 19.
47. NARG 24, deck logs of *Cyane* dated June 6, July 12 and 13, plus September 6, 1854.
48. Ordnance Instructions for the U.S. Navy, C. Alexander, Printer, 1852, Washington, D.C.
49. NARG 74-1.
50. NARG 24, deck logs of *Constitution* dated June 6, 1855, and RG 74, #19 letter from New York Navy Yard of April 2, 1855.
51. NARG 24, deck logs of *Saratoga* of June 8, 20 and July 6, 1853.
52. *Ibid.*, *John P. Kennedy*, dated October 30, 1855.
53. NARG 74-5.
54. NARG 74-1.
55. NARG 74-5, Morris to Ames, March 31, 1852 and April 6 to Morris.
56. NARG 74-19, Boston Navy Yard.
57. NARG 74-5.
58. NARG 74-19, Boston Navy Yard.
59. *Ibid.*

Chapter 2

1. NARG 127-4, letter dated October 17, 1859.
2. NARG 74-1, report dated January 7, 1859.
3. Hay, Warren H., "More on the Plymouth Rifle," *The Gun Report*, January 1965, p. 8.
4. *Ibid.*, p. 9.
5. NARG 74-18.
6. Hay, Warren H., *op. cit.*, p. 9. Henry Schively is listed in directories at 1229 Spruce Street and is described in the 1860s as "late instruments," which means he used to be an instrument maker. (Information from Bruce Bazelon)
7. NARG 156-21, letter of September 9, 1856, Clove to Craig.
8. NARG 74-201, entry 5.
9. Dahlgren to Ames dated May 23, 1857, letter collection of Steven Selenfriend.
10. NARG 74-5.
11. NARG 74-5, Howard Michael Madaus, Part 1, "The Percussion Martial Longarms of the Eli Whitney, Jr.," *Armax*, Volume 2, Number 1, 1988, p. 61.
12. Dahlgren to Ames of May 23 letter in the collection of Steve Selenfriend.
13. NARG 74-201, entry 5.
14. NARG 156-3, Volume 49.
15. NARG 24, deck logs of the USS *Plymouth* dated December 24, 1858.
16. *Ibid.*, entries dated August 11 and 12.
17. *Ibid.*, dated August 30, 1858.
18. NARG 74-1, March 14, 1856.
19. NARG 156-3, Volume 46, p. 425.
20. *Ibid.*, Volume 47, pp. 270–271.
21. NARG 74-19, Philadelphia Navy Yard.
22. NARG 24, deck logs of Portsmouth dated November 20, 1856.
23. *Ibid.*, deck logs of *St. Mary's* dated September 29, 1856.
24. NARG 74-18, letters from the *St. Mary's* dated July 18 and November 7, 1856.
25. NARG 24, deck logs of the *Portsmouth* of November 20–22, 1856.
26. NARG 156-3, Volume 48, pp. 123–124.
27. NARG 24, deck logs of the *Wabash* dated May 25, 1858.
28. *Ibid.*, July 30, 1858.
29. NARG 74-19, Philadelphia Navy Yard.
30. NARG 74-18.
31. NARG 156-3, and 74-3.
32. NARG 156-3, Volume 48, dated May 23, 1857.
33. *Ibid.*, Craig to Sutherland dated January 7, 1858.
34. NARG 74-1.
35. NARG 74-18, Henderson to Ingraham January 20, 1858.
36. NARG 24, deck logs dated February 24, 1858, of the *Niagara* and *Merrimack* dated October 19, 1858.
37. NARG 156-3, Volume 49.
38. NARG 74-1, June 5, 1860.
39. NARG 127-4, Volume 8.
40. NARG 156-3, Volume 51.
41. NARG 127-4, Volume 8.
42. *Ibid.*, Harris to Toucey of May 3, 1860.

43. NARG 156-3, Craig to Toucey of May 3, 1860.
44. NARG 127-125.
45. NARG 74-19, New York Navy Yard.
46. NARG 127-125.
47. NARG 127-4.
48. NARG 74-19, Philadelphia Navy Yard.
49. NARG 24, deck logs of the *Colorado* of May 17, 1858, and 74-1.
50. *Ibid.*, deck logs of the *Iroquois* of May 29, July 2, September 10 and 12, 1860, and June 16, 1861.
51. NARG 74-145.
52. McAulay, John D., *Civil War Carbines, Volume 2, The Early Years*, Andrew Mowbray Inc., Publishers, Lincoln, RI, 1991, p. 97.
53. *Ibid.*, pp. 97–99.
54. McAulay, John D., *Civil War Breechloading Rifles*, Andrew Mowbray Inc., Lincoln RI, 1987, pp. 67–70.
55. McAulay, John D., *Civil War Carbines, Volume 2, The Early Years*, *op. cit.*, pp. 107–109.
56. NARG 24, deck logs *Merrimack* dated September 7 and 8 and October 5, 1857.
57. NARG 24, deck logs of *Sabine* dated December 13, 1858, January 20, March 4 and December 29, 1859.
58. NARG 74-18 and 19, Portsmouth Navy Yard.
59. NARG 74-145.
60. Hull, Edward A., *The Burnside Breechloading Carbines*, Man at Arms Monograph Series, Andrew Mowbray Inc., Lincoln, RI, 1986, pp. 37–38; John D. McAulay, *Civil War Breechloading Rifles*, Andrew Mowbray, Inc., *op. cit.*, 1987, pp. 55–57; Earl J. Coates & John D. McAulay, *Civil War Sharps Carbines & Rifles*, Thomas Publications, Gettysburg, PA, 1996, p. 40, and John D. McAulay, *Civil War Carbines Volume 2, The Early Years*, Andrew Mowbray, Inc., *op. cit.*, 1991, pp. 81–83.
61. NARG 74-19, Philadelphia Navy Yard dated November 1, 1860.
62. Lederer, Paul S., "How the Navy Drifted into Buying Navies," *American Rifleman*, March 1973, pp. 30–31, and NARG 74-1.
63. NARG 74-18.
64. NARG 74-5.
65. Pachanian, Sam, "U.S. Navy Markings & Their Variations on Colts 1851 & 1861 Navy Model Revolvers, Percussion & Conversion," The American Society of Arms Collectors Bulletin #65, September 4–8, 1991, p. 39.
66. *Ibid.*, p. 40.
67. NARG 74-1, letter of May 28, 1859, from Ingraham to the Secretary of the Navy.
68. *Ibid.*
69. NARG 74-18, Henderson to Ingraham dated September 30, 1858.
70. NARG 74-19, Pensacola and Philadelphia Navy Yards.
71. NARG 74-5.
72. NARG 74-19, Philadelphia Navy Yard.
73. NARG 74-5.
74. NARG 127-125.
75. *Ibid.*
76. *Ibid.*
77. *Ibid.*, letter to Maddax from Slack dated October 15, 1859.
78. *Ibid.*, Slack to Ames of November 22, 1859.

Chapter 3

1. Miller, Francis Trevlyan, *The Photographic History of the Civil War — The Navies*, Castle Books, New York, 1957, pp. 46–54
2. Lindert, A.W., "U.S. Naval Martial Sidearms 1775–1875, Part 2" (conclusion), *The Gun Report*, January 1970, pp. 13–16.
3. NARG 74-19, letters from New York and Philadelphia Navy Yards.
4. NARG 74-201, Entry 7.
5. ORN Series 1, Volume 12, pp. 330–331.
6. Wise, Stephen R., *Lifeline of the Confederacy Blockade Running During the Civil War*, University of South Carolina Press, Columbia, SC, 1988, pp. 53–55.
7. *Ibid.*, pp. 58–60 and ORN Series 1, Volume 6, pp. 454 and 455.
8. ORN Series 1, Volume 6, pp. 56–59.
9. ORN Series 1, Volume 4, p. 579.
10. NARG 127-125, telegram from Slack to Headquarters of July 15, 1861.
11. Sullivan, David, "Uncommon Soldiers" *Military Images*, September/October 1990, p. 21.
12. ORN Series 1, Volume 4, p. 581.
13. Silverstone, Paul H., *Warships of the Civil War Navies*, Naval Institute Press, Annapolis, MD, 1989, p. 76.
14. NARG 74-22.
15. *Ibid.*, and The Union Defense Committee of the City of New York, Minutes, Reports, and Correspondence, The Union Defense Committee, New York, 1885, pp. 142–145.
16. NARG 74-19, letter of May 18, 1864 from New York and 74-18 volume 70.
17. NARG 156-7.
18. NARG 74-201 entry 7.
19. NARG 74-18.
20. NARG 156-7.
21. ORN series 1, Volume 12, p. 436.
22. Hay, Warren H., "More on the Plymouth Rifle", *The Gun Report*, January 1965, p. 11 and Howard Michael Madaus, Part 1, "The Percussion Martial Longarms of Eli Whitney Jr.," *Armax*, Volume 2, November 1, 1988, The Buffalo Bill Historical Center, Cody, WY, pp. 62 and 63.
23. *Ibid.*
24. NARG 127-4, Harris to Welles May 9, 1861.
25. ORN Series 1, Volume 4, p. 693.
26. ORN Series 1, Volume 12, pp. 209 and 210.
27. NARG 127-4.
28. *Ibid.*
29. *Ibid.*
30. ORN Series 1, Volume 12, pp. 217 and 223.
31. *Ibid.*, pp. 233–235.
32. NARG 127-125.
33. NARG 74-3.
34. NARG 74-19, letters from Philadelphia Navy Yard.
35. NARG 74-19, letter from Mare Island dated July 22, 1861.
36. NARG 127-4.
37. *Ibid.*
38. NARG 127-4, September 5, 1861.
39. ORN Series 1, Volume 6, pp. 134–135.
40. *Ibid.*, p. 130.
41. NARG 74-5 and 145 plus John D. McAulay, *Civil War Carbines, Volume 2, The Early Years*, Andrew Mowbray Inc., Lincoln, RI, 1991, pp. 82 and 83.
42. NARG 74-18.
43. *Ibid.*
44. Silverstone, Paul H., *op. cit.*, pp. 24 and 38.
45. NARG 74-201, letters from Dahlgren.
46. NARG 74-19.
47. Joint Committee on the Conduct of the War, Congressional Series, No. 1142, p. 238.
48. NARG 74-5.
49. NARG 24, ship logs of the USS *Brooklyn*.
50. NARG 74-3, Volume 10, pp. 199–203.
51. NARG 74-201, entry 7, letters from Commander R.B. Hickcock.
52. NARG 74-19, letter from Dahlgren and ORN series 1, Volume 4, pp. 284–292.
53. ORN *Ibid.*, pp. 537–546.
54. NARG 74-165.
55. NARG 74-201, entry 7, letter dated July 2, 1861. Chart of Mitchell Contract Sharps rifles is from entry 21, box 17, letter dated August 7, 1861.
56. NARG 74-18.
57. NARG 156-7.
58. *Ibid.*
59. Silverstone, Paul H., *op. cit.*, pp. 88 and 89.
60. NARG 74-18, and ORN Series 1, Volume 5, p. 736.
61. NARG 74-157.
62. NARG 74-22.
63. ORN Series 1, Volume 16, pp. 755–762.
64. *Ibid.*, and pp. 864–865, Paul H. Silverstone, *op. cit.*, p. 235.
65. NARG 74-145.
66. NARG 74-18.
67. NARG 74-156.
68. McAulay, John D., *Civil War Pistols*, Andrew Mowbray, Inc., Lincoln, RI, 1992, p. 102.

69 NARG 74-6.
70 NARG 74-19.
71 NARG 74-5.
72 *Ibid.*
73 NARG 74-22.
74 Hickox, Ron G., *Collector's Guide to Ames U.S. Contract Military Edge Weapons*, 1832–1906, Pioneer Press, Union City, TN, 1992, p. 43.
75 NARG 74-5 and 22.
76 NARG 127-125, Slack to Horstmann of June 3, 1861.
77 *Ibid.*
78 NARG 74-5 and 22.
79 *Ibid.*
80 ORN Series 1, Volume 15, p. 623.
81 NARG 74-5.
82 NARG 74-22.
83 NARG 74-5 and 22.

Chapter 4

1 Musicant, Ivan, *Divided Waters — The Naval History of the Civil War*, Harper Collins Publishers, New York, 1995, p. 151.
2 *Ibid.*, p. 151.
3 *Ibid.*, p. 162.
4 NARG 45, Appendix D, Entry 110, Log of the *Monitor* dated May 18, 1862.
5 ORN Series 1, Volume 19, p. 40.
6 *Ibid.*, p. 43.
7 NARG 74-18, and RG 24 deck logs of *Sophronia* dated November 14, 1862.
8 *Ibid.*, requested June 23, 1862.
9 NARG 74-2, dated June 2, 1862.
10 NARG 74-19, letters from New York Navy Yard.
11 NARG 74-2.
12 NARG 156-7.
13 NARG 74-2.
14 NARG 74-18.
15 ORN Series 1, Volume 13, p. 94.
16 ORN Series 1, Volume 17, pp. 125–126.
17 ORN Series 1, Volume 12, p. 689.
18 NARG 24, deck logs of the *Commodore Perry* dated January 12, 1862, and NARG 74-18, May 1862.
19 ORN Series 1, Volume 19, p. 23.
20 NARG 127-125.
21 *Ibid.*, letter to Ripley dated July 30, 1862.
22 NARG 74-2, 3, 18 and ORN Series 1, Volumes 12, 18, and 19.
23 ORN Series 1, Volume 18, pp. 471 and 687.
24 NARG 74-18.
25 NARG 74-19, Letters from the Western Flotilla.
26 ORN Series 1, Volume 19, pp. 201 and 360–361, plus Vol. 23, pp. 545–547.
27 NARG 74-22, letter from John Palmer dated July 21, 1862.
28 NARG 74-5.
29 ORN Series 1, Volume 8, pp. 204–205.
30 NARG 74-22, letter to Harwood dated March 11th.
31 Silverstone, Paul H., *Warships of the Civil War Navies*, Naval Institute Press, Annapolis, Md., 1989, pp. 49–52.
32 NARG 74-22, letter to Dahlgren dated November 19, 1862.
33 Marcot, Roy M., *Spencer Repeating Firearms*, Northwood Heritage Press, Irvine, CA, 1983, p. 45.
34 *Ibid.*, pp. 42–43
35 NARG 74-5.
36 NARG 74-19, Box 130, Washington Navy Yard report of July 3, 1862.
37 *Ibid.*
38 NARG 74-5.
39 NARG 74-3, Philadelphia Navy Yard.
40 NARG 74-2.
41 ORN Series 1, Volume 19, pp. 364–368.
42 NARG 74-158, Volume 9.
43 NARG 74-18.
44 NARG 74-18, letter from Sanford to Harwood dated July 12.
45 NARG 74-145.
46 NARG 74-5 and 156-7.
47 *Ibid.*
48 NARG 74-3, Philadelphia Navy Yard and ORN Series 1, Volume 23, pp. 418–419.
49 NARG 24, deck logs of the USS *Constellation* and *Galena*.
50 ORN Series 1, Volume 19, pp. 396–398.
51 NARG 74-158, Volume 9 and 74-22.
52 NARG 74-19, letters from the Western Flotilla dated November 13 and RG 156-7.
53 NARG 74-5.
54 NARG 74-22, Reynolds bill dated October 1, 1862.
55 *Ibid.*
56 NARG 24, deck logs of the *Minnesota* and *Constellation*.
57 ORN Series 1, Volume 18, pp. 169–170.

Chapter 5

1 ORN Series 1, Volume 24, pp. 325–326, 621 and Volume 25, p. 208.
2 ORN Series 1, Volume 24, p. 453.
3 NARG 24, USS *Champion* dated July 4, 1863.
4 NARG 156-7.
5 NARG 74-19, letters from Western Flotilla dated March 11 and May 1, 1863.
6 NARG 74-3, letters dated March 17 from the Philadelphia Navy Yard.
7 NARG 74-19, letter dated February 11 from the Western Flotilla.
8 NARG 24, deck logs of the ships named.
9 NARG 74-3, letters from Philadelphia Navy Yard.
10 NARG 24, deck logs of the *Mound City*, *Benton* and *Conestoga*.
11 NARG 74-18, Porter to Dahlgren June 12, 1863.
12 NARG 74-19, Reports from Western Flotilla for July, August and September.
13 *Ibid.*
14 ORN Series 1, Volume 5, pp. 332–345.
15 NARG 74-19, letter from Washington Navy Yard dated January 1, 1863.
16 ORN Series 1, Volume 14, pp. 278–279 and 696.
17 Ex. Doc. No.16-2, 39th Congress (December 31, 1866), p. 24.
18 Silverstone, Paul H., *Warships of the Civil War Navies*, Naval Institute Press, Annapolis, Maryland, 1989, p. 203.
19 NARG 74-19, letters dated April 27 and July 20 from Mare Island.
20 *Ibid.*, dated July 1863.
21 NARG 74-3, letters to the Washington Navy Yard.
22 NARG 74-5.
23 NARG 74-2.
24 NARG 74-22.
25 NARG 74-22, Warner to Dahlgren of June 25.
26 NARG 74-3, letter to Washington Navy Yard dated June 25, 1863.
27 NARG 74-3, letters dated August 4 and August 11 to Philadelphia, NARG 74-2.
28 NARG 74-3, letters from both Philadelphia and Washington.
29 NARG 74-158, Volume 9.
30 NARG 74-18, letter dated April 25, 1863.
31 NARG 74-18, letter dated June 23, 1863.
32 ORN Series 1, Volume 13, p. 801 and NARG 74-19, Boston Navy Yard.
33 NARG 74-19, New York letter dated November 18, 1863.
34 ORN Series 1, Volume 15, p. 72 and NARG 24 deck log USS *Catskill*.
35 NARG 74-18.
36 ORN Series 1, Volume 20, pp. 167–169.
37 NARG 24, deck logs of the *New Ironsides* dated April 6, 1865 and Paul H. Silverstone *op. cit.*, p. 15.
38 NARG 74-3, letters to the Washington Navy Yard.
39 NARG 74-19, letters from the Washington Navy Yard.
40 ORN Series 1, Volume 5, pp. 605–606.
41 NARG 74-18, letter dated November 4, 1864.
42 NARG 74-22, letter from Spencer dated August 17, 1863.

43 *Ibid.*, letter dated September 7, 1863.
44 NARG 74-19, Box 193, letters from the Washington Navy Yard dated October 10, 1863.
45 NARG 24, deck logs of USS *Yankee* dated November 17, 1863.
46 ORN Series 1, Volume 15, pp. 148–149.
47 NARG 127-129.
48 NARG 74-158, Volumes 2 and 9.
49 ORN Series 1, Volume 14, pp. 622–625.
50 *Ibid.*, pp. 620 and 632–633, plus NARG 74-18.
51 NARG 74-19, Box 192 letters from Washington Navy Yard.
52 NARG 74-2.
53 NARG 74-158, Volume 9.
54 ORN Series 1, Volume 9, pp. 166–169.
55 NARG 74-19, letters from Boston Navy Yard.
56 NARG 74-5.

Chapter 6

1 ORN Series 1, Volume 21, p. 820.
2 NARG 74-19, Report of April 20, 1864, from the New York Navy Yard.
3 ORN Series 1, Volume 21, p. 553.
4 NARG 24, deck logs of the USS *Richmond* dated August 6, 1864.
5 ORN Series 1, Volume 10, pp. 202–206.
6 *Ibid.*, pp. 611–620.
7 Roske, Ralph J. and Charles Van Doren, *Lincoln Commando: The Biography of Commander W.B. Cushing*, USN, Harper Brothers, New York, 1957.
8 NARG 74-19, reports from the various navy yards.
9 Ordnance Instructions, Appendix D, Table of Allowance of Ordnance Equipment and Stores, Washington, GPO, 1864.
10 NARG 74-19, letters from Boston.
11 NARG 127-129, dated March 26 and 27, 1864.
12 Inspection Circular 1864.
13 NARG 156-3.
14 NARG 74-18, June 1864.
15 NARG 24, deck log of the USS *Pittsburg* dated July 5 and the deck logs of the *Winnebago* dated May 5.
16 NARG 74-18.
17 NARG 24, deck log of the *Yankee* dated May 3, 1864.
18 ORN Series 1, Volume 10, p. 388.
19 NARG 74-18.
20 NARG 127-129.
21 Heinl, Colonel Robert Debs, Jr., USMC, *Soldiers of the Sea, The United States Marine Corps 1775–1962*, The Nautical & Aviation Publishing Co. of America, Inc., Baltimore, Md., 1991, pp. 85 and 98.
22 NARG 74-19, letters from Philadelphia dated June 8, 1864.
23 ORN Series 1, Volume 10, pp. 539–541.
24 ORN Series 1, Volume 26, pp. 542–548.
25 NARG 74-19, letter from New York dated January 21, 1864.
26 NARG 74-19, letters from Washington dated April 9 and 19.
27 NARG 74-158, Volume 9.
28 ORN Series 1, Volume 9, pp. 748–749 and Volume 11, pp. 18–19.
29 *Ibid.*, Series 1, Volume 16, pp. 67, 87, 99–102.
30 *Ibid.*, Series 1, Volume 21, pp. 248–249.
31 NARG 24, deck log dated April 14, 1864, USS *Kearsage*.
32 Silverstone, Paul H., *Warships of the Civil War Navies*, Naval Institute Press, Annapolis, Md., 1989, p. 38.
33 NARG 74-158, Volume 9.
34 NARG 74-19, letter dated June 22, 1864, from the Philadelphia Navy Yard.
35 *Ibid.*, letters from Mare Island.
36 NARG 24, deck logs of the *Malvern* dated May 20, 1864.
37 ORN Series 1, Volume 10, p. 63 and NARG 74-18. and 24 deck logs *Meteor* dated May 12, 1864.
38 *Ibid.*, Series 1, Volume 15, pp. 342–345.
39 NARG 74-19, letter from the Western Flotilla of June 25, 1864.
40 NARG 74-18.
41 ORN Series 1, Volume 15, pp. 484–486.
42 NARG 24, deck logs of the USS *Pittsburg* and the *Lafayette*.
43 NARG 74-18.
44 NARG 24, deck logs of the *Ella, Fuchsia* and *Coeur de Lion*.
45 NARG 74-19, letter from New York Navy Yard.
46 *Ibid.*
47 NARG 24, deck logs of the USS *Choctaw*.
48 NARG 74-19.
49 *Ibid.*, letters from Philadelphia.
50 NARG 24, deck logs of the *Winnebago*.
51 Silverstone, Paul H., op. cit., pp. 149.
52 NARG 74-19, letter from Washington.
53 *Ibid.*
54 NARG 74-148.
55 NARG 74-5.
56 *Ibid.*
57 NARG 74-18, Volume 65.
58 NARG 24, deck logs of the *Paul Jones*.
59 NARG 127-129.

Chapter 7

1 ORN Series 1, Volume 11, p. 427.
2 *Ibid.*, p. 446.
3 *Ibid.*, p. 514.
4 *Ibid.*, p. 543 and NARG 24 ship logs of the *Ticonderoga* dated January 11, 1865.
5 *Ibid.*, p. 498 and NARG 74-18, Volume 65.
6 *Ibid.*, p. 578.
7 *Ibid.*, p. 444.
8 *Ibid.*, p. 435.
9 NARG 74-18, and NARG 24 various ship logs and ORN.
10 NARG 24, Ship logs.
11 NARG 74-18, date January 3 from the *Vincennes* and NARG 24 ship logs from the *Silver Cloud* and the *Kickapoo*.
12 NARG 74-18, Volume 64.
13 NARG 127-134.
14 NARG 127-129.
15 ORN Series 1, Volume 11, p. 516.
16 NARG 74-18, and entry 19 letters from Philadelphia Navy Yard.
17 NARG 24, ship logs of the *Chillicothe*.
18 NARG 74-18, Box 22 dated April 4, 1865.
19 Musicant, Ivan, *Divided Waters — Naval History of the Civil War*, Harper Collins Publishers, New York, 1995, p. 431.
20 NARG 74-19, letters from Mare Island.
21 NARG 74-19, letters from Boston of August 26, 1865.
22 NARG 74-18, box 22, letter of February 15, 1865.
23 NARG 24, deck logs USS *Choctaw*.
24 NARG 74-158.
25 NARG, letters from New York and Philadelphia Navy Yards.
26 NARG 74-18.
27 ORN Series 1, Volume 12, pp. 90–91.
28 NARG 24, deck logs of the USS *Brooklyn*.
29 NARG 74-18, Volume 68, and 74-158, Volume 2.
30 NARG 24, log books of the USS *Oriole* dated March 22, 1865.
31 NARG 127-129.
32 ORN Series 1, Volume 16, pp. 154, 267, 352; Volume 17, p. 859 and Volume 27, p. 206.
33 NARG 74-18, and various ship logs.
34 NARG 74-18, Volume 69.
35 NARG *Ibid.*, Volume 70.
36 NARG 74-19, letters from Western Flotilla.
37 NARG 127-134.
38 Urick, William J., III, *Small Arms Development In The United States Navy*, "The Remington Rolling Block Action 1865–1880," *The Gun Report*, January 1995, p. 23.
39 Schulimson, Jack, *The Marine Corps Search For a Mission*, University Press of Kansas, Lawrence, Kansas, 1993, p. 162.
40 39th Congress, 2nd Session, House of Representatives, Ex. Document No. 16.

Bibliography

Coates, Earl, J. and John D. McAulay, *Civil War Sharps Carbines and Rifles*, Thomas Publications, Gettysburg, PA, 1996.

Civil War Naval Chronology 1861–1865, Naval History Division Navy Department, Washington, 1971, Executive House Document 16-2, 39th Congress, 2nd Session.

Hays, Warren H., "More on Plymouth Rifles," *The Gun Report*, January 1965.

Heinl, Robert Debs, Col. USMC, *Soldiers of the Sea the United States Marine Corps 1775–1962*, The Nautical and Aviation Publishing Co. of America, Inc., Baltimore, MD, 1991.

Hickox, Ron G., *Collector's Guide to Ames U.S. Contract Military Edge Weapon, 1832–1906*, Pioneer Press, Union City, TN, 1992.

Hull, Edward A., *The Burnside Breech Loading Carbines*, Man at Arms Monograph Series, Andrew Mowbray Publishers, Inc., Lincoln, RI, 1986; "Perry Carbines," *Man at Arms*, March/April 1986.

Kimbrough, Robert E., *The Gun Collector Magazine*, Vol. 33, September 1950.

Lederer, P.S., "How the Navy Drifted into Buying Navies," *American Rifleman*, March 1973.

Lindert, A.W., "U.S. Naval Martial Sidearms 1775–1875," *The Gun Report*, August and September 1971; May 1972; September, October, November 1973; "The Colt Model 1851 Navy 'Navy Re-Appraised,' " *The Gun Report*, October 1988.

Love, Robert W., Jr., *History of the U.S. Navy Vol. One: 1775–1941*, Stackpole Books, Harrisburg, PA, 1992.

Madaus, Howard Michael, Part I, "The Percussion Martial Longarms of Eli Whitney, Jr.," *Armax*, Vol. 2, No. 1, The Buffalo Bill Historical Center, Cody, WY, 1988.

Marcot, Roy M., *Spencer Repeating Firearms*, Northwood Heritage Press, Irvine, CA, 1983.

McAulay, John D., *Civil War Breechloading Rifles*, Andrew Mowbray, Inc., Lincoln, RI, 1987; *Civil War Carbines Vol. II, The Early Years*, Andrew Mowbray, Inc., Lincoln, RI, 1991; *Civil War Pistols*, Andrew Mowbray, Inc., Lincoln, RI, 1992.

Miller, Francis Trevlyan, *The Photographic History of the Civil War — The Navies*, Castle Books, NY, 1957.

Musicant, Ivan, *Divided Waters — The Naval History of the Civil War*, Harper Collins Publishers, NY, 1995.

Nalty, Bernard C., "United States Marines at Harpers Ferry and in the Civil War," History and Museums Division, Headquarters U.S. Marine Corps, Washington, D.C., 1983.

Official Records of the Union and Confederate Navies in the War of the Rebellion, GPO, 1927.

Ordnance Instructions, Table of Allowances of Ordnance Equipment and Stores, C. Alexander, Printer, Washington, 1852.

Ordnance Instructions, Appendix D, Table of Allowance of Ordnance Equipment and Stores, GPO, 1864.

Pachanian, Sam, "U.S. Navy Markings and Their Variations on Colts 1851 and 1861 Navy Model Revolvers, Percussion and Conversion," *The American Society of Arms Collectors Bulletin #65*, September 4–8, 1991.

Rankin, Robert H., Col. USMC (Ret.), *Small Arms of the Sea Service*, N. Flayderman & Co., New Milford, CT, 1972.

Reed, Rowena, *Combined Operations in the Civil War*, Naval Institute Press, Annapolis, MD, 1978.

Reilly, Robert M., *United States Military Small Arms 1816–1865*, The Eagle Press Inc., Baton Rouge, LA, 1970.

Roske, Ralph J. and Charles Van Doren, *Lincoln's Commando — The Biography of Commander W.B. Cushing, USN*, Harper and Bros., NY, 1957.

Schmidt, Peter A., *Hall's Military Breechloaders*, Andrew Mowbray Publishers, Inc., Lincoln, RI, 1996.

Schneller, Robert J. Jr., *A Quest for Glory — A Biography of Rear Admiral John A. Dahlgren*, Naval Institution Press, Annapolis, MD, 1996.

Senate Executive Document, 33rd Congress, 1st Session, Vol. 3, 1853–1854.

Shulimson, Jack, *The Marine Corps' Search for a Mission, 1880–1898*, University Press of Kansas, Lawrence, KS, 1993.

Silverstone, Paul H., *Warships of the Civil War Navies*, Naval Institute Press, Annapolis, MD, 1989.

Sullivan, David, "Uncommon Soldiers," *Military Images*, September/October 1990.

Todd, Frederick, *American Military Equipage 1851–1872, Vol. 1*, Charles Scribner's Sons, NY, 1980.

The Union Defense Committee of the City of New York, Minutes, Reports, and Correspondence, The Union Defense Committee, NY, 1885.

Urick, William J. III, *Small Arms Development in the United States Navy — The Remington Rolling Block Action 1865–1880*, The Gun Report, January 1995.

Winter, Fredrick R., *U.S. Naval Handguns 1808–1911*, Andrew Mowbray Publishers, Inc., Lincoln, RI, 1990.

Wise, Stephen R., *Lifeline of the Confederacy Blockade Running During the Civil War*, University of South Carolina Press, Columbia, SC, 1988.

National Archives
Record Group #24
List of Logbooks of U.S. Navy Ships 1801–1947

Abeona	*Commodore Morris*	*General Bragg*	*Little Ada*	*Niagara*	*Sassacus*
Adirondack	*Commodore Perry*	*General Lyon*	*Little Rebel*	*Nymph*	*Selma*
Agamenticus	*Commodore Read*	*General Price*	*Louisville*	*Octorara*	*Seminole*
Agawam	*Conemaugh*	*General Sherman*	*Malvern*	*Ohio*	*Shenandoah*
Alabama (u)	*Conestoga*	*Gertrude*	*Manhattan*	*Oriole*	*Silver Cloud*
Atlanta	*Congress*	*Gettysburg*	*Maratanza*	*Owasco*	*Silver Lake*
Avenger	*Constellation*	*Harcourt*	*Marblehead*	*Passaic*	*Sophronia*
Banshee	*Constitution*	*Hartford*	*Marmora*	*Patapsco*	*South Carolina*
Bat	*Cricket*	*Harvest Moon*	*Mendota*	*Paul Johns*	*Stepping Stone*
Benton	*Cumberland*	*Hastings*	*Merrimack*	*Paw Paw*	*St. Louis*
Brooklyn	*Currituck*	*Hunchback*	*Metacomet*	*Pawtuxet*	*St. Mary's*
Canonicus	*Cyane*	*Huron*	*Meteor*	*Pembina*	*Supply*
Carondelet	*Dacotah*	*Independence*	*Michigan*	*Pensacola*	*Susquehanna*
Catskill	*Dai-Ching*	*Iroquois*	*Minnesota*	*Perry*	*Teaser*
Champion	*Dragon*	*Itasca*	*Mississippi*	*Pittsburg*	*Ticonderoga*
Chenango	*Eastport*	*Iuka*	*Mist*	*Plymouth*	*Tristram Shandy*
Cherokee	*Elk*	*John P. Kennedy*	*Moccasin*	*Porpoise*	*Tuscumbia*
Chickasaw	*Ella*	*Juliet*	*Monadnock*	*Portsmouth*	*Tyler*
Chillicothe	*Essex*	*Kanawha*	*Mound City*	*Powhatan*	*Vandalia*
Choctaw	*Exchange*	*Katahdin*	*Mingoe*	*Reindeer*	*Vermont*
Cincinnati	*Fairplay*	*Kearsarge*	*Nahant*	*Richmond*	*Vincennes*
Clyde	*Fawn*	*Kenwood*	*Nansemond*	*Roanoke*	*Wabash*
Coeur de Lion	*Fenimore Cooper*	*Kickapoo*	*Nantucket*	*Romeo*	*Wachusett*
Collier	*Forest Rose*	*Lafayette*	*Naumkeag*	*Sabine*	*Wando*
Colorado	*Fuchsia*	*Lancaster*	*New Era*	*Saco*	*Water Witch*
Colossus	*Galena*	*Levant*	*New Ironsides*	*San Jacinto*	*Winnebago*
Commodore Hull	*Gamage*	*Linda (Delta)*	*Niad*	*Saratoga*	*Wilderness*
					Yankee

Record Group #45
Collection of the Office of Naval Records and Library

Entry
- 110 Appendix C, Log of the *Monitor*
- 464 Subject File CA 1775–1900 Appendix F

Record Group #74
Record of the Bureau of Ornance

- 1 Letters Sent to the Secretary of the Navy 1842–82
- 3 Letters Sent to the Navy Yards 1842–84
- 5 Miscellaneous Letters Sent 1842–83
- 6 Letters and Telegrams Sent 1861–1911
- 18 Letters Received from Naval Officers 1842–84
- 19 Letters Received from Navy Yards 1842–84
- 22 Miscellaneous Letters Received 1842–84
- 145 Correspondence Regarding the Examination of Inventions 1851–80
- 158 Record of Accounts Approved for Payment 1842–1903
- 165 Record of Ordnance Contracts 1861
- 201 Correspondence and Reports #5 and #7

Record Group #127
Records of the United States Marine Corps

Entry
- 4 Letters Sent by the Commandant 1798–1884
- 125 Letters Sent by the Quartermaster — Various Periods
- 129 Press Copies of Letters Sent by Quartermaster 1860–1903
- 134 Letters Received by Quartermaster 1861–1872

Record Group #156
Records of the Chief of Ordnance

Entry
- 3 Miscellaneous Letters Sent 1812–189
- 21 Letters Received 1812–94

Index

A

Abbott, Capt., 17
Abeona, 165, 178
Acacia, 165
Accessory Transit Company, 28
Ada, 163
Adams, John Q., 71
Adamson, Pvt. B., 22
Adirondack, 165, 178
Adolph Hugel, 86
Agamenticus, 165, 178
Agawam, 123–125, 141, 165, 178
Aiken, Gov. (SC), 65
Alabama, 107, 135, 164, 165, 178
Albany, 24, 54, 55
Albemarle, 123, 124, 134, 164
Aleutian Islands, 21
Alexandria, Egypt, 25
Allegheny, 45
Allegheny Arsenal, 38, 44, 129
Allen & Wheelock, 94
Alvarado, 61
American Volunteer Company, 15
Ames, 37, 55, 72, 73, 78, 82, 86, 99, 100, 115, 142, 153, 160
Ames Bayonets, 36, 72, 73, 82
Ames Cutlasses, 86–88, 95, 99, 100, 102, 103, 105, 106, 108, 109, 111, 113, 115, 118, 123–125, 135, 142, 154, 156–158, 160
Ames Model 1842 Boxlock Pistol, 28, 29
Ames Swords, 19, 32, 55, 78, 153
Ames, T.J., 31
Ammunition, 15–18, 21, 22, 28, 33, 40, 42, 44, 45, 46, 67, 69, 87, 88, 91, 94, 100, 103, 105, 106, 108, 111, 113, 119, 130, 132, 134, 137–139, 144, 152
Amphibious Landing, 59, 69
Anaconda Plan, 59
Anacostia, 72, 163, 165
William G. Anderson, 74, 111, 172
Andersonville, 137
Ariel, 165
Aries, 165
Arkansas, 85
Arletta, 165
Aroostook, 165
Arthur, 90, 165
Artillery Swords, 14, 17, 74, 85, 98, 100
Ascutney, 133, 165
Aston Pistols, 28, 95, 153
Atlanta, 52, 105, 106, 165, 178
Atlantic Blockading Squadron, 35, 64, 65, 67, 68, 76, 87, 88, 91, 100, 107, 108, 118, 136, 141, 142, 154, 156
Augusta, 87, 90, 156, 165
Austrian Rifles, 163
Avenger, 133, 165, 178

B

Back River, 138
Badger, Lt. Cmdr. Oscar C., 95, 98, 99, 103
Baltimore, 113, 165
Baltimore, Maryland, 69, 93, 97, 106, 108, 118, 129, 153
Banshee, 153, 165, 178
Baron deKalb, 74, 101, 165
Barrett, Lt. Cmdr. Edward, 155
Barron, Samuel, 41
Bat, 165
Battle Axe Frogs, 126
Battle Axes, 19, 20, 27, 32, 34, 35, 45, 47, 50, 52, 53, 60, 63, 81, 86, 93, 100, 106, 108, 119, 123–126, 136, 141, 150, 152, 156, 158
Bay of Panama, 132
Bayon Gara, Louisiana, 152
Bayonets, 13, 16, 18–20, 29, 36, 37, 39, 45, 47, 53, 66, 71–73, 81, 82, 87–89, 91, 92, 99, 103, 107, 108, 110, 111, 114, 123, 129, 131–133, 138, 142, 144, 146, 156, 158, 163
Bayonet Belts, 54, 116
Bayonet Frogs, 128
Bayonet Scabbards, 54, 79, 98, 116, 128, 148

Beals Revolvers, 94, 95, 118
Beauregard, 165
Bell, George, 74
Bell, Joseph T., 31
Belts, 16, 22, 29, 82, 117, 139
   Bayonet, 116
   Cartridge Box, 31, 114, 128, 148, 150
   Pistol, 20
   Sword, 31, 153
   Waist, 85, 126, 128, 148, 150
Bent & Bush, 98, 115, 142, 154
Benton, 94, 101, 103, 104, 156, 157, 163, 165, 178
Bering Strait, 21
Beta, 165
Blenville, 165
Black Hawk, 104, 132, 137, 165
Blakely River, 150
Blockade, 59–62, 84, 87, 88, 94, 118, 121, 142
Blunderbusses, 19, 34
Boarding Pikes, 16, 19, 20, 52, 53, 60, 63, 74, 81, 85, 86, 88, 91, 98, 99, 104–106, 113, 119, 123–125, 129, 135, 136, 154, 158
Boarding Pistols, 86, 90, 91, 104, 105, 140, 156
Boarding Swords, 63
Bohio, 165
Booth, John Wilkes, 151
Boston, Massachusetts, 21, 24, 26, 27, 32, 42, 47, 48, 50–52, 55, 61, 67, 69, 72, 74, 92, 93, 98, 103, 107, 108, 113, 115, 118, 126, 128, 129, 132–134, 136, 140, 142, 146, 154, 163
Boston Navy Yard, 22, 25, 31, 32, 37, 43, 50, 60, 61, 68, 72, 73, 76, 78, 82, 90, 92, 93, 95, 106, 111, 118, 126, 127, 135, 147
Bowie Knife Pistols, 13
Bowie Knives, 35, 36, 43, 75, 81, 82, 115, 142, 156, 158
Boxlock Pistol, 28, 29
Boxer, 165
Boyd, Lt. William, 42
Brandywine, 165
Braun, Pvt. Henry L., 22
Breast Plates, 89, 116
Breese, Lt. Cmdr. Kidder R., 144
Brilliant, 165
Brooklyn, 59, 71, 90, 153, 165
Brooklyn Navy Yard, 20, 42, 47, 51, 84, 109, 128, 132, 148
Brooklyn, New York, 31
Brown, John, 33, 34
Brown, Lt. Isaac, 85
Bull Run, 62, 132
Burnside Rifles, 49, 50

C

Cadet Muskets, 1859 Pattern, 22, 87
Cairo, 90, 94, 165, 166
Cairo, Illinois, 87, 90, 94, 95, 103–105, 119, 128, 154, 157
Calcasieu Pass, Louisiana, 134
Caledonia, 52, 55
Calypso, 166
Cambridge, 163, 166
Cannon, 63, 127
Canonicus, 124, 134, 141, 166, 178
Canteens, 67, 89, 98, 116, 128, 148
Cap Boxes, 123
Cap Pouches, 89, 107, 116, 128, 148
Cape Fear River, 124
Carbine Ball Cartridges, 22
Carondelet, 85, 94, 101, 166, 178
Carrabasset, 166
Cartridge Box Belts, 31, 54, 128, 148
Cartridge Box Plates, 116
Cartridge Boxes, 16, 17, 21, 22, 29, 31, 32, 40, 54, 79, 82, 89, 98, 103, 107, 109, 111, 114–116, 123, 126–129, 132, 136, 137, 139, 140, 142, 146, 148, 150, 151, 160, 163
Cartridges, 14, 17, 22, 24, 25, 28, 33, 39, 40, 42–44, 48, 51, 52, 60, 62, 65, 68, 69, 71, 87, 91–93, 95, 99, 103, 105–107, 113, 114, 117–120, 123, 125, 129, 130, 132, 134–142, 146, 150, 152, 156, 162
Casco, 153, 166
Catskill, 111, 112, 155, 166, 178
Cavalry, 1st U.S., 33
Cayuga, 166
Ceder, James, 111
Champion, 102, 166, 178
Charleston and Savannah Railroad, 134
Charlestown, Massachusetts, 31
Chase, Anthony, 93, 94
Chauncey, Capt. John S., 92
Chenango, 148, 156, 166, 178
Cherbourg, France, 135
Cherokee, 145, 166, 178
Chickasaw, 166, 178
Chicopee, 166
Chicopee, Massachusetts, 37, 50, 54, 55, 72, 82
Chillicothe, 146, 150, 166
Chimo, 166
China, 15–18, 24, 39, 40, 42, 50
Chippewa, 145, 163, 166
Choctaw, 103, 140, 152, 163, 166
Chocura, 166
Church, Lt. Frank, 132
Cimarron, 166
Cincinnati, 74, 94, 103, 104, 166, 178
Cincinnati, Ohio, 73, 95
Circassian, 167
Clarendon, Arkansas, 147
Cleaning Rods, 92
Clifford, Sgt. Thomas, 125
Clove, Henry W., 36
Clyde, 167, 178
Coes, Isaac, 22
Coeur de Lion, 114, 139, 167
Coffman, Inspector John M., 135
Cohen, Capt. D.M., 132
Collier, 167, 178
Collins & Co., 108
Colorado, 45, 55, 65, 71, 157, 158, 167
Colossus, 146, 154, 167
Colt Dragoons, 30
Colt New Model Holster Revolvers, 74
Colt Revolvers, 16–18, 20, 21, 29, 30, 34, 40, 41, 47, 48, 50–53, 55, 56, 60, 61, 68, 71, 74, 84–88, 93–95, 99, 105, 106, 111, 113, 115, 117, 118, 124, 129, 135, 142, 145, 150, 153, 156, 157, 163, 164
Colt Revolving Rifles, 49, 130
Colt Rifles, 49, 50, 160
Colt, Samuel, 15
Columbia, 22, 55
Columbine, 167
Commodore Hull, 167
Commodore McDonough, 167
Commodore Morris, 167
Commodore Perry, 88, 167
Commodore Read, 114, 139, 167
Conemaugh, 133, 167
Conestoga, 103, 167
Congress, 24, 27, 42, 44, 45, 55, 83, 163, 167
Connecticut, 167
Constellation, 44, 68, 97, 100, 167
Constitution, 23, 27, 28, 55, 76
Cooper Rifle, 19
Cornubia, 124, 167
Corpus Christi, Texas, 98
Corrotoman Creek, 163
Corwin, 167
Covington, Capt., 132
C.P. Williams, 167
Craig, Col. H.K., 37, 38, 43–45
Cricket, 167
Crusader, 48, 52, 55, 167
Crystal River, 107
Cumberland, 22, 45, 50, 56, 83, 163
Currituck, 115, 130, 139, 167
Cushing, William Barker, 123, 124, 164
Cutlasses, 16, 19, 20, 28, 29, 34, 52, 55, 59, 63, 74, 78, 87, 88, 90, 91, 98–100, 106, 108, 87, 91–93, 95, 99, 103, 105–107, 113, 114, 117–120, 123, 125, 129, 130, 132, 134–142, 146, 150, 152, 156, 162

110, 119, 123, 126, 129, 135, 142, 144, 145, 153–158, 163, 164
Cyane, 27, 28, 45, 56, 106, 167

D

Dacotah, 137, 167
Dahlgren, 25, 35–38, 46, 47, 53, 69, 72, 76, 77, 81, 84, 90, 104, 107, 109, 110, 115, 117, 119, 134, 138, 142, 154
Dahlgren Bowie Knife, 75, 82
Dahlgren, John, 34
Dai-Ching, 167
Dale, 65, 106, 133, 167
Dan Smith, 86, 167
Darey, James, 23
Darien, Georgia, 138
Dart, 167
David, 111
Dawn, 74, 167
Dawson, L.L., 144
Daylight, 90, 167
DeSoto, 76, 88, 156, 167
Decatur, 40, 56
Delta, 167
Dictator, 167
Dingee, Henry A., 54, 79, 98
Dobbin, James, 30
Dolphin, 56
Don, 133, 167
Doriss, Sgt. Bernard, 15, 16
Dragon, 114, 115, 139
Drayton, Capt., 139
Drewry's Bluff, 96
Drums, 79, 107
DuPont, Rear Adm., 87
DuPont, Samuel F., 67
Dyer, Brig. Gen. A.B., 147

E

E.B. Hale, 167
East China Sea, 42
East Gulf Blockading Squadron, 100, 154
East India Squadron, 13, 27
Eastman, A.M., 71
Eastman, T.W., 138
Eastport, 167
Edisto River, 65
Elgin Cutlass Pistols, 13
Elk, 137, 167
Ella, 114, 133, 138, 139, 167
Ellen, 87, 167
Ellet Marine Brigade, 156
Ellis, 167
Emperor of Japan, 17
Empire Tool Co., 81
Enfield, 85, 90, 105, 124, 129
Enfield Artillery Carbines, 158
Enfield Rifles, 60, 61, 65, 84, 86, 87, 90, 91, 101–106, 110, 124, 129, 132, 133, 140, 142, 145, 147, 152, 156–158, 160, 163–172
England, 50
Erie, Pennsylvania, 129, 137, 141
Essex, 74, 94, 167
Ethan Allen, 167
Eureka, 167
Eutaw, 108, 114, 120, 152, 167
Evans, Rodney R., 145
Exchange, 147, 167

F

Fagan, 1st Lt. Lewis, 144, 148
Fairplay, 167
Fairy, 167
Farrallones, 133, 167
Farragut, Rear Adm. David, 25, 90, 92, 93, 100, 111, 118, 120, 121, 123, 139
Fawn, 103, 167
Fencing Swords, 153
Fenimore Cooper, 20, 28, 56, 178
Fernandina, 167
Field Pieces, 28
Fife, 79, 107

Fillmore, President, 17
Fingal, 60, 61
First Model Maynard Carbines, 69
Flag, 167
Flambeau, 133, 167
Flint, 21, 56
Flintlock Pistols, 61, 106, 129
Flintlocks, 158
Florida, 167
Flour Bluffs, Texas, 90
Flusser, Lt., 61
Foote, A.H., 40
Forest Rose, 103, 167
Fort Clark, 69
Fort Fisher, 113, 118, 124, 142–145, 148, 154
Fort Hatteras, 69
Fort Henry, 107, 167
Fort Hindman, 167
Fort Jackson, 88
Fort Jackson, 145, 156, 163, 167
Fort Monroe, 93, 95, 118
Fort Morgan, 121
Fort Moultrie, 137
Fort Sumter, 59, 111, 117, 118, 137, 142, 145, 154
Fowling Pieces, 20
Fox, Gustavas, 113
France, 50
Frankford Arsenal, 14, 36, 39, 40, 129
Franklin Expedition, 19
Freeborn, 167
Fremont, John C., 99
Frogs, 16, 43, 82, 89, 114, 116, 122, 126, 128, 142, 148, 163
Fuchsia, 114, 133, 139, 167
Fulton, 48, 52, 56

G

Galatea, 167
Galena, 84, 95–97, 167
Gallager Carbine, 156
Gamage, 146, 154, 167
Gamma, 167
Gardner, 130
Gaylord, Emerson, 54
Gem of the Sea, 163, 167
General Bragg, 146, 167
General Lyon, 167
General Price, 103, 167
General Rusk, 74
General Sherman, 167
Genesee, 90, 167
George Mangham, 86, 167
George Washington, 90, 167
Georgetown, South Carolina, 150
Georgia, 5th Infantry, 134
Germantown, 42
Gettysburg, 167
Gladiator, 60, 61
Glasgow, 167
Glenney, Daniel W., 132
Glide, 167
Goldsborough, Lt., 65, 67, 74
Good, Sgt. Major Henry, 63
Gosport Navy Yard, 59
Gosport, Virginia, 31
Governor, 67
Governor Buckingham, 167
Grand Gulf, 167
Grand Gulf, Mississippi, 104, 132, 138
Granite City, 134
Grant, Gen. U.S., 101, 104, 151
Great Western, 168
Greene, First Lt. Israel, 33
Greene, Samuel D., 84
Greenville, North Carolina, 91
Greytown, Nicaragua, 27, 28, 48
Griffin, Charles, 62
Griffith, John H., 92, 107
Guest, Lt., 18
Gunpowder, 60

H

Hagner, Maj., 39
Haiti, 106
Hall Carbines, 13, 18, 25, 34, 39, 56, 63, 87, 106, 157
Hall Rifles, 14, 17–19, 22, 24, 25
Halsey, James A., 22
Hampton Roads, Virginia, 65, 67, 72, 76, 83, 84, 134, 151
Harcourt, 168
Harding, Maj. Edward, 22
Harpers Ferry, 18, 33, 36–40, 42, 44, 45, 89, 129, 130, 156, 163
Harriet Lane, 52, 69, 168
Harris, Col. John, 33, 43–45, 59, 62, 66, 68, 132
Hartford, 71, 78, 98, 100, 121, 122, 138, 139, 168, 178
Hartford, Connecticut, 108
Harvest Moon, 129, 133, 142, 168
Harwood, Capt. Andrew A., 60, 69, 87, 114
Hastings, 168
Hatchets, 32
Hatteras, 168
Haversacks, 62, 67, 89, 98, 116, 128, 148
Hawaii, 27, 42, 47, 48
Hebe, 118
Henderson, Archibald, 33, 42, 43, 55
Henderson, Charles, 23
Henderson, James L., 51
Hendrick Hudson, 110, 168
Henry Janes, 90, 168
Henry Rifle, 19
Hetzel, 168
Hitchcock, Capt. 65, 76
Hitchcock, Lt. Robert B., 31
Hitchcock, 2nd Lt. Robert E., 62
Hoftman, William, 124
Hollins, George, 27, 28
Holsters, 140, 142
Home Guard, 132
Honduras, 48, 168
Hong Kong, 15, 21, 22, 29
Hopkins, Townsend, 140
Horace Beals, 168
Horstmann Bros. & Co., 54, 55, 79
House of Russel & Co., 15
Howitzers, 115, 124, 134
Hunchback, 168, 178
Huntington, Lt. Robert W., 62, 63, 67
Huron, 87, 145, 168
Hurricane Island, Louisiana, 138
Hydrangea, 124, 168

I

Ice Boat, 168
Illinois, 20th Infantry, 101
Illinois, 39th Infantry, 101
Illinois, 101st Infantry, 101
Independence, 50, 56
Indiana, 145
Indianola, 95, 168
Ingraham, Duncan N., 43
Iosco, 145, 163, 168
Iroquois, 44, 45, 46, 56, 73, 133, 168
Itasca, 168
Iuka, 168

J

J.C. Kuhn, 168
Jacob Bell, 133, 168
James Alger, 76, 168
James River, 132, 137, 152
James River Fleet, 106
Jamestown, 27, 56, 61, 71, 168
Japan, 13, 16, 17, 18, 25, 29, 43, 59
Jason, 172
Jeffers, William, 141
Jefferson Barracks, Missouri, 156
Jefferson Davis, 61
Jenks, 15, 19, 25, 26, 29, 39, 45, 47, 69

Index

Jenks Carbines, 13, 21, 25–28, 34, 41, 45–48, 52, 55, 56, 60, 71, 87, 106, 160
Jenks Long Carbines, 70
Jenks Old Style, 70
Jenks Rifles, 26, 60
Jenks-Merrill Carbines, 46, 51, 69, 70, 129, 137
John Adams, 27, 40, 44, 56, 168
John Griffith, 168
John Hancock, 20, 56
John Lockwood, 168
John P. Jackson, 156, 168
John P. Kennedy, 20, 29, 56
Johnson and Dow, 118
Johnson's Island, 129
Johnson, Joseph, 97
Jones, 130
Jones, James, 69
Joslyn Revolver, 76, 114, 153
Joslyn Rifles, 49, 71, 100, 160
Jouett, Lt. James, E., 74
Juliet, 168
Juniata, 150, 168

K

Kanawha, 168
Kansas, 145, 163, 165, 168
Katahdin, 168
Kearsarge, 73, 81, 93, 135, 168
Kelly, Cmdr. John, 18
Kennebec, 92, 168
Kensington, 168
Kentucky, State of, 102
Kentucky Rifles, 157
Kenwood, 168
Kerr Revolvers, 160
Ketland & Co., 19
Key West, Florida, 65, 85, 133
Keystone State, 168
Kickapoo, 146, 168
Kineo, 168
Kingfisher, 168
Knapsacks, 67, 98, 116, 148
Knives, 19, 81, 82, 115, 142, 156, 158
Korea, 157

L

Lackawanna, 111, 121, 168
Lafayette, 103, 138, 168
Lake Erie, 129
Lancaster, 44–46, 56, 68, 69, 89, 132, 151, 159, 168
Lancaster, A.M., 165
Lances, 104, 157
Lay, John L., 91
Lee, Robert E., 33
Lee, S.P., 136
Lehigh, 168
LeMat revolvers, 106
Levant, 27, 40, 44, 56
Lewis, H.H., 49
Lexington, 168
Light Cavalry Sabers, 14
Lincoln, President, 62, 150, 151
Linda, 167
Linden, 101, 168
Lindsay, George F., 40, 42
Lindsay, M1863 Double Rifle Musket, 129
Little Rebel, 146, 163, 168
Lodona, 117, 168
Logbooks, 161
Logowitz, J., 98
Loo Choo, 21
Louisiana, 91, 168
Louisville, 74, 94, 101, 103, 168, 178
Lowrey, Capt. H.B., 66
Lynch, Commander, 141, 150

M

Macao, 16
Macedonian, 29, 42, 45, 48, 56, 168
Mackie, John F., 97
Mackinaw, 145, 168

Maddox, 55, 115, 128
Mahaska, 168
Malta, 25
Malvern, 136, 143, 150, 151, 168
Manassas, Virginia, 62
Manchester, New Hampshire, 71
Manhattan, 168
Maratanza, 168, 169
Marblehead, 168
Mare Island, 68, 89, 106, 128, 135, 136, 140, 150, 151
Maria A. Wood, 93, 168
Maria J. Carlton, 168
Marine Corps Swords, 54
Marine Corps, 23, 24, 27, 32, 33, 40–45, 52, 54, 59, 61, 62, 64–69, 79, 89, 96, 97, 101, 105–107, 111, 113, 115, 117, 121, 123, 125, 131, 132, 134, 136, 140, 144, 145, 147, 148, 151, 154, 157
Marion, 56
Marmora, 90, 91, 168
Marquette, Michigan, 129
Marseilles, France, 25
Marston Carbine, 20
Marston Revolvers, 34
Massachusetts, State of, 21, 56, 114
Massasoit, 125, 168
Matagorda, Texas, 90
Mathias Point, Virginia, 72
Mattabesett, 125, 134, 168
Matthew Vassar, 168
May, Richard L., 107
Maynard, 14, 26, 36
Maynard Carbines, 49, 50, 56, 60, 106, 109, 160
Maynard Muskets, 17, 42
Maynard Percussion Locks, 14
Maynard Rifle, 61
Maynard Tape Priming System, 20, 26, 36, 40–42, 44, 45, 67
McCorkle, George, 18
McDowell, Brig. Gen., 62
Medal of Honor, 107, 124, 148
Mediterranean, 97
Mediterranean Squadron, 41, 46
Memphis, 133, 168
Mendenhall, Jones and Gardner Rifles, 130
Mendota, 127, 133, 136, 151, 168
Mercury, 133, 168
Merrill, James H., 69, 129
Merrill Breechloading System, 46
Merrimack, 39, 42, 45, 47, 48, 50, 56, 59, 72, 83, 163
Metacomet, 154, 178
Meteor, 137, 168
Mexican War, 43
Miami, 99, 117, 168
Michigan, 69, 129, 130, 137, 141, 151, 154, 168
Midnight, 140, 168
Miller, Samuel, 92
Miller, W. Angus, 102
Milwaukee, 150, 168
Mingoe, 133, 168
Minnesota, 41, 45, 47, 50, 56, 68, 69, 84, 100, 113, 144, 145, 163, 168
Mississippi, 13–17, 30, 42, 47, 50, 56, 68, 71, 169, 178
Mississippi Fleet, 73, 103
Mississippi Flotilla, 94
Mississippi River, 59, 74, 85, 88, 94, 100, 101, 104, 132, 138
Mississippi Sound, 94
Mississippi Squadron, 65, 74, 90, 94, 95, 98, 100–103, 115, 129, 137, 138, 140, 146, 152, 154, 156, 166
Mist, 169
Mitchell Contract, 73, 114
Mitchell's Sharps Rifles, 73, 82
Mitchell, John, 72, 82
Mitchell, William, 94
Mobile Bay, 121, 140
Mobile Harbor, 111
M1822 Remington/Maynard Conversions, 44
M1832 Foot Artillery Swords, 100
M1833, 25
M1840 Muskets, 38

M1840 NCO and Musician Swords, 54
M1841 Cutlasses, 41, 55, 132
M1841 Naval Cutlasses, 31, 78
M1841 Officer's Swords, 31
M1842, 40
M1842 Muskets, 24, 43, 62, 146
M1842 Percussion Locks, 36
M1842 Percussion Muskets, 42, 44
M1842 Rifled Muskets, 85
M1846 Carabine a Tige, 36
M1847 Sappers and Miners, 63
M1849 Colt Revolvers, 125
M1849 Revolvers, 64
M1850 Foot Officer's Swords, 54, 79
M1851 Colt Navy Revolvers, 74
M1851 Colt Revolvers, 50, 52
M1851 Colts, 51
M1851 Revolvers, 30
M1852 Officer's Swords, 31, 32
M1855, 43
M1855 .58 Caliber Pistol Carbine, 62
M1855 Colt Revolving Rifles, 49
M1855 Joslyn Rifles, 71
M1855 Rifle Muskets, 36, 42, 44, 45, 54, 61, 66, 67, 68, 79, 88
M1855 Sharps, 110
M1855 Sharps Carbines, 47, 48, 134
M1855 Sharps Rifles, 41, 48
M1858 Plymouth Rifles, 71
M1859 Rifle, 66
M1861 Ames Cutlass, 84, 99, 164
M1861 Ames Naval Cutlass, 78
M1861 Colt Revolvers, 93, 135
M1861 Cutlasses, 153, 154
M1861 Rifle Muskets, 68
M1861 Springfield Rifle Muskets, 87, 111, 151
Mohawk, 44
Mohican, 169
Monadnock, 169
Monitor, 83, 84, 85, 169
Monongahela, 169
Monongahela, Texas, 110
Montgomery, 169
Monticello, 69, 71, 169
Moose, 169
Morcteniga, 169
Morris, Commadore Charles, 15, 28, 31
Morris Island, 111
Mound City, 74, 94, 101, 103, 138, 139, 169, 178
Mound City, Illinois, 108, 118, 126, 133, 137, 140–142, 146, 152, 156
Mount Vernon, 72, 93, 169
Mount Washington, 110
Mullaney, James R. Madison, 51
Mullards, Samuel, 22
Musician's Swords, 54, 55, 79, 98, 115, 142, 154
Musket Ball Cartridges, 22, 28
Musket Slings, 79, 98
Musketoons, 63, 74
Muskets, 16, 17, 19, 22, 24, 28, 29, 39, 41, 55, 56, 59, 65, 71, 73, 85, 86, 88, 98–100, 105–107, 119, 124, 126, 129, 130, 136, 142, 146, 153, 156, 157, 160, 164
Mystic, 44

N

Naha, Okinawa, 16
Nahant, 105, 117, 162, 169
Nansemond, 108, 169
Nansemond River, 110
Nantucket, 169
Napa Roads, 29
Narragansett, 44, 169
National Archives, 161
Naubuc, 169
Naumkeag, 169
Naval Academy, 22, 74, 76, 87, 118, 123, 124, 129, 142
Nelson, William, 73
Neosho, 103, 169
Nereus, 124, 169
Neuse River, 76
New Era, 169
New Hampshire, 64, 96, 169

New Inlet, North Carolina, 130, 137
New Ironsides, 84, 93, 111, 113, 169
New London, 134, 169
New Orleans, Louisiana, 71, 86, 88, 92, 93, 100, 111, 118, 137, 150, 156, 157
New York, 23, 26, 46, 76, 93, 97, 111, 126, 133, 135, 137, 140, 142, 148
New York Arsenal, 14
New York Navy Yard, 13, 19, 21, 25–27, 38, 52, 60, 64, 65, 71, 88, 93, 95, 98, 106, 107, 109–111, 118, 123, 132, 140, 142, 156
New York Zouaves, 62
Newport, Rhode Island, 76
Niad, 133, 146, 169
Niagara, 42, 45, 52, 56, 59, 169
Nichols, Richard M., 81, 93
Nicholson, Commander, 109
Nina, 170
Niphon, 118, 119, 130, 140, 170
Nipsic, 137, 170
Nita, 170
NM1859 Sharps Rifles, 48, 69, 82, 91, 110, 135, 158
NM1861 Colt Revolvers, 74
Norfolk, Virginia, 19, 21, 25, 26, 32, 46, 50, 59, 128, 150
Norfolk Navy Yard, 19, 21, 25, 48, 141, 163
Norfolk Packet, 170
North, Simeon, 18
North Atlantic Blockading Squadron, 118, 136, 141
North Carolina, State of, 21, 23, 29, 56, 67
North Carolina, 51st Infantry, 153
North's Patent Pistols, 53
North-Savage .36 Caliber Six-Shot Revolver, 53
North-Savage Revolvers, 76
Norwich, 170
Norwich University, 62
Nugent, Christopher, 107
Nyack, 153, 170
Nymph, 170, 171

O

Octorara, 146, 156, 170
Official Records of the Union and Confederate Navies in the War of the Rebellion, 161
Ohio, 67, 148
Ohio, 58th Infantry, 101
Okinawa, 29
Olive Branch, 138
Oliver H. Lee, 170
Onachita, 138
Oneida, 86, 88, 170
Onondaga, 124, 125, 162, 170
Oriole, 146, 154, 170
Orvetta, 170
Osage, 103, 170
Osceola, 145, 170
Ossipee, 94, 170
Otsego, 133, 170
Ottawa, 120, 170
Ouachita, 170
Owasco, 110, 170
Ozark, 103, 170

P

Pacific Squadron, 151
Paicchan Shells, 28
Panama, 27, 39, 40, 46, 50
Para, 86, 170
Paraguay Expedition, 47, 48, 51, 52
Parrott Guns, 129
Pascagoule, Mississippi, 94
Passaic, 170
Patapsco, 170
Patroon, 170
Paul Jones, 99, 100, 142, 152, 170
Paulding, Hiram, 48
Paw Paw, 170
Pawnee, 52, 53, 55, 56, 67, 68, 72, 79, 133, 170
Pawtuxet, 170
Payne, Lewis, 149
Peddie, Thomas B., 116, 148

Pembina, 170
Pennsylvania, 170
Pennsylvania, 45th Infantry, 65
Penobscot, 170
Pensacola, 45, 72, 73, 78, 128, 155, 170
Pensacola Naval Yard, 138
Peosta, 170
Pepper, John, 22
Pequot, 170
Percussion Caps, 22, 60, 65, 77, 103, 105, 123, 132, 135, 139, 140, 142
Percussion Cap Pouches, 128
Percussion Muskets, 27
Percussion Rifled Muskets, 34
Perry, Matthew C., 13, 15, 17, 25, 28, 30
Perry, 56, 61, 170
Perry Carbines, 34, 46, 87, 160
Perry's East India Squadron, 13–15, 21
Peru, 151
Phelps, J.S., 34
Philadelphia, 87, 170
Philadelphia Depot, 55, 67, 69, 115
Philadelphia Navy Yard, 26, 40–42, 48, 52, 60, 65, 78, 70–74, 76, 78, 82, 92–95, 103, 106, 108, 111, 113, 116, 118, 128, 132, 133, 140, 141, 150, 152, 153, 156, 163
Philadelphia, Pennsylvania, 18, 23, 27, 31, 36, 54, 71, 79, 106, 153
Phlox, 170
Pickering, Lt., 28
Picket Boat #1, 170
Picket Boat #5, 170
Pikes, 27, 29, 34, 81, 98, 106, 156, 157
Pinola, 170
Pinta, 170
Pirates, 22
Pistol Ball Cartridges, 22
Pistol Cases, 98
Pistols, .54 cal. Army, 60
Pittsburg, 74, 94, 101, 103, 104, 129, 138, 163, 170
Plymouth, 15, 17, 18, 36–38, 48, 56
Plymouth Rifles, 34, 36–38, 43, 56, 61, 65, 71, 81, 89, 90, 106–109, 124–126, 129, 130, 133, 134, 136, 138, 139, 142, 153, 156–158, 160, 165
Plymouth, North Carolina, 123, 134
Pocahontas, 72, 170
Pontiac, 133, 150, 151, 170
Pontoosuc, 125, 145, 170
Pope's Creek, Virginia, 113
Porpoise, 20, 56
Port Royal, 170
Port Royal, South Carolina, 66–68, 87–89, 110, 111, 120, 156
Port-au-Prince, 45
Porter Mortor Squadron, 65, 74, 85, 86, 90
Porter, Benjamin H., 145
Porter, Adm. David D., 85, 101, 104, 137, 138, 143–145, 150, 151
Porto Grande, 23
Portsmouth, 21, 22, 39, 40, 45, 56, 170, 178
Portsmouth Navy Yard, 24, 26, 48, 67, 73, 74, 78, 89, 93, 94, 97, 106, 111, 118, 125, 128, 135, 141, 156, 163
Potomac, 60, 68, 69, 170
Potomac Flotilla, 76, 82, 100, 113, 118, 133, 139
Potomska, 138, 170
Powers, John, 153
Powhatan, 15, 17, 18, 22, 24, 29, 42, 56, 117, 145, 170
Prairie Bird, 170
Preble, 41, 45, 52, 56, 71, 170
Preston, Samuel W., 144, 145
Primer Boxes, 126
Primrose, 113, 114, 170
Princess Royal, 170
Princeton, 22, 56, 170
Proteus, 124, 170
Prussian Muskets, 156
Pursuit, 170
Putnam, 163

Q

Quaker City, 62, 63, 64, 170
Queen of the West, 85
Quimby, J.M., 46

R

Racer, 170
Ramsey, Maj. George, 42, 45, 65, 88
Ranson, George M., 51
Rappahannock, Virginia, 113
Rattler, 132, 170
Reid, 2nd Lt. George C., 158
Reindeer, 170
Reliance, 105
Relief, 59
Remington & Sons, 36, 40, 94, 106, 118, 164
Remington .36 Caliber Beals Revolvers, 94
Remington Revolvers, 103, 105, 106, 110, 118, 119, 124, 125, 134, 140, 142, 147, 152, 153, 156, 160, 163
Remington Rolling Block Rifles, 157, 160
Remington/Jenks Carbines, 25, 26, 45, 70
Remington/Maynard Conversion, 40, 41
Remington/Maynard Rifled Muskets, 41, 42, 52, 54
Resolute, 170
Restless, 90, 170
Reynolds, Maj., 62, 68, 88
Reynolds, Daniel, 99
Reynolds, William W., 64
Rhode Island, 170
Rice, Dr., 138
Richmond, 69, 70, 90, 123, 164, 170
Richmond, Virginia, 85, 151
Rickett, Capt. 62
Ringgold, Commander, 20, 21, 30
Ringgold China Sea Expedition, 20
Ripley, Maj. James W., 73, 87, 107
Roanoke, 46, 56, 60, 111, 120, 170
Rodgers, Lt., 21
Rodgers, George W., 52
Rodgers, John, 24
Roman Swords, 60, 78, 87, 105, 142, 154, 156, 158, 164
Romeo, 170
Roncador Reef, 135
Rowan, Stephen C., 47, 51
Royal Yacht, 74
Rudd, John, 23
Russell, John H., 92
Russell, William, 33

S

Saber Bayonets, 66, 71, 81, 82, 92, 99, 132, 142, 156
Sabers, 17, 18, 60
Sabine, 48, 52, 56, 67, 68, 153, 170
Sachem, 98, 170
Saco, 133, 170
Sacramento, 94, 170
Sagamore, 170
Saginaw, 150, 170
St. Andrews Sound, Georgia, 107
St. Joseph's Island, Texas, 111
St. Lawrence, 40, 60, 73, 76, 171
St. Louis, 23, 56, 94, 98, 110, 133, 171
St. Louis Arsenal, 44, 95, 102, 129
St. Mary's, 25, 39, 40, 45, 50, 56, 68, 171
St. Phillip, 88
St. Vincent, 23
Samuel Rotan, 88, 170
San Francisco Bay, 106
San Jacinto, 27, 40, 44, 56, 171
Sanford, Lt. Joseph P., 65, 74, 87, 94, 119
Sangamon, 170
Santee, 74, 171
Santiago de Cuba, 171
Sappers & Miners, 63
Sarah Bruen, 171
Saranac, 42, 45, 56, 106, 133, 171
Saratoga, 15, 16, 28, 29, 42, 50, 56, 133, 142,

Index

171
Sassacus, 171
Satellite, 105, 171
Saugus, 171
Savage Revolving Fire-Arms Co., 76, 164
Savage Revolvers, 27, 60, 63, 76, 77, 87, 118, 127, 140, 156, 160, 163, 164
Savage, Edward, 53
Savannah, 21, 56, 60, 61, 171
Savannah River, 150
Savannah, Georgia, 61
Scabbards, 89, 92, 163
Schively (of Phila./manufacturer), 36
Schofield, John, 153
Schoolmaker, Lt. Cornelius, 155
Sciota, 88, 171
Scott, Winfield, 59
Screwdrivers, 92, 103
Sea Foam, 171
Sebago, 171
Selma, 123, 171
Seminole, 48, 56, 163, 171
Semmes, Raphael, 135
Seneca, 145, 171
Shamokin, 171
Shamrock, 171
Shanghai, 15, 24
Shark, 171
Sharps, 48, 109, 130, 139
Sharps & Hankins, 93, 106, 135, 150, 160, 164
Sharps & Hankins Carbines, 92, 93, 102, 103, 108, 110, 111, 118, 120, 123–125, 134–137, 145, 150–152, 160
Sharps & Hankins Rifles, 71, 92, 99, 111, 158, 163
Sharps Carbines, 20, 28, 34, 47, 55, 60, 106, 134, 163
Sharps Rifles, 20, 29, 34, 41, 47–49, 51, 52, 56, 60, 61, 63, 65, 71–73, 76, 85–87, 91, 93, 95, 105, 109, 111, 124, 130, 135, 137, 144, 145, 153, 156, 163
Shawsheen, 171
Shenandoah, 145, 171
Sherman, William T., 153
Ship Island, Mississippi, 146
Shotguns, 157
Shuttleworth, W.L., 68, 69
Sibyl, 133, 171
Sidney C. Jones, 171
Signal, 90, 101, 171
Silver Cloud, 146, 171
Silver Lake, 171
Single Sticks, 41, 91, 100, 104, 123–126, 154, 156, 163
Slack, Maj. Wm. B., 55, 66, 67, 79, 88, 98, 115, 132, 142
Slack, W.M., 131
Slings, 89, 116, 148
Smalley, E.A., 88
Smith & Sons, Thomas, 79
Smith Carbines, 137, 138
Somerset, 88, 171
Sommers, Rudolph, 105
Sonoma, 133, 171
Sophronia, 86, 171
South Atlantic Blockading Squadron, 67, 87, 100, 107, 142, 154, 156
South Carolina, State of, 55, 171
South Carolina, 4th Infantry, 65
Southfield, 124
Spencer Rifles, 71, 92, 103–105, 109, 113–115, 119, 123–126, 130, 133, 138–140, 144, 145, 152, 156, 158, 160
Springfield Armory, 18, 36, 40, 42–44, 66, 67, 87, 107, 129
Springfield Bayonets, 114
Springfield, Massachusetts, 28, 29
Springfield Muskets, 123, 146, 156, 163
Springfield Muzzleloaders, 157
Springfield Rifle Muskets, 42, 43, 66, 67, 87, 89, 104, 107, 111, 113, 129, 131, 132, 145, 147–149, 151, 163, 164
Springfield Rifled Muskets, 150
Springfield Smoothbore Muskets, 104
Springfield .50/.70 Rifles, 157

Starr Revolvers, 73, 76–78, 100, 157, 160, 164
Stars & Stripes, 76, 171
Stepping Stone, 99, 100, 161, 171
Stoddard, George, 134
Storms, C.S., 116, 128, 148
Stuart, Jeb, 33
Sumter, 44, 171
Supply, 17, 29, 178
Susquehanna, 15–17, 29, 39, 45, 56, 71, 145, 171
Sutherland, Maj. D.J., 42–44
Suwanee, 164, 171
Swann, R.P., 138
Sword Bayonets, 36, 103
Sword Frogs, 79
Swords, 31, 34, 39, 45, 54, 55, 60, 73, 78, 80, 86, 89, 98–100, 106, 107, 115, 116, 126, 135, 142, 153–155, 163
Syms, W.J., 63

T

T.A. Ward, 90, 171
Tacony, 137, 145, 163, 171
Tahoma, 171
Tansill, Robert, 52
Teaser, 114, 133, 171
Tecumseh, 121, 123, 171
Tennessee, 90, 121, 123, 171
Texas, 8th Volunteer Infantry, 111
Thatcher, Henry K., 97
Thomas Freeborn, 72, 153
Ticonderoga, 109, 144, 145, 172
Tilton, Capt. McLane, 115, 157, 158
Tokyo, 17
Tokyo Bay, 28
Tomlin, Corp. Andrew, 148
Toucey, Isaac, 40, 44
Tower Muskets, 19
Trefoil, 172
Tristram Shandy, 172
Truxtun, Lt., 65
Tulifinny Crossroads, 134
Tulip, 172
Tuscarora, 145, 172
Tuscumbia, 103, 104, 172
Ty-Ho Bay, 22
Tyler, 85, 172

U

U.S. Model 1822, 36
Unadilla, 76, 133, 140, 172
Underhill Edge Tool Company, 32
Underwriter, 76, 172
Union, 172
Union Defense Committee (UDC), 62–64

V

Valley City, 76, 172
Valley Forge, 18
Vandalia, 56, 178
Vanderbilt, 28
Vanderbilt, 143, 145, 163, 172
Varuna, 88
Vermont, 172
Vicksburg, 172
Vicksburg, 85, 88, 92, 100, 101, 104
Victoria, 172
Victory, 172
Vincennes, 20, 21, 28, 56, 71, 146, 172
Vindicator, 133, 152, 172
Virginia, 48, 72, 76, 83, 84
Virginia, State of, 31, 34, 59, 60, 61, 65, 72, 83, 105, 110, 112, 117, 132, 151, 163
Virginia Home Guard, 132

W

Wabash, 40–42, 45, 47, 48, 56, 60, 61, 66, 67, 69, 87, 93, 100, 120, 144, 148, 172
Wachusett, 163, 172
Wainwright, Lt. Richard, 69, 74
Waist Belts, 54, 85, 123, 126, 132, 148, 160
Waist Plates, 54, 89, 116, 148

Walker, William, 48
Wallace, Bvt. Capt. Wm., 158
Walter, Thomas, 89
Wando, 172
Ward, J.H., 72
Warner, Franklin, 107
Warrington, Florida, 44
Washington Arsenal, 14, 24, 38, 42–45, 65, 66, 74, 88, 89, 94, 107, 129, 147
Washington, D.C., 27, 31, 62, 71, 72, 151
Washington Navy Yard, 19, 25, 36–39, 42, 43, 46, 48–50, 63, 69, 71–74, 76–78, 82, 90–93, 99, 104, 106, 108, 111, 113–115, 118, 120, 124, 131–133, 138, 140, 141, 152, 163
Wassaw Sound, Georgia, 105
Water Witch, 27, 51, 52, 56, 172
Wateree, 151, 172
Watertown Arsenal, 22, 24, 25
Watervliet Arsenal, 14, 22, 87
Weaverton, Maryland, 33
Weehawken, 105
Welles, Gideon, 66, 67, 85
West Gulf Blockading Squadron, 90, 92, 111, 134, 140
Westernport, 52, 56
White, Rollin, 47
Whiting, Wm., 24
Whitney, Eli, 18, 34–36, 65, 66, 89, 107, 108, 119, 120
Whitney Revolvers, 102–104, 106, 109, 114, 119–121, 123–125, 128, 129, 136, 140–142, 145, 152–154, 156, 157, 160, 163, 164
Wickham, M.T., 18
Wicomico Bay, Virginia, 132
Wild Cat, 172
Wilderness, 172
William Bacon, 108, 114, 172
William Putnam, 172
Williams, Charles F., 144
Williams, George F., 152
Wilmington, North Carolina, 153
Winnebago, 129, 140, 172
Winona, 133, 172
Winslow, John, 135
Wiping Rods, 103
Wisconsin, 4th Infantry, 85
Wise, Henry A., 31, 99, 115, 128, 137, 138
Wise, W.A., 147
Wissahickon, 133, 156, 172
Worden, John L., 84
Wyalusing, 172
Wyandank, 172
Wyandotte, 44, 172
Wyoming, 56, 153, 172

Y

Yankee, 76, 114, 130, 139, 153, 172
Yantic, 145, 163, 172
Yazoo, 172
Yazoo River, 85, 101
Yokohama, 17
Young, Capt., 45
Young Rover, 76, 163, 172
Young, George W., 153
Young, Jas B., 111
Yucca, 172

Z

Zeilin, Jacob, 41, 60, 62, 63, 76, 87, 91, 131, 132, 140
Zeta, 172

Other Civil War Titles

Andrew Mowbray Inc.,/Publishers
P.O. Box 460 • Lincoln, RI 02816
1-800-999-4697 • 401-726-8011
Fax 401-726-8061 • email: manatarms@ids.net

Carbines of the U.S. Cavalry 1861–1905

By John D. McAulay. The carbines used by the U.S. Cavalry have always been of special interest to both historians and collectors. And this exhaustively researched book covers the period from the beginning of the Civil War to the end of the cavalry carbine era in 1905. These innovative carbines played pivotal roles in some of the most exciting episodes in American history, including the War Between the States, the Indian Campaigns, Custer's Last Stand, the Rough Riders in Cuba, the Philippine Insurrection and the Boxer Rebellion. Every one of these topics is covered in this entertaining and informative book — all illustrated with period and modern photos. 144 pp., 127 black & white photos, 8½" x 11". Hardcover. $35 + $4.50 p/h

Civil War Pistols of the Union

By John D. McAulay. This book, by an authority in the field, covers the handguns of the War between the States, pistol by pistol, including government procurement information, issue details and historical background. From common types like Colt, Remington and Smith & Wesson, to obscure makers such as Allen & Wheelock, North-Savage and exotic imports. Black & white photos. 166 pp., 8½" x 11". Softcover. $24; Hardcover. $36 + $4.50

Civil War Breech Loading Rifles

By John D. McAulay. *2nd Printing.* Although only about 35,000 of these rifles were purchased by the Union during the Civil War, their effect was enormous. All the major breech loading rifles of the Civil War — and most, if not all, of the obscure types — are detailed, illustrated and set in their historical context. 144 pp., 8½" x 11". Softcover. $15 + $4.50 p/h

Civil War Cartridge Boxes of the Union Infantryman

By Paul D. Johnson. There were four patterns of infantry cartridge boxes used by Union forces. Quoting original Ordnance Department letters, the author describes the development and subsequent pattern changes to these cartridge boxes that were made throughout the rifle-musket percussion era. Using 175+ photos from extant examples, Johnson has finally answered many of the questions concerning these cartridge boxes. This information will be a must for collectors and reenactors alike. The author has also found new information on government production records as well as contractor production and contracts during the first nine months of the Civil War. Also, there is never-before-released information on the inspection procedures of Civil War accouterments, as well as newly found information on the operation of the Ordnance Department just before and during the Civil War. Original artwork by George Woodbridge. 7"x10" • 352 pgs. Hardcover. $45 + $4.50 p/h

Civil War Arms Makers and Their Contracts

A facsimile reprint of the Report by the Commission on Ordnance and Ordnance Stores, 1862. The historical report reprinted in this book is perhaps the most important arms-related document of the Civil War. It includes the correspondence, testimony and decisions of the Commission on Ordnance and Ordnance Stores, which met in 1862 to review (and in many cases rewrite) all Federal contracts for guns, carbines, pistols, ammunition, swords and many other military items. The case histories, covering over 107 manufacturers and suppliers, are remarkably in-depth. Terms of contracts are outlined, factories described, machinery listed, and the fairness of prices is debated. The amount of material covered is astounding — almost 600 pages in all. 6" x 9". Hardcover. $39.50 + $4.50 p/h

     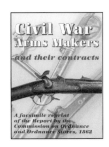

Subscribe to Man at Arms magazine!

Get all the news and information you need from the world's leading source on antique gun collecting.

Six times a year, *Man at Arms* magazine brings the whole world of gun collecting right into your home, with entertaining and authoritative articles, and lots of large color pictures of your favorite antique firearms. And, as the NRA's official "Journal for the American Arms Collector," we can give you special, exclusive features like NRA Collector News and the NRA's nationwide Gun Show Calendar. New subscribers also receive a discount on the purchase of available back issues. Don't get left behind...get *Man at Arms* today!

$32 FOR ONE YEAR • $62 FOR TWO YEARS

Send check or money order to:
MAN AT ARMS
P.O. Box 460
Lincoln, Rhode Island 02865 U.S.A.

VISA and MasterCard accepted
CALL TOLL FREE 1-800-999-4697
Outside the U.S. Call **401-726-8011** • *Fax* **401-726-8061**